# Buffy THE VAMPIRE SLAYER™

## A STAKE TO THE HEART

# Buffy the Vampire Slayer™

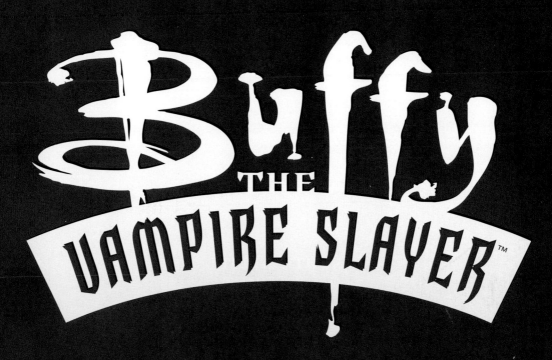

## A Stake to the Heart

*based on the television series created by*
**JOSS WHEDON**

*writer* **FABIAN NICIEZA**

*penciller* **CLIFF RICHARDS**

*painted pages by* **BRIAN HORTON**

*inker* **WILL CONRAD**

*colorist* **MICHELLE MADSEN**

*letterer* **CLEM ROBINS**

*Malignancy Demons designed by* **BRIAN HORTON**

*cover art* **BRIAN HORTON**

*This story takes place before Buffy the Vampire Slayer's first season.*

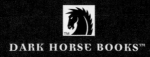

DARK HORSE BOOKS™

*publisher*
# MIKE RICHARDSON

*editor*
## SCOTT ALLIE
*with* MATT DRYER

*designer*
## LANI SCHREIBSTEIN

*special thanks to*
DEBBIE OLSHAN, CRYSTAL YANG, AND ALISON WALLACE AT FOX LICENSING
AND DAVID CAMPITI AT GLASS HOUSE GRAPHICS

PUBLISHED BY
DARK HORSE BOOKS
A DIVISION OF DARK HORSE COMICS, INC.
10956 SE MAIN STREET
MILWAUKIE, OR 97222

FIRST EDITION
MARCH 2004
ISBN: 1-59307-012-8

1 3 5 7 9 10 8 6 4 2

PRINTED IN CHINA

# INTRODUCTION

BUFFY SUMMERS, the Chosen slayer of vampires, has discovered that one's own family can be more dangerous than any shadows in the night! First, to avoid the burden of her school expulsion and her parents' disintegrating marriage, Buffy ran away to Las Vegas. She ashed a casino full of vampires, lost a sort-of boyfriend, and returned to Los Angeles...

...only to learn that her sister Dawn had read her diary—and told their parents about the strange things Buffy had been writing about. Things like vampires, Watchers, crosses, and stakes. So Joyce and Hank Summers did the only thing they could do: they had Buffy committed!

At the institution, Buffy encountered a new kind of danger—a demon who was feasting on the tormented souls of the girls at the rehabilitation facility. Having vanquished the demon and been released from the institute, Buffy has come to accept the reality of her job as a Slayer. But does that mean she wants to do the job?

Back home, Buffy is trying to find the answer, but she now has to face an even greater threat...

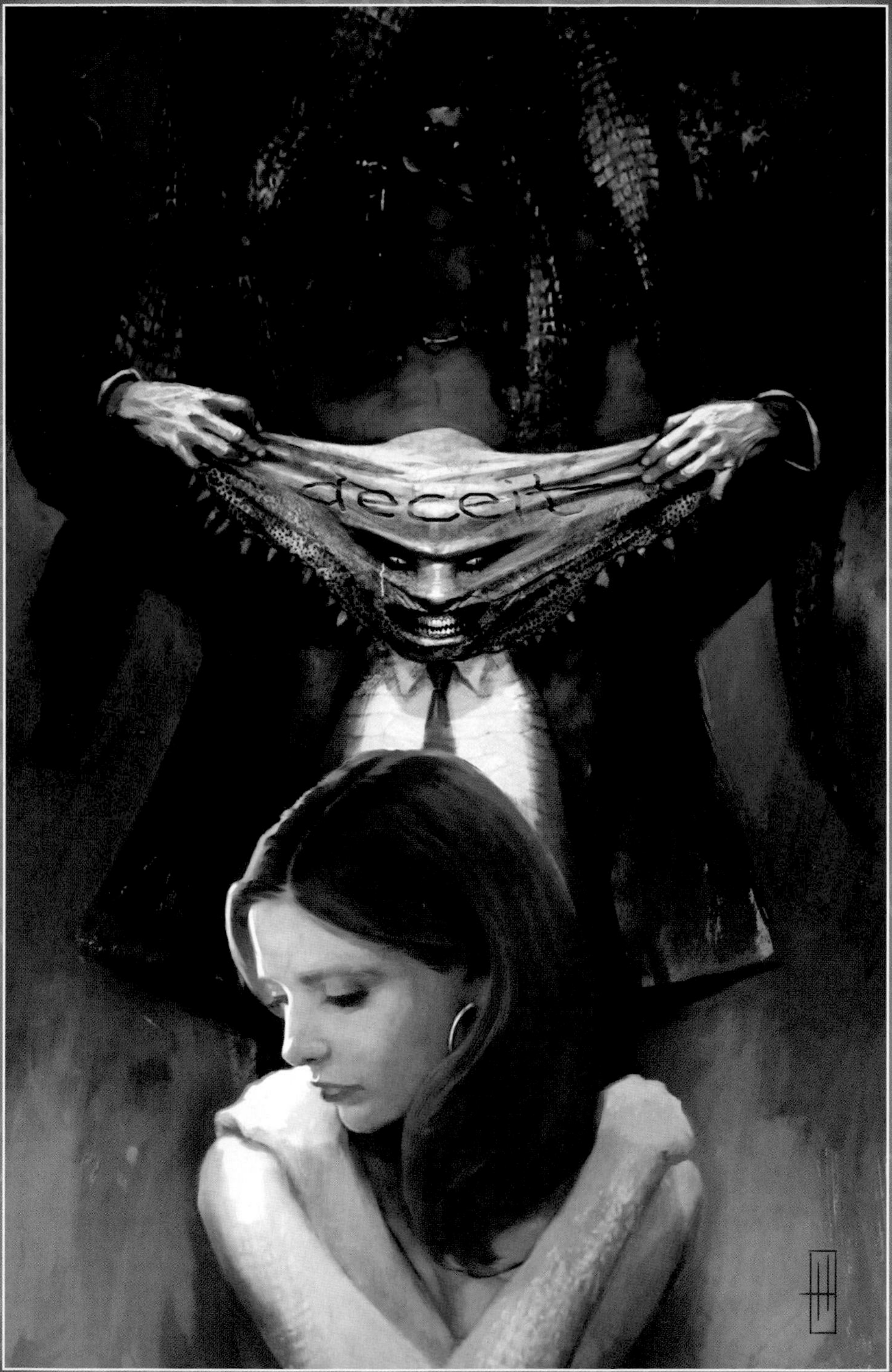
deceit

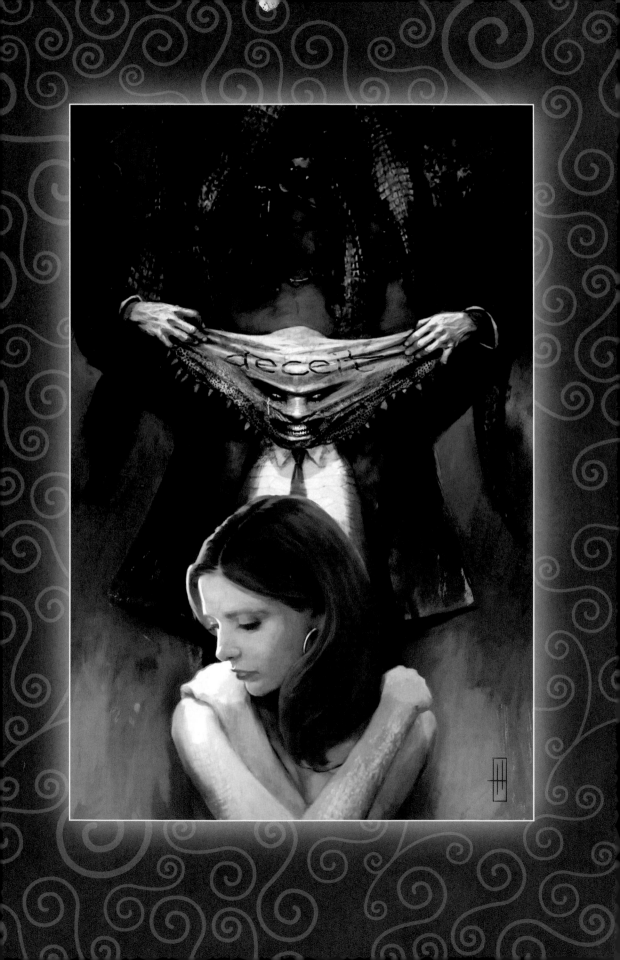

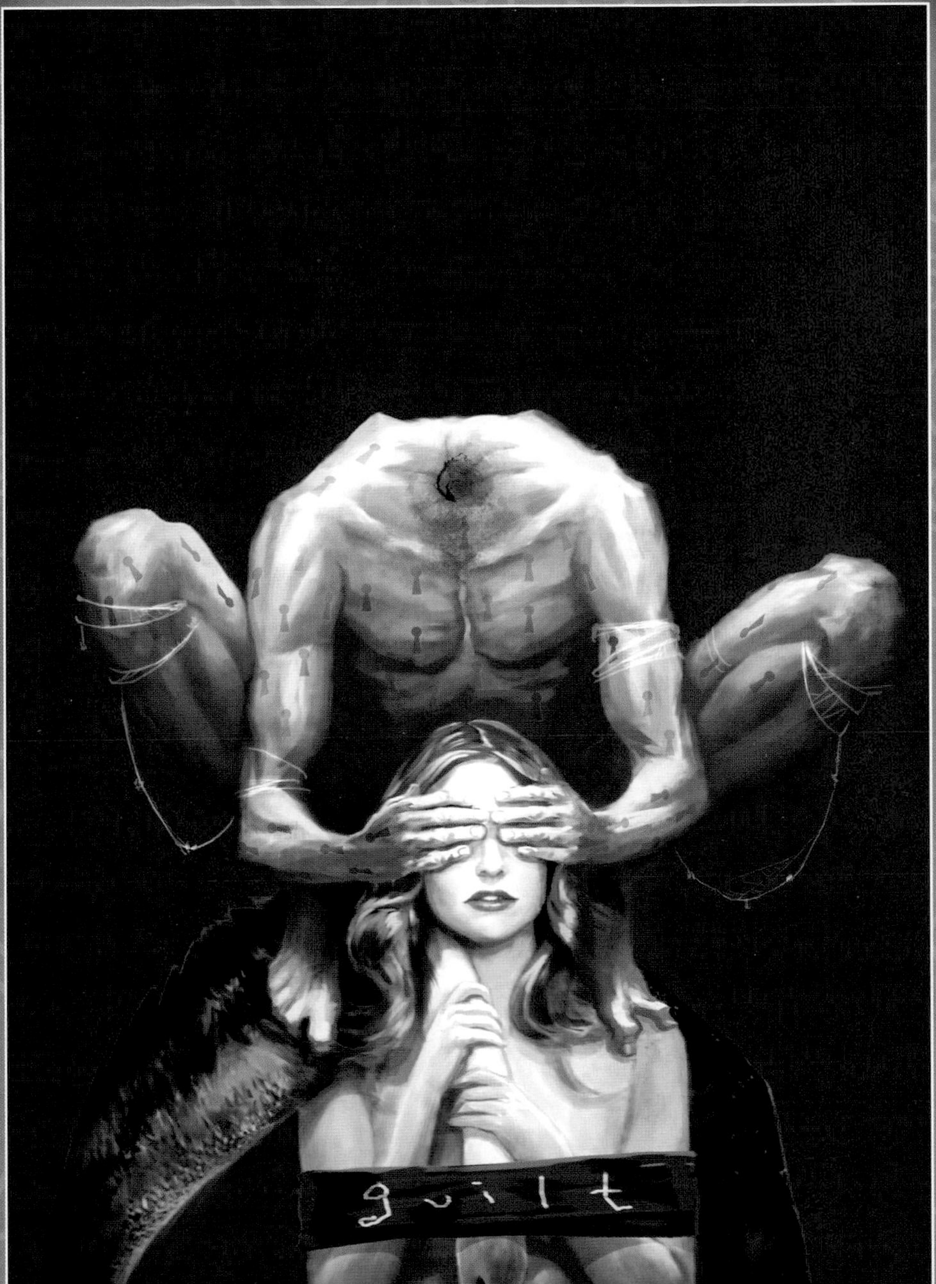
guilt

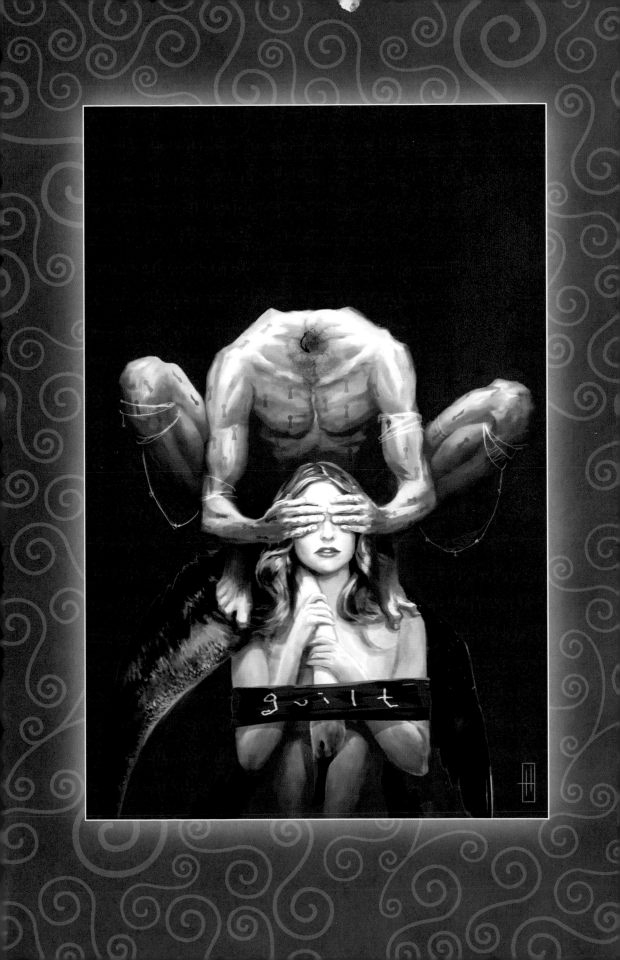

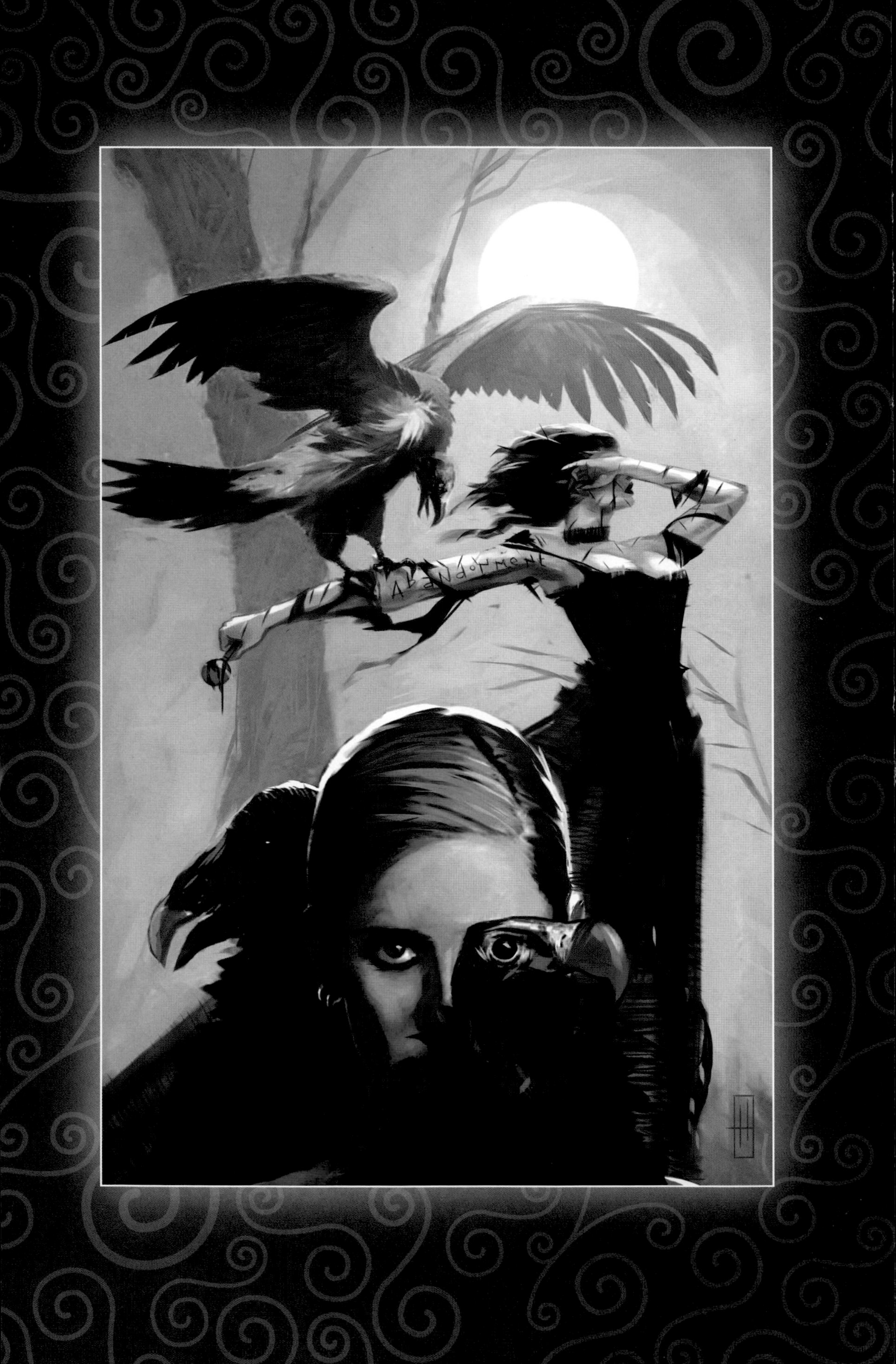
ABANDONMENT

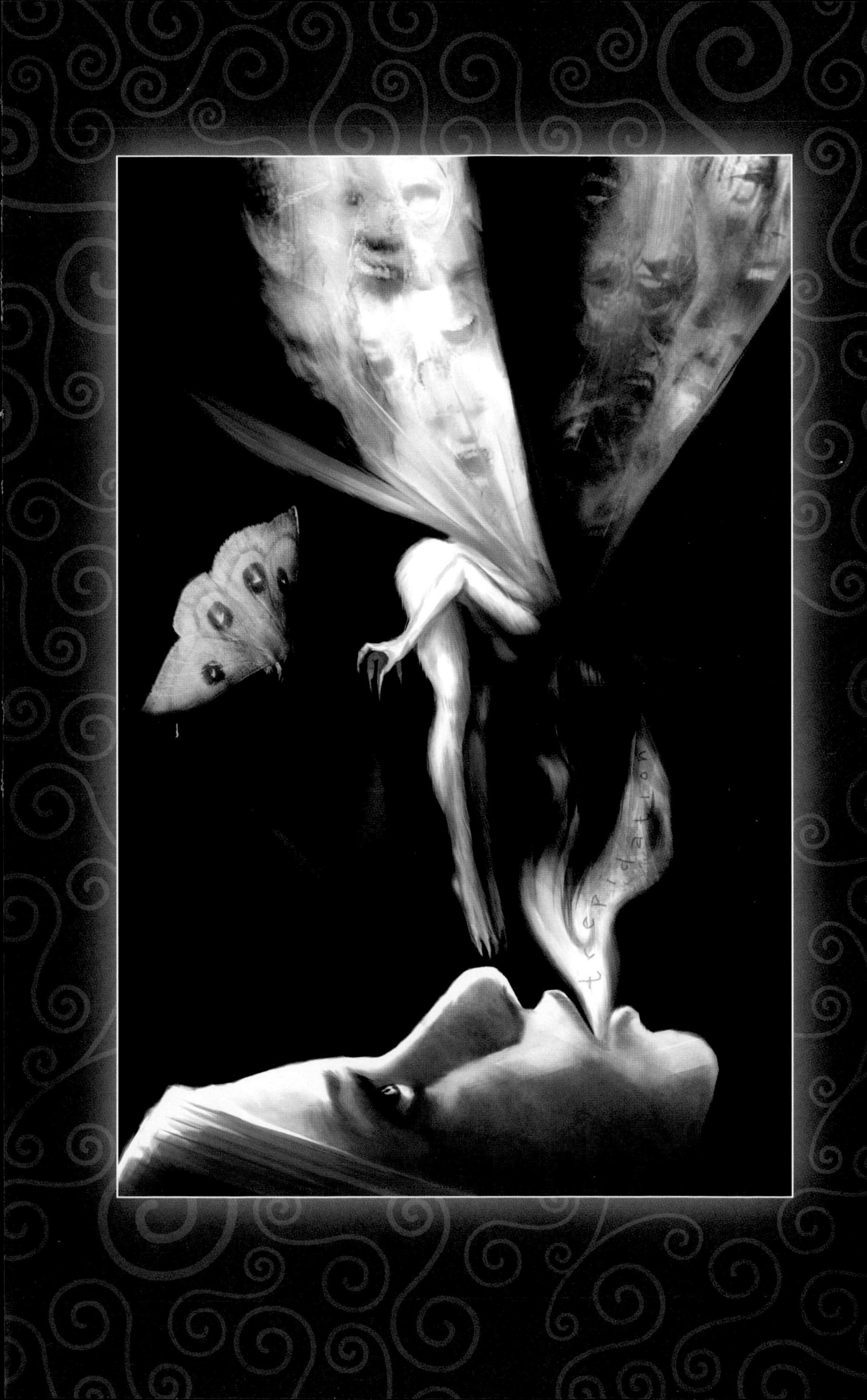
trepidation

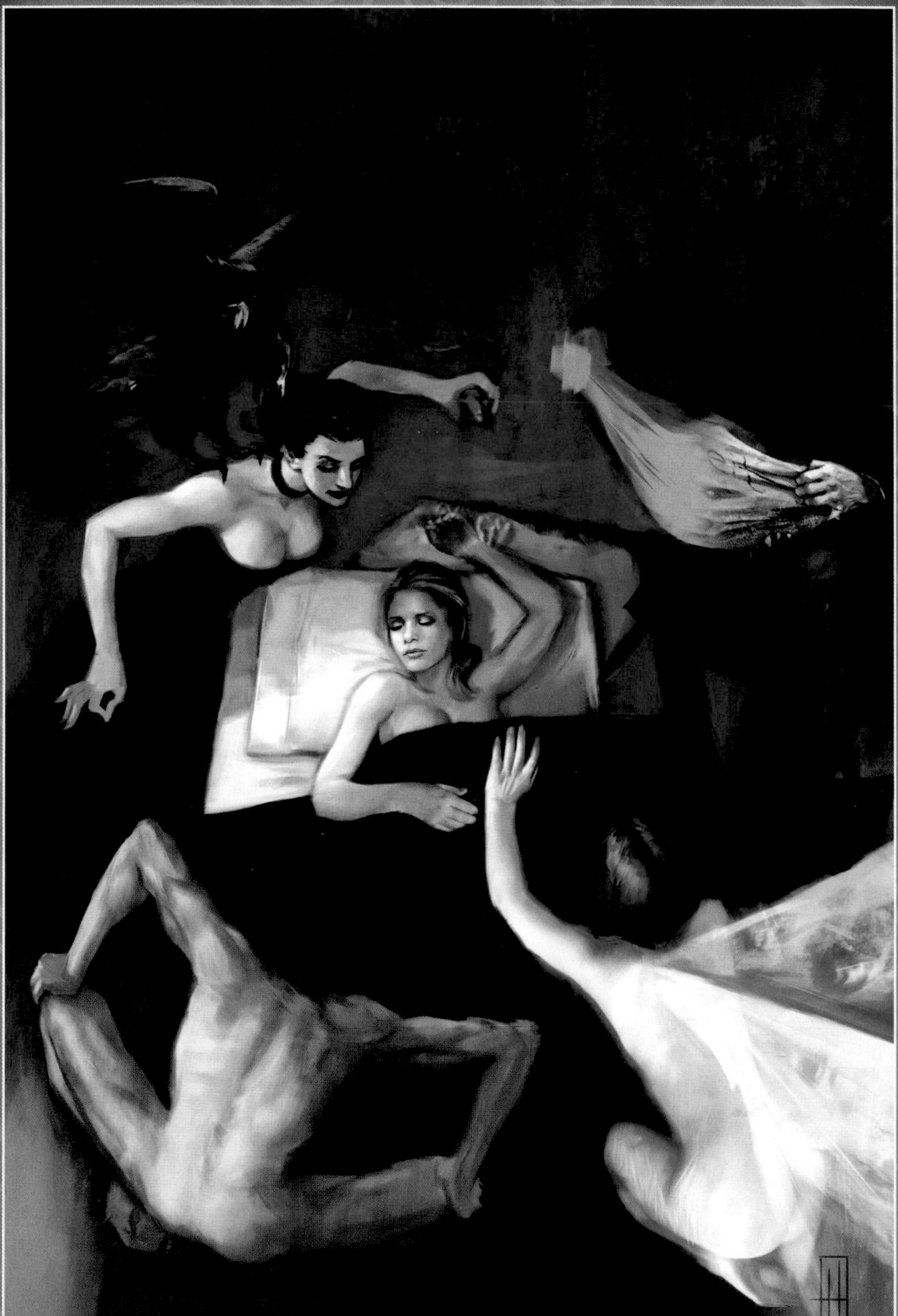

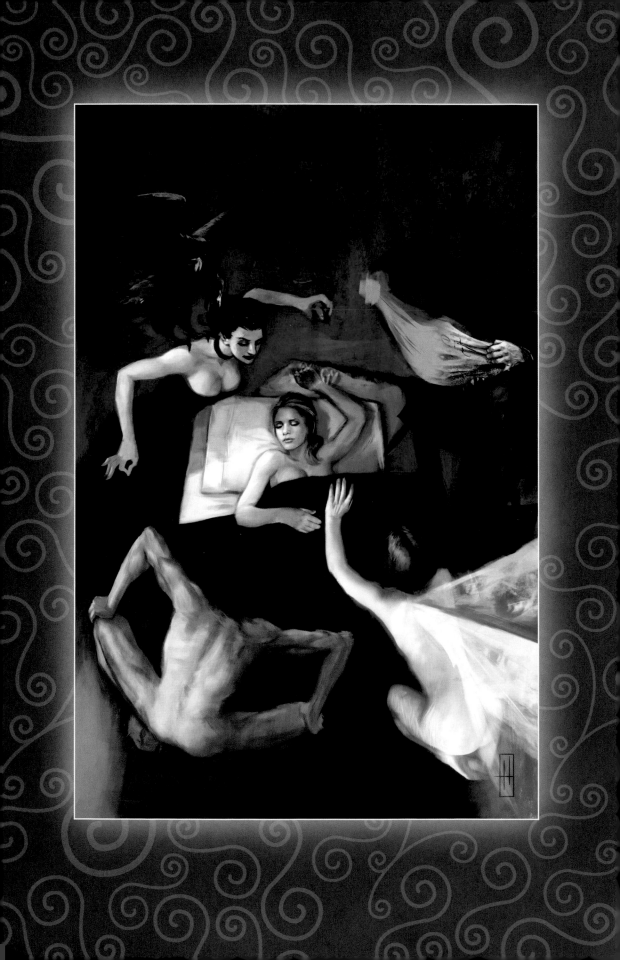

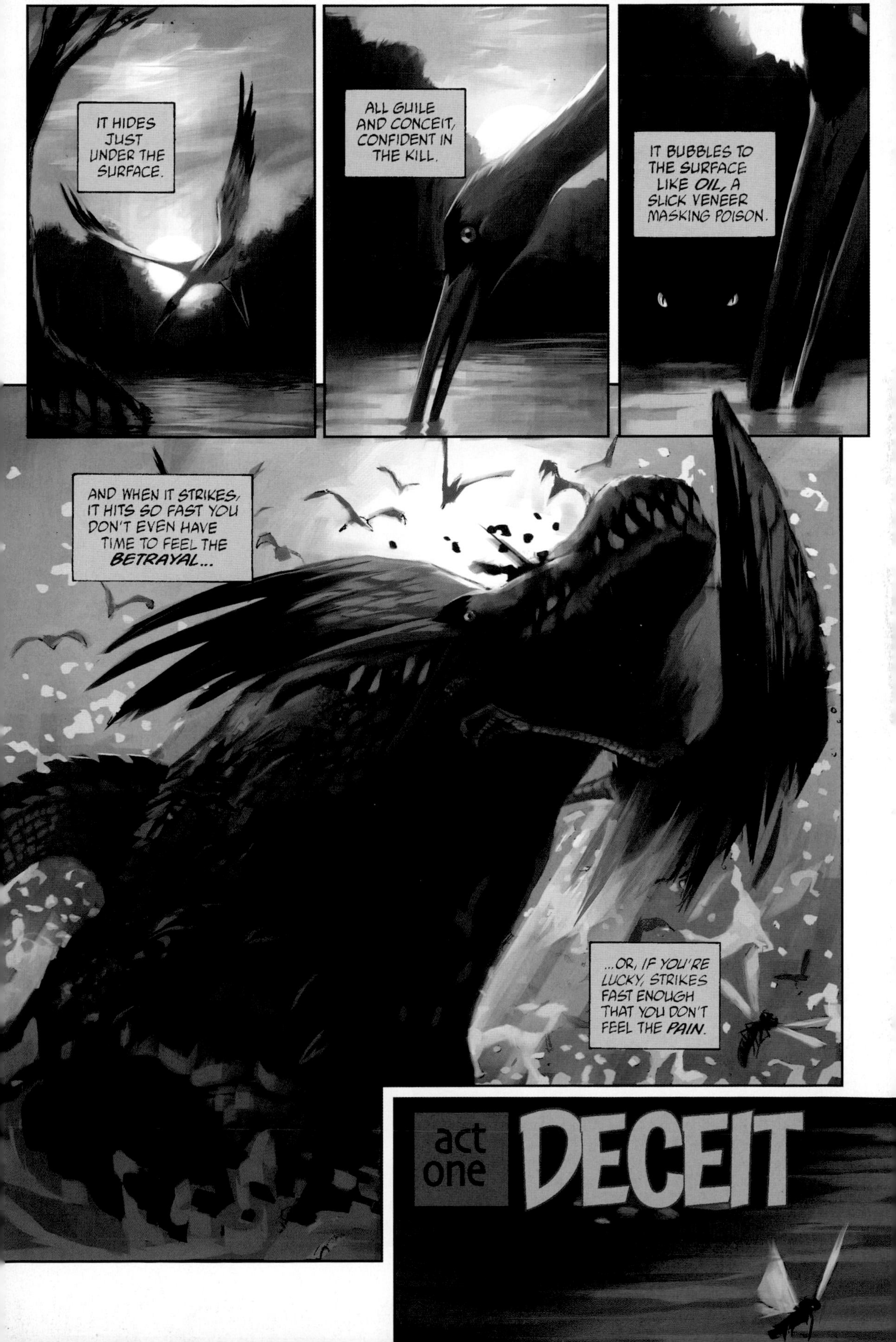
IT HIDES JUST UNDER THE SURFACE.
ALL GUILE AND CONCEIT, CONFIDENT IN THE KILL.
IT BUBBLES TO THE SURFACE LIKE OIL, A SLICK VENEER MASKING POISON.
AND WHEN IT STRIKES, IT HITS SO FAST YOU DON'T EVEN HAVE TIME TO FEEL THE BETRAYAL...
...OR, IF YOU'RE LUCKY, STRIKES FAST ENOUGH THAT YOU DON'T FEEL THE PAIN.
act one
DECEIT

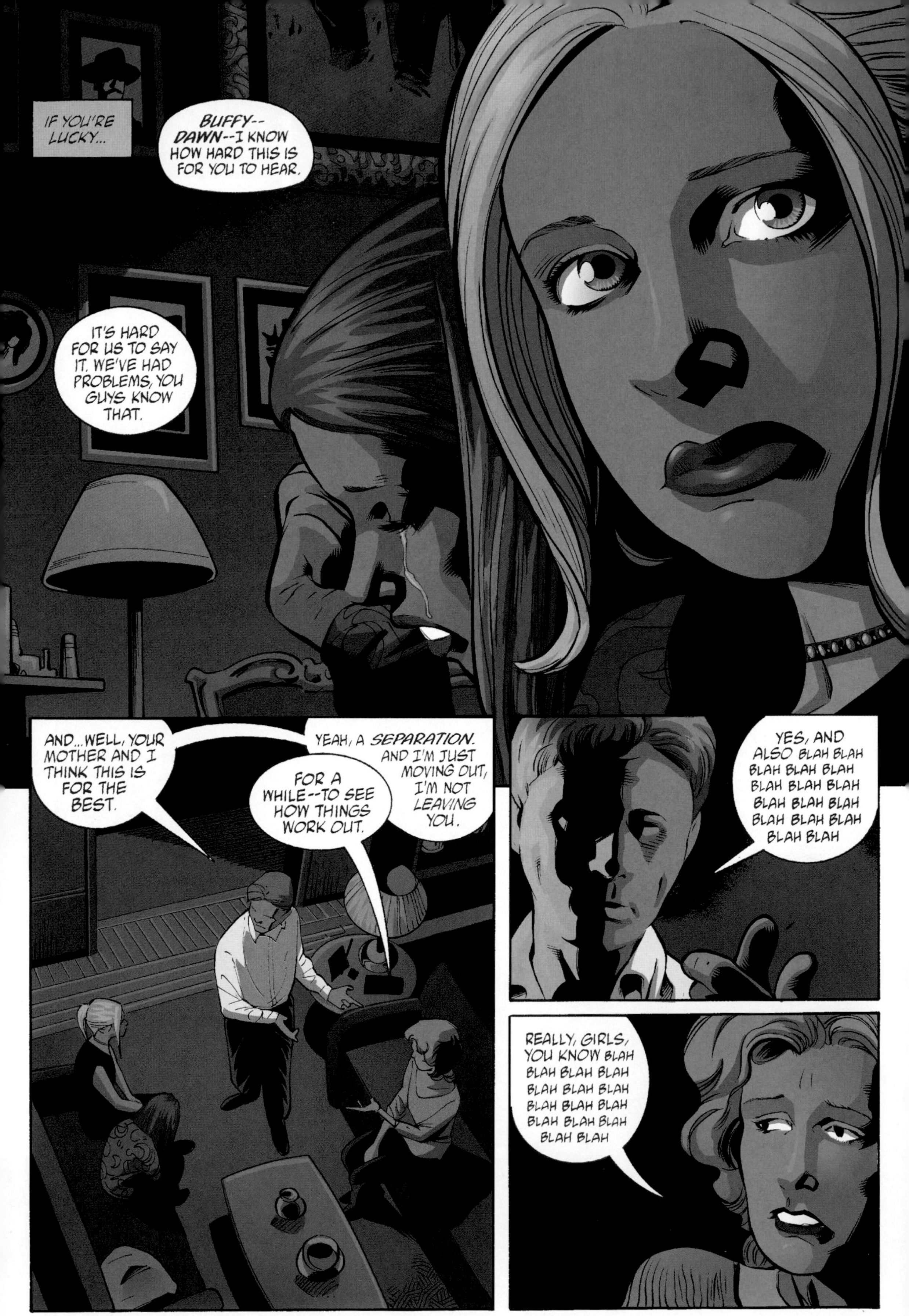
IF YOU'RE LUCKY...
BUFFY-- DAWN--I KNOW HOW HARD THIS IS FOR YOU TO HEAR.
IT'S HARD FOR US TO SAY IT. WE'VE HAD PROBLEMS, YOU GUYS KNOW THAT.
AND...WELL, YOUR MOTHER AND I THINK THIS IS FOR THE BEST.
YEAH, A SEPARATION. AND I'M JUST MOVING OUT, I'M NOT LEAVING YOU.
FOR A WHILE--TO SEE HOW THINGS WORK OUT.
YES, AND ALSO BLAH BLAH BLAH BLAH BLAH BLAH BLAH BLAH BLAH BLAH BLAH BLAH BLAH BLAH BLAH BLAH
REALLY, GIRLS, YOU KNOW BLAH BLAH BLAH BLAH BLAH BLAH BLAH BLAH BLAH BLAH BLAH BLAH BLAH BLAH BLAH

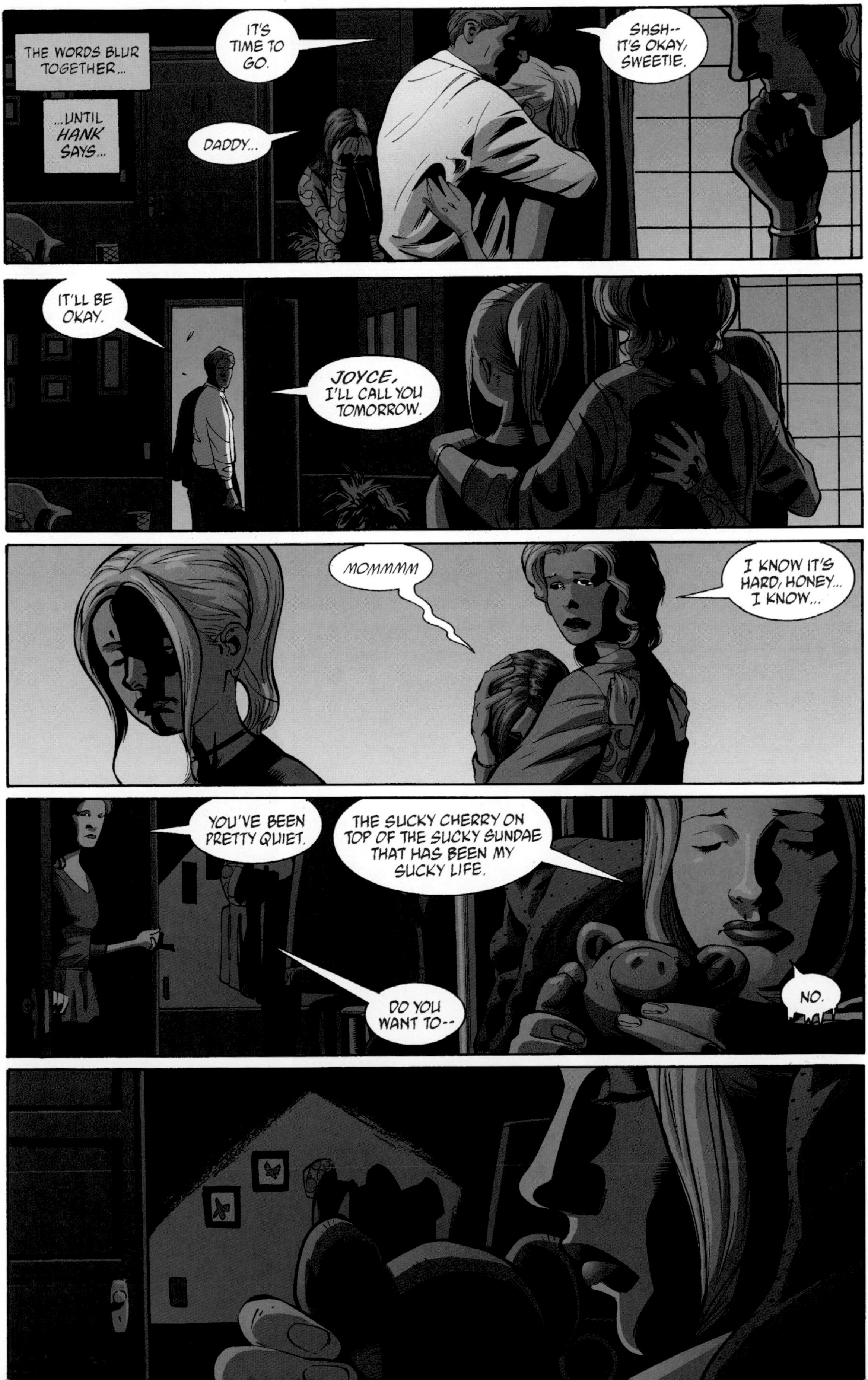
THE WORDS BLUR TOGETHER...
...UNTIL HANK SAYS...
IT'S TIME TO GO.
DADDY...
SHSH-- IT'S OKAY, SWEETIE.
IT'LL BE OKAY.
JOYCE, I'LL CALL YOU TOMORROW.
MOMMMM
I KNOW IT'S HARD, HONEY... I KNOW...
YOU'VE BEEN PRETTY QUIET.
THE SUCKY CHERRY ON TOP OF THE SUCKY SUNDAE THAT HAS BEEN MY SUCKY LIFE.
DO YOU WANT TO--
NO.

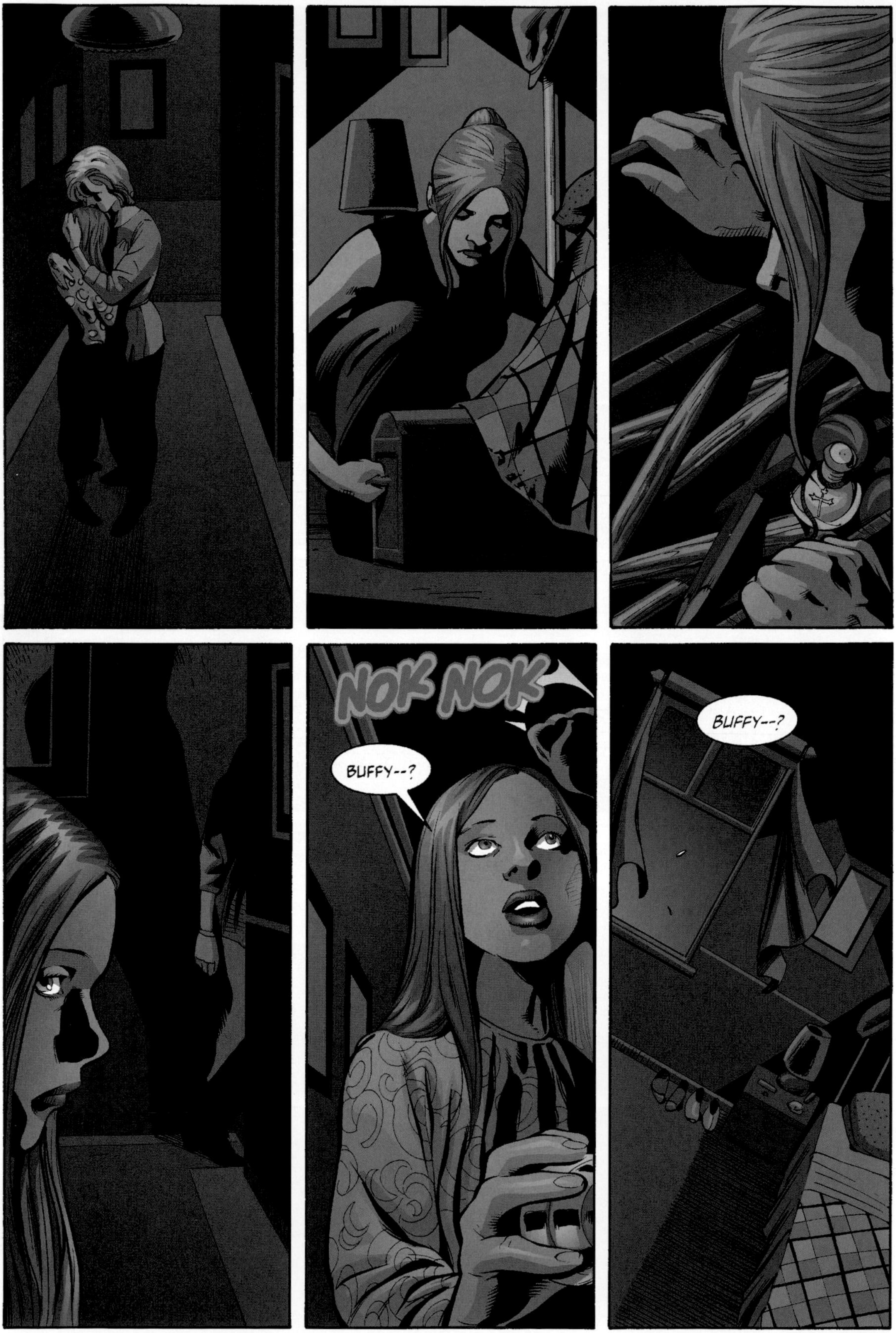
NOK NOK
BUFFY--?
BUFFY--?

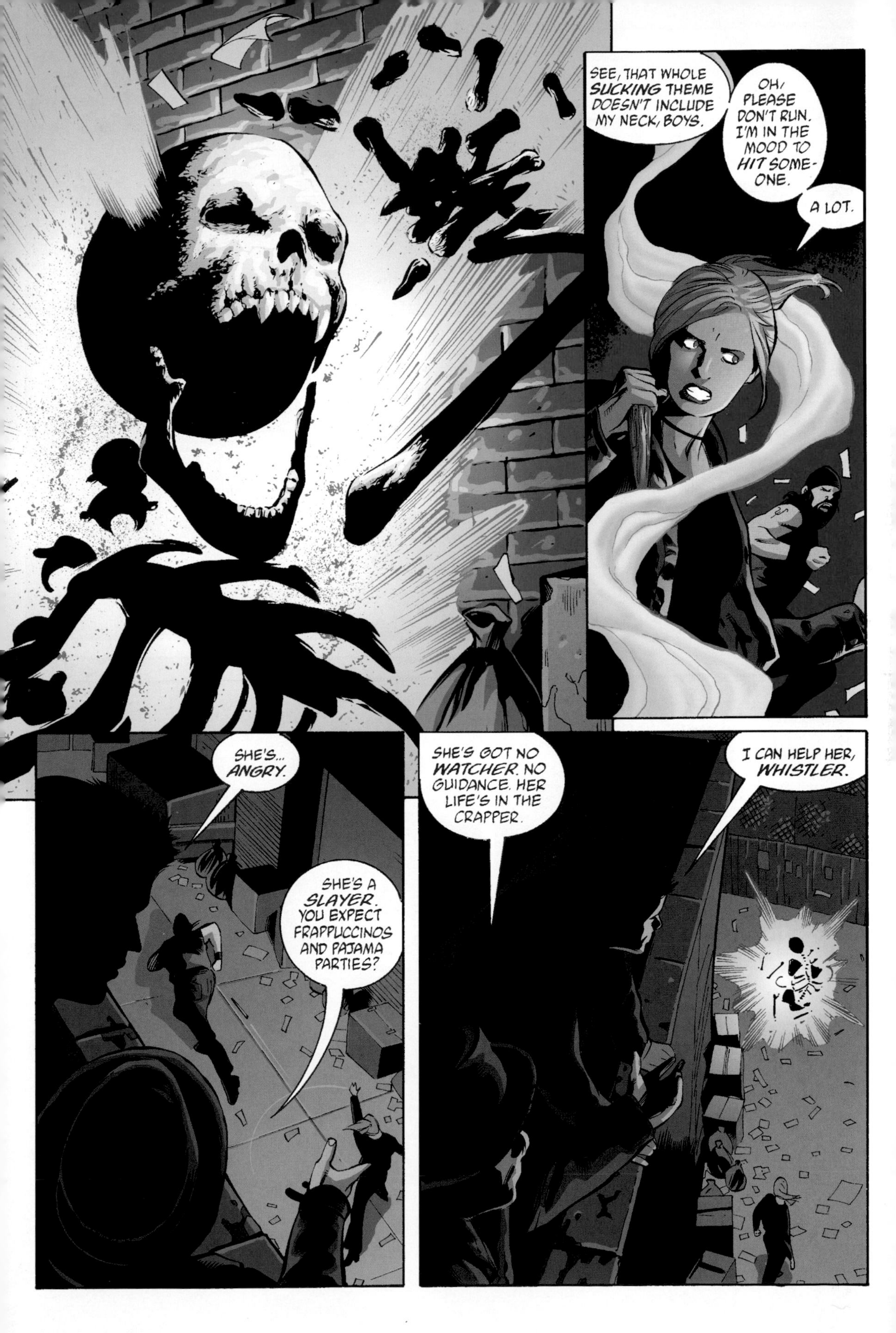
SEE, THAT WHOLE SUCKING THEME DOESN'T INCLUDE MY NECK, BOYS.
OH, PLEASE DON'T RUN. I'M IN THE MOOD TO HIT SOME-ONE.
A LOT.
SHE'S... ANGRY.
SHE'S A SLAYER. YOU EXPECT FRAPPUCCINOS AND PAJAMA PARTIES?
SHE'S GOT NO WATCHER. NO GUIDANCE. HER LIFE'S IN THE CRAPPER.
I CAN HELP HER, WHISTLER.

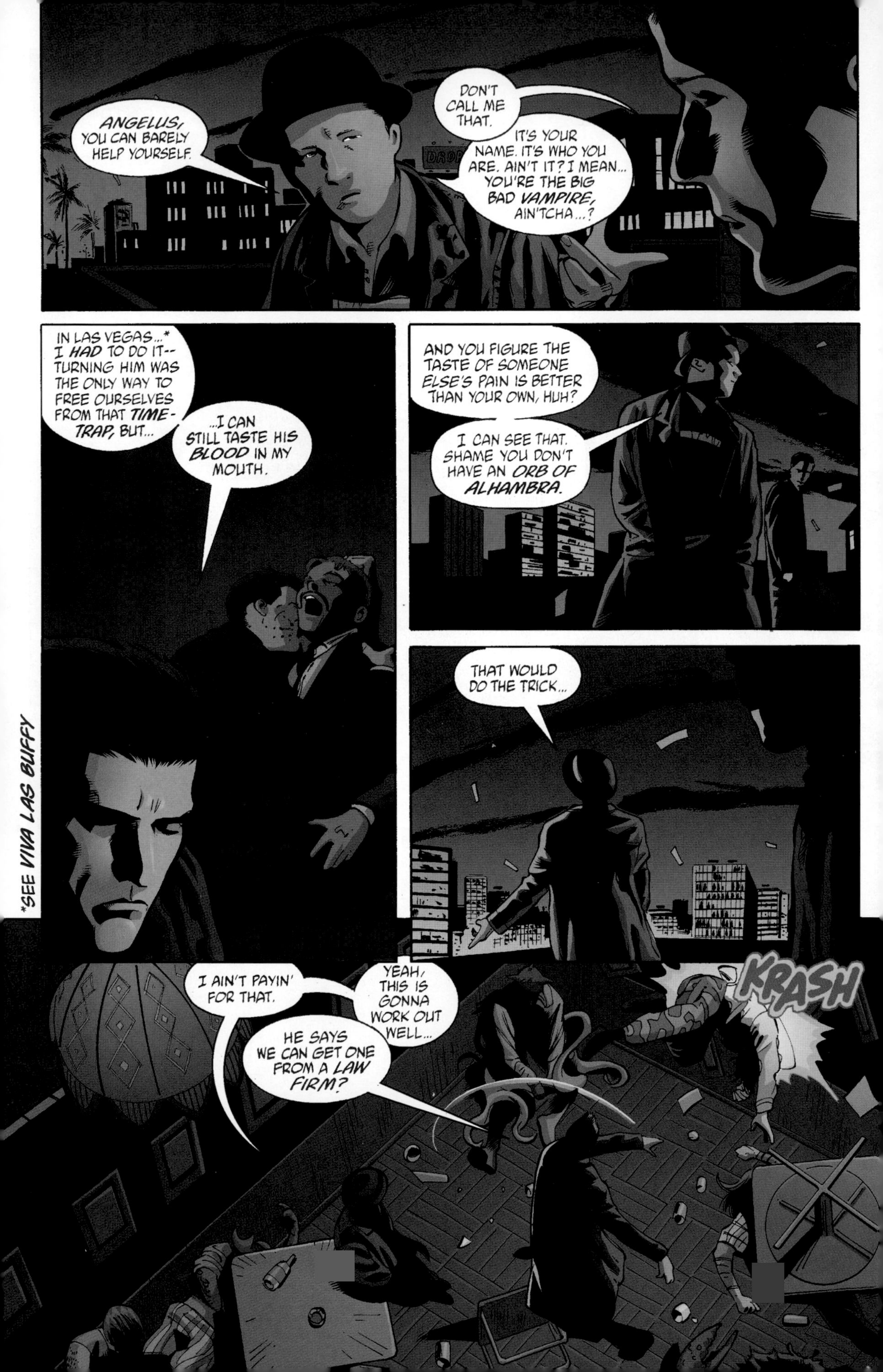
ANGELUS, YOU CAN BARELY HELP YOURSELF.
DON'T CALL ME THAT.
IT'S YOUR NAME. IT'S WHO YOU ARE. AIN'T IT? I MEAN... YOU'RE THE BIG BAD VAMPIRE, AIN'TCHA...?
IN LAS VEGAS...* I HAD TO DO IT-- TURNING HIM WAS THE ONLY WAY TO FREE OURSELVES FROM THAT TIME-TRAP, BUT...
...I CAN STILL TASTE HIS BLOOD IN MY MOUTH.
AND YOU FIGURE THE TASTE OF SOMEONE ELSE'S PAIN IS BETTER THAN YOUR OWN, HUH?
I CAN SEE THAT. SHAME YOU DON'T HAVE AN ORB OF ALHAMBRA.
THAT WOULD DO THE TRICK...
I AIN'T PAYIN' FOR THAT.
YEAH, THIS IS GONNA WORK OUT WELL...
HE SAYS WE CAN GET ONE FROM A LAW FIRM?
KRASH

*SEE VIVA LAS BUFFY

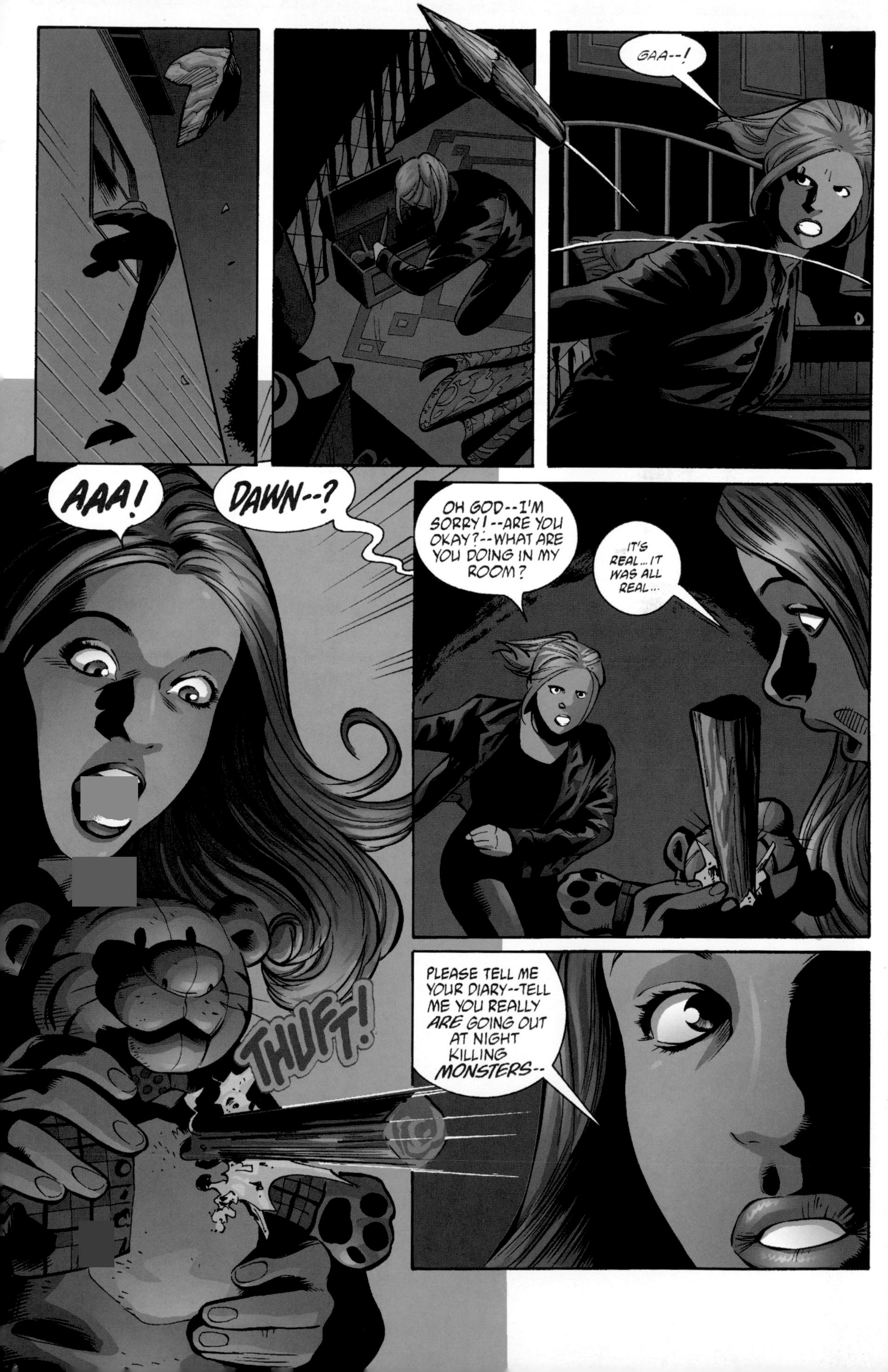
GAA--!
AAA!
DAWN--?
OH GOD--I'M SORRY!--ARE YOU OKAY?--WHAT ARE YOU DOING IN MY ROOM?
IT'S REAL...IT WAS ALL REAL...
THUFT!
PLEASE TELL ME YOUR DIARY--TELL ME YOU REALLY *ARE* GOING OUT AT NIGHT KILLING *MONSTERS*--

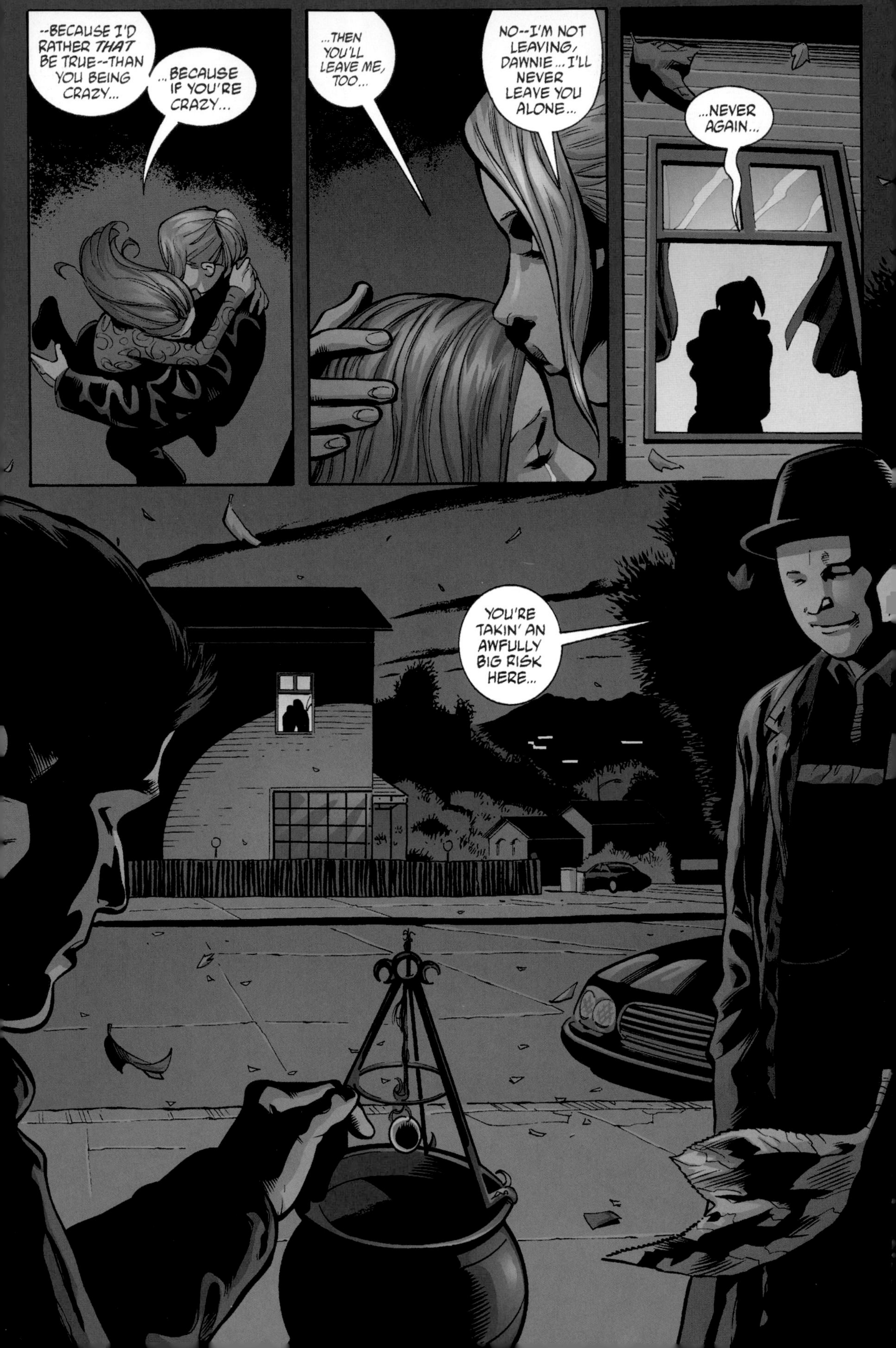
--BECAUSE I'D RATHER *THAT* BE TRUE--THAN YOU BEING CRAZY...
...BECAUSE IF YOU'RE CRAZY...
...THEN YOU'LL LEAVE ME, TOO...
NO--I'M NOT LEAVING, DAWNIE... I'LL NEVER LEAVE YOU ALONE...
...NEVER AGAIN...
YOU'RE TAKIN' AN AWFULLY BIG RISK HERE...

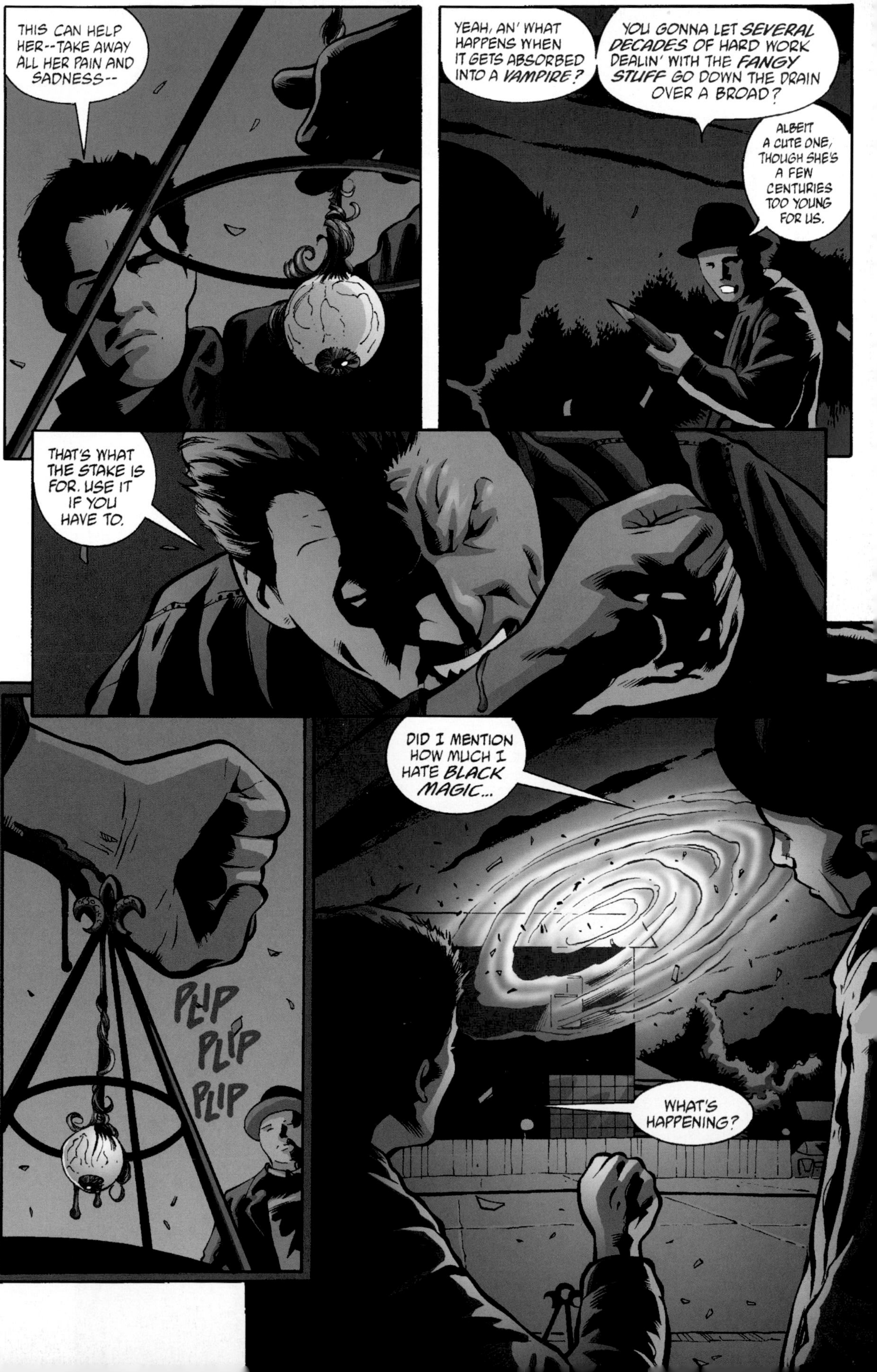
THIS CAN HELP HER--TAKE AWAY ALL HER PAIN AND SADNESS--
YEAH, AN' WHAT HAPPENS WHEN IT GETS ABSORBED INTO A VAMPIRE?
YOU GONNA LET SEVERAL DECADES OF HARD WORK DEALIN' WITH THE FANGY STUFF GO DOWN THE DRAIN OVER A BROAD?
ALBEIT A CUTE ONE, THOUGH SHE'S A FEW CENTURIES TOO YOUNG FOR US.
THAT'S WHAT THE STAKE IS FOR. USE IT IF YOU HAVE TO.
PLIP PLIP PLIP
DID I MENTION HOW MUCH I HATE BLACK MAGIC...
WHAT'S HAPPENING?

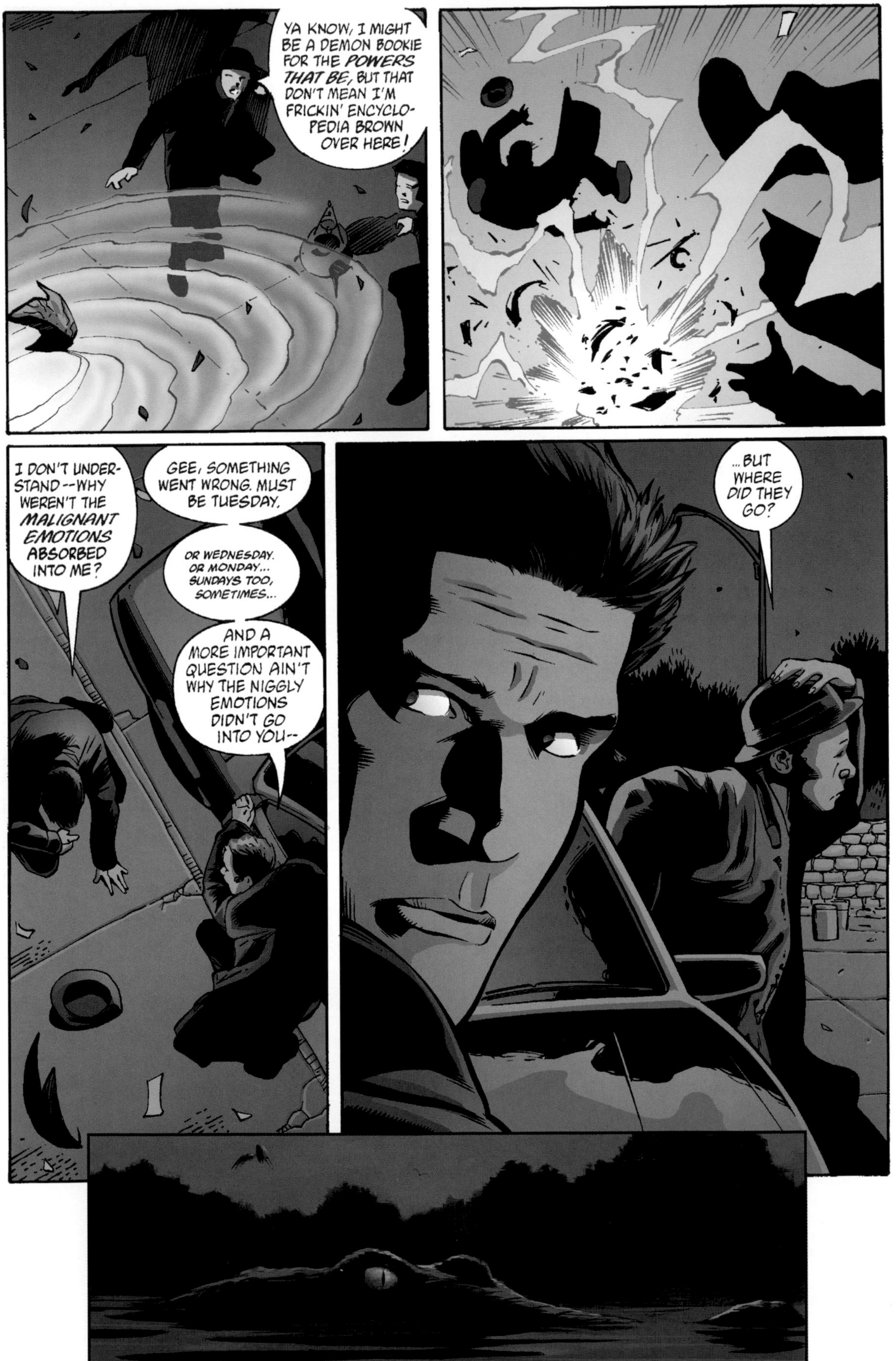
YA KNOW, I MIGHT BE A DEMON BOOKIE FOR THE *POWERS THAT BE*, BUT THAT DON'T MEAN I'M FRICKIN' ENCYCLOPEDIA BROWN OVER HERE!
I DON'T UNDERSTAND--WHY WEREN'T THE *MALIGNANT EMOTIONS* ABSORBED INTO ME?
GEE, SOMETHING WENT WRONG. MUST BE TUESDAY.
OR WEDNESDAY. OR MONDAY... SUNDAYS TOO, SOMETIMES...
AND A MORE IMPORTANT QUESTION AIN'T WHY THE NIGGLY EMOTIONS DIDN'T GO INTO YOU--
...BUT WHERE DID THEY GO?

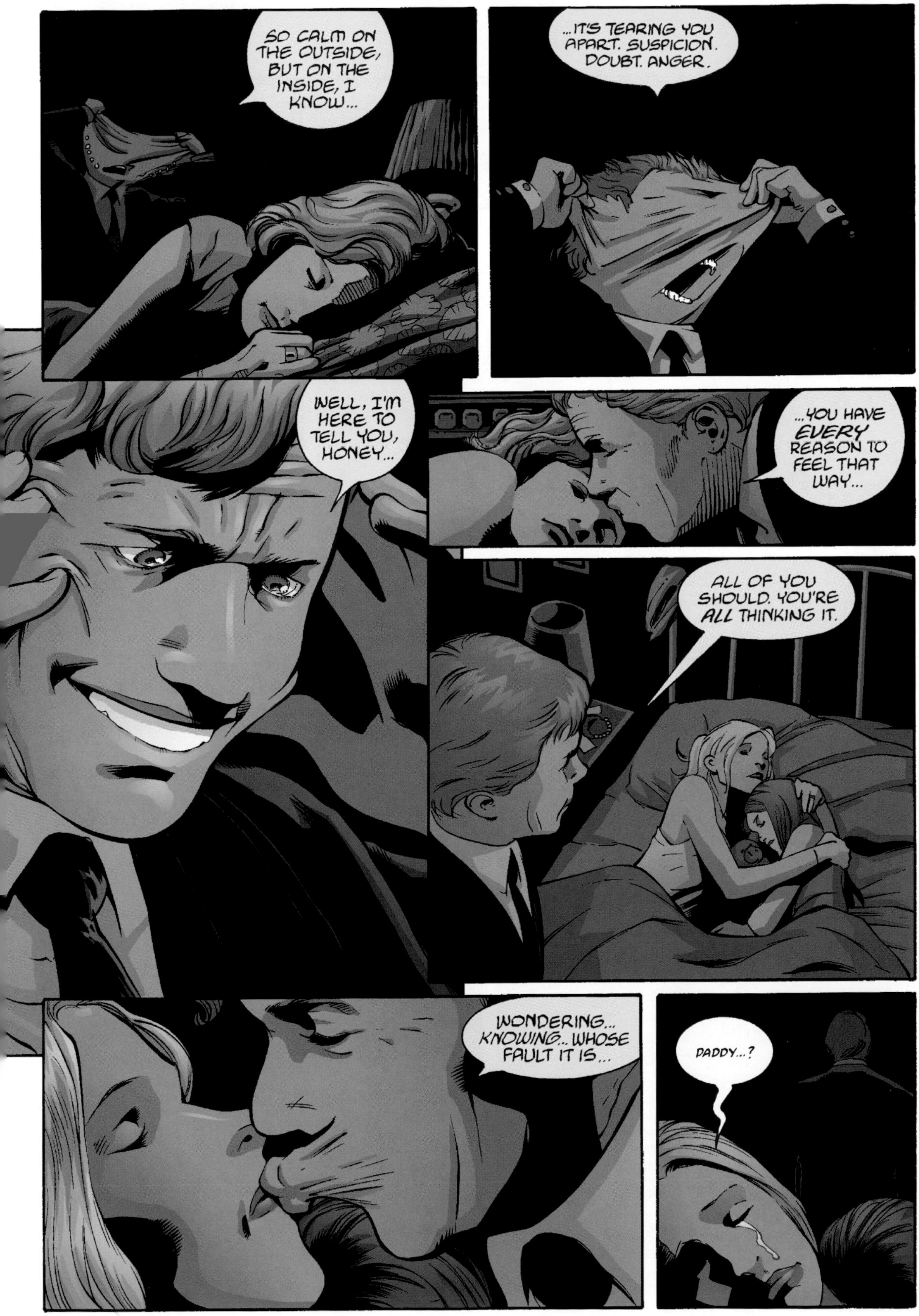
SO CALM ON THE OUTSIDE, BUT ON THE INSIDE, I KNOW...
...IT'S TEARING YOU APART. SUSPICION. DOUBT. ANGER.
WELL, I'M HERE TO TELL YOU, HONEY...
...YOU HAVE EVERY REASON TO FEEL THAT WAY...
ALL OF YOU SHOULD. YOU'RE ALL THINKING IT.
WONDERING... KNOWING... WHOSE FAULT IT IS...
DADDY...?

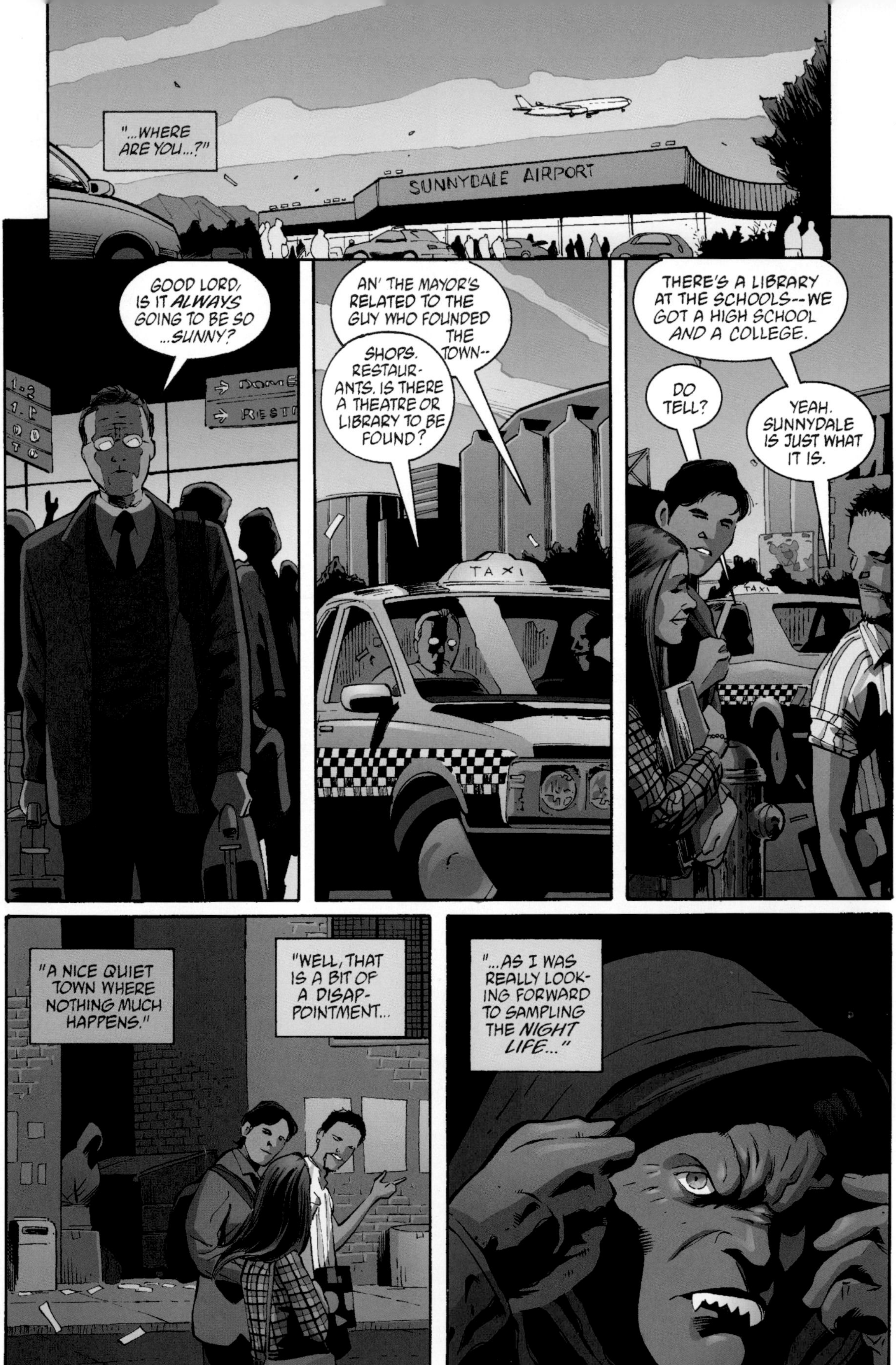
"...WHERE ARE YOU...?"
SUNNYDALE AIRPORT
GOOD LORD, IS IT ALWAYS GOING TO BE SO ...SUNNY?
AN' THE MAYOR'S RELATED TO THE GUY WHO FOUNDED THE TOWN--
SHOPS. RESTAUR-ANTS. IS THERE A THEATRE OR LIBRARY TO BE FOUND?
TAXI
THERE'S A LIBRARY AT THE SCHOOLS--WE GOT A HIGH SCHOOL AND A COLLEGE.
DO TELL?
YEAH. SUNNYDALE IS JUST WHAT IT IS.
"A NICE QUIET TOWN WHERE NOTHING MUCH HAPPENS."
"WELL, THAT IS A BIT OF A DISAP-POINTMENT...
"...AS I WAS REALLY LOOK-ING FORWARD TO SAMPLING THE NIGHT LIFE..."

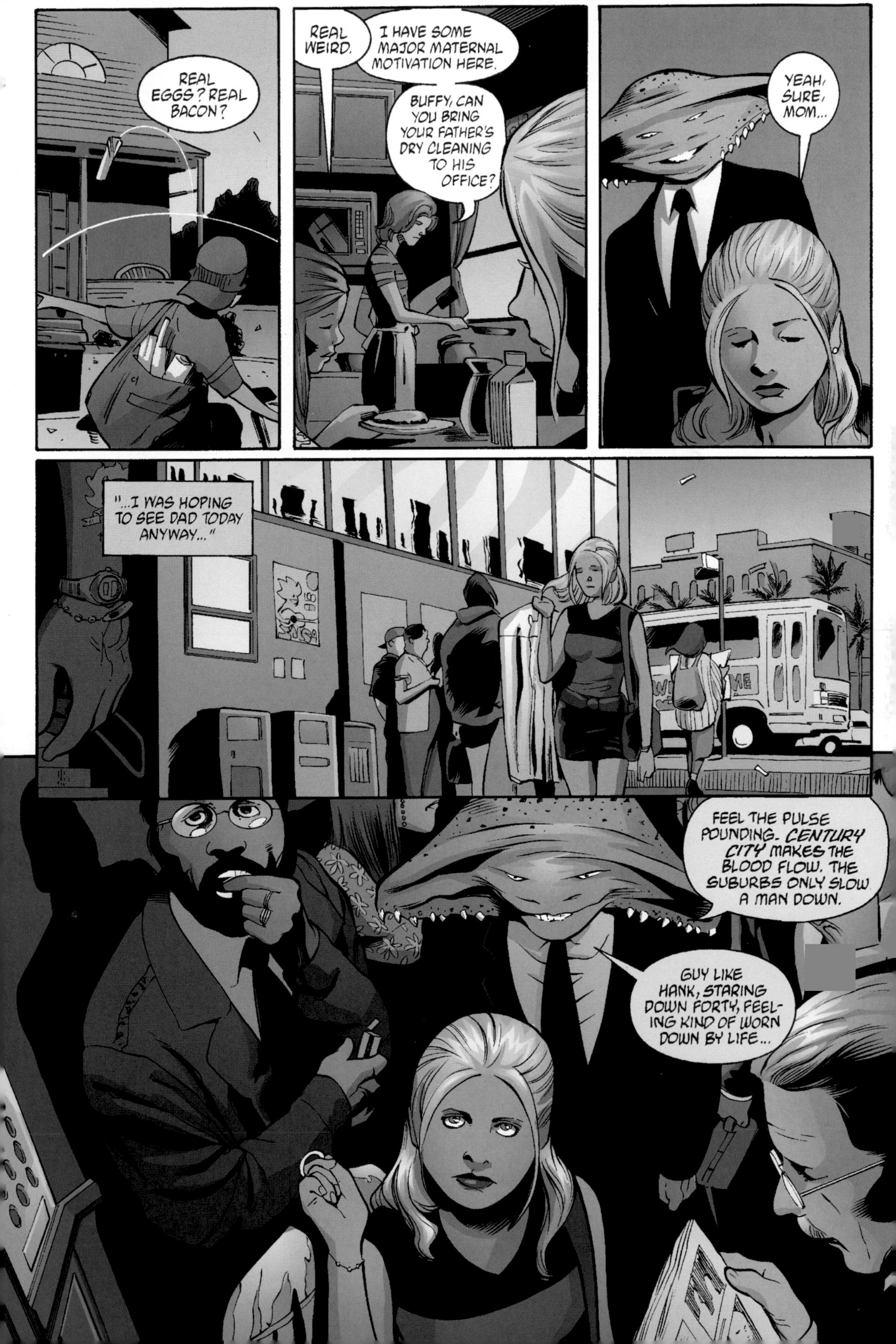
REAL EGGS? REAL BACON?
REAL WEIRD.
I HAVE SOME MAJOR MATERNAL MOTIVATION HERE.
BUFFY, CAN YOU BRING YOUR FATHER'S DRY CLEANING TO HIS OFFICE?
YEAH, SURE, MOM...
"...I WAS HOPING TO SEE DAD TODAY ANYWAY..."
FEEL THE PULSE POUNDING. CENTURY CITY MAKES THE BLOOD FLOW. THE SUBURBS ONLY SLOW A MAN DOWN.
GUY LIKE HANK, STARING DOWN FORTY, FEEL-ING KIND OF WORN DOWN BY LIFE...

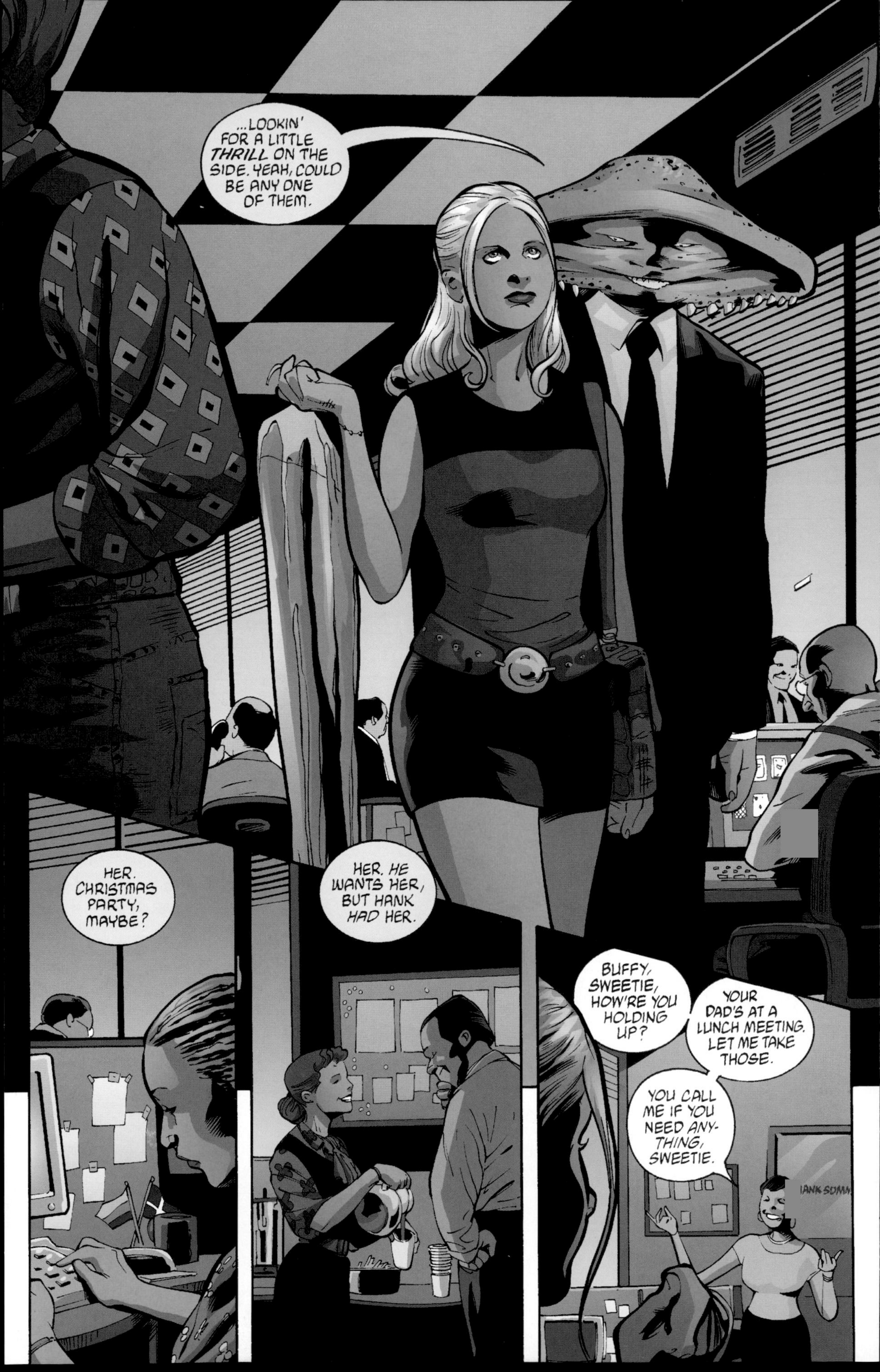
...LOOKIN' FOR A LITTLE *THRILL* ON THE SIDE. YEAH, COULD BE ANY ONE OF THEM.
HER. CHRISTMAS PARTY, MAYBE?
HER. *HE* WANTS HER, BUT HANK *HAD* HER.
BUFFY, SWEETIE, HOW'RE YOU HOLDING UP?
YOUR DAD'S AT A LUNCH MEETING. LET ME TAKE THOSE.
YOU CALL ME IF YOU NEED *ANY-THING*, SWEETIE.

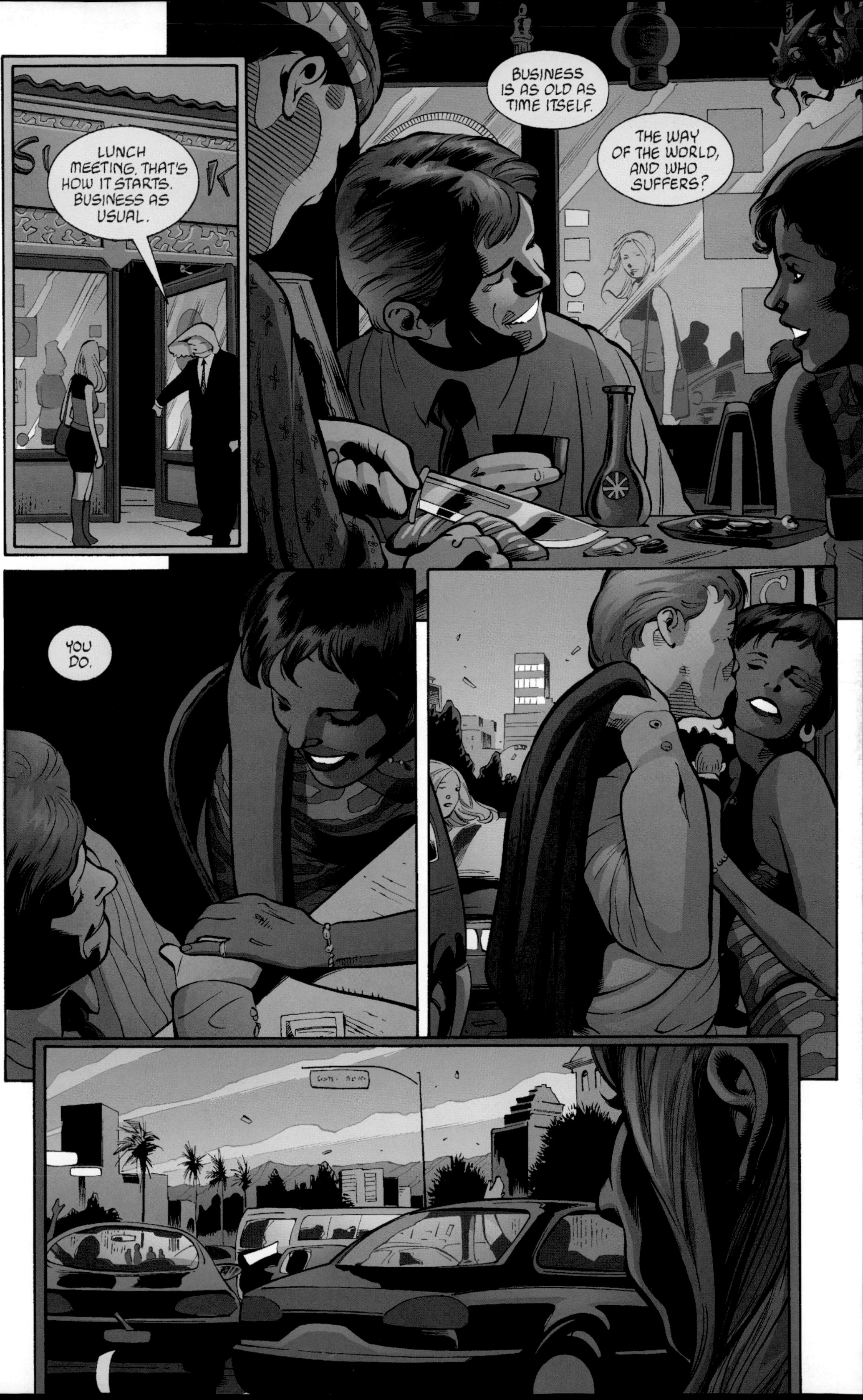
LUNCH MEETING. THAT'S HOW IT STARTS. BUSINESS AS USUAL.
BUSINESS IS AS OLD AS TIME ITSELF.
THE WAY OF THE WORLD, AND WHO SUFFERS?
YOU DO.

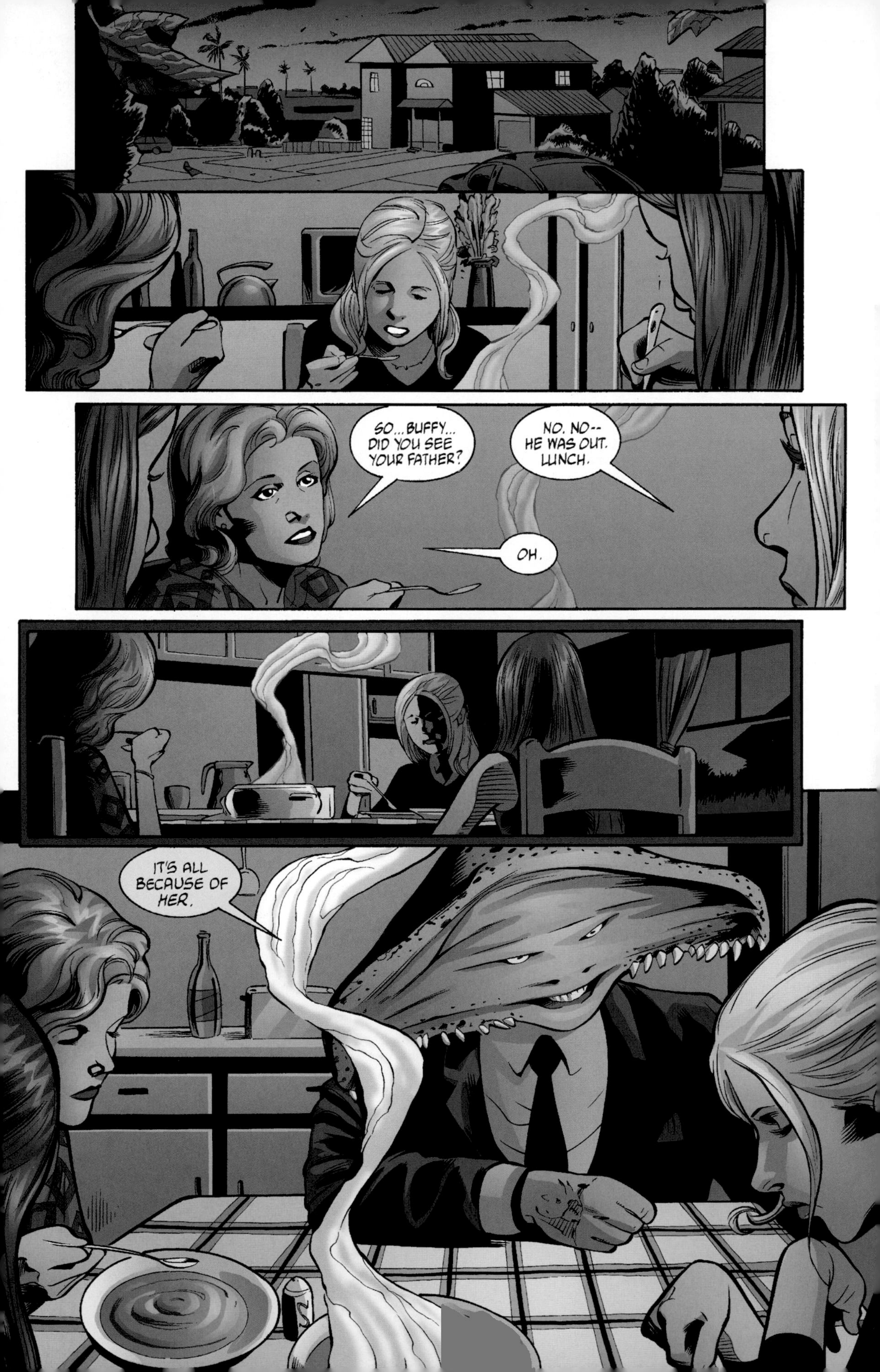
SO...BUFFY...
DID YOU SEE
YOUR FATHER?
NO. NO--
HE WAS OUT.
LUNCH.
OH.
IT'S ALL
BECAUSE OF
HER.

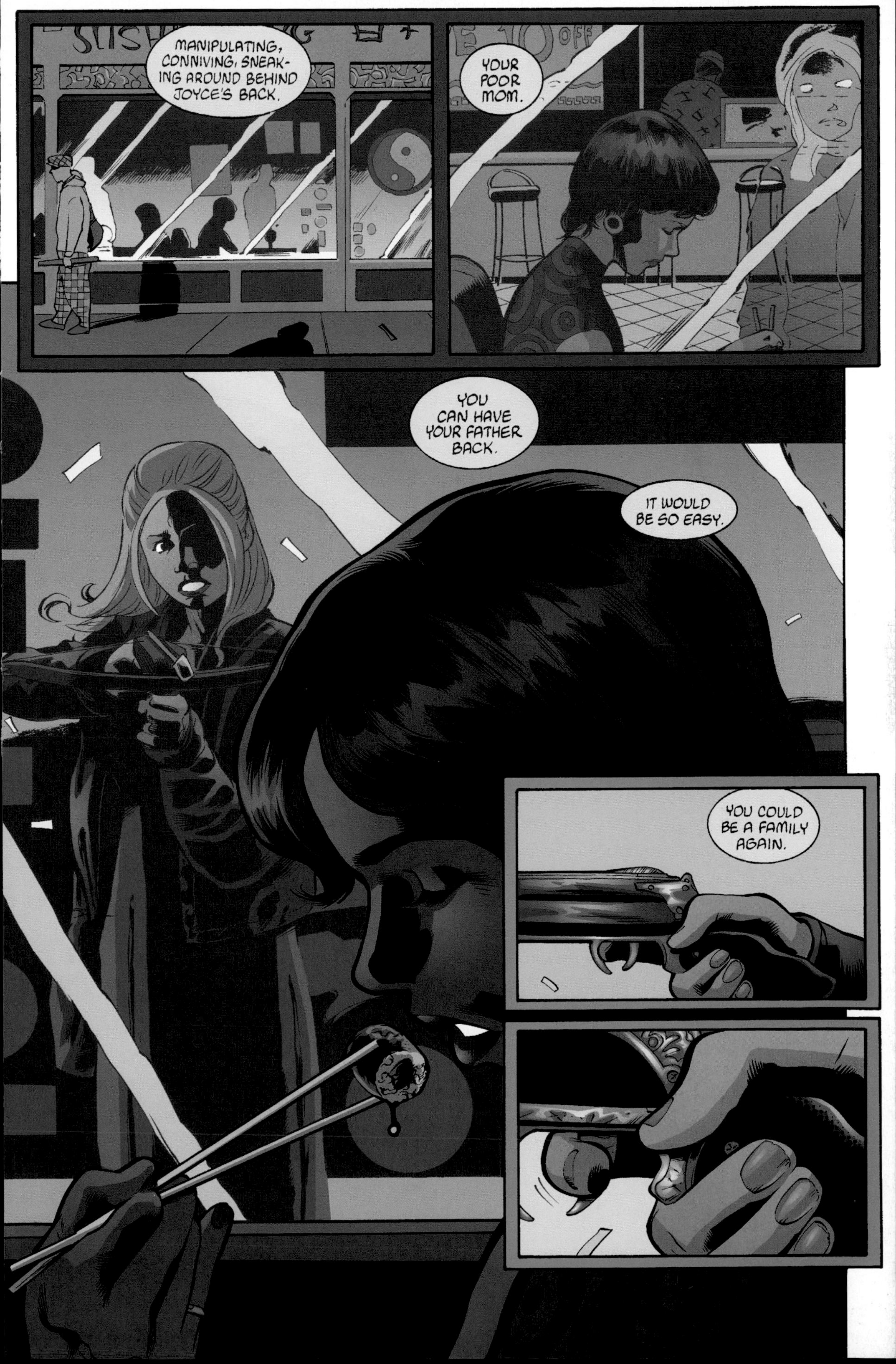
MANIPULATING, CONNIVING, SNEAK-ING AROUND BEHIND JOYCE'S BACK.
YOUR POOR MOM.
YOU CAN HAVE YOUR FATHER BACK.
IT WOULD BE SO EASY.
YOU COULD BE A FAMILY AGAIN.

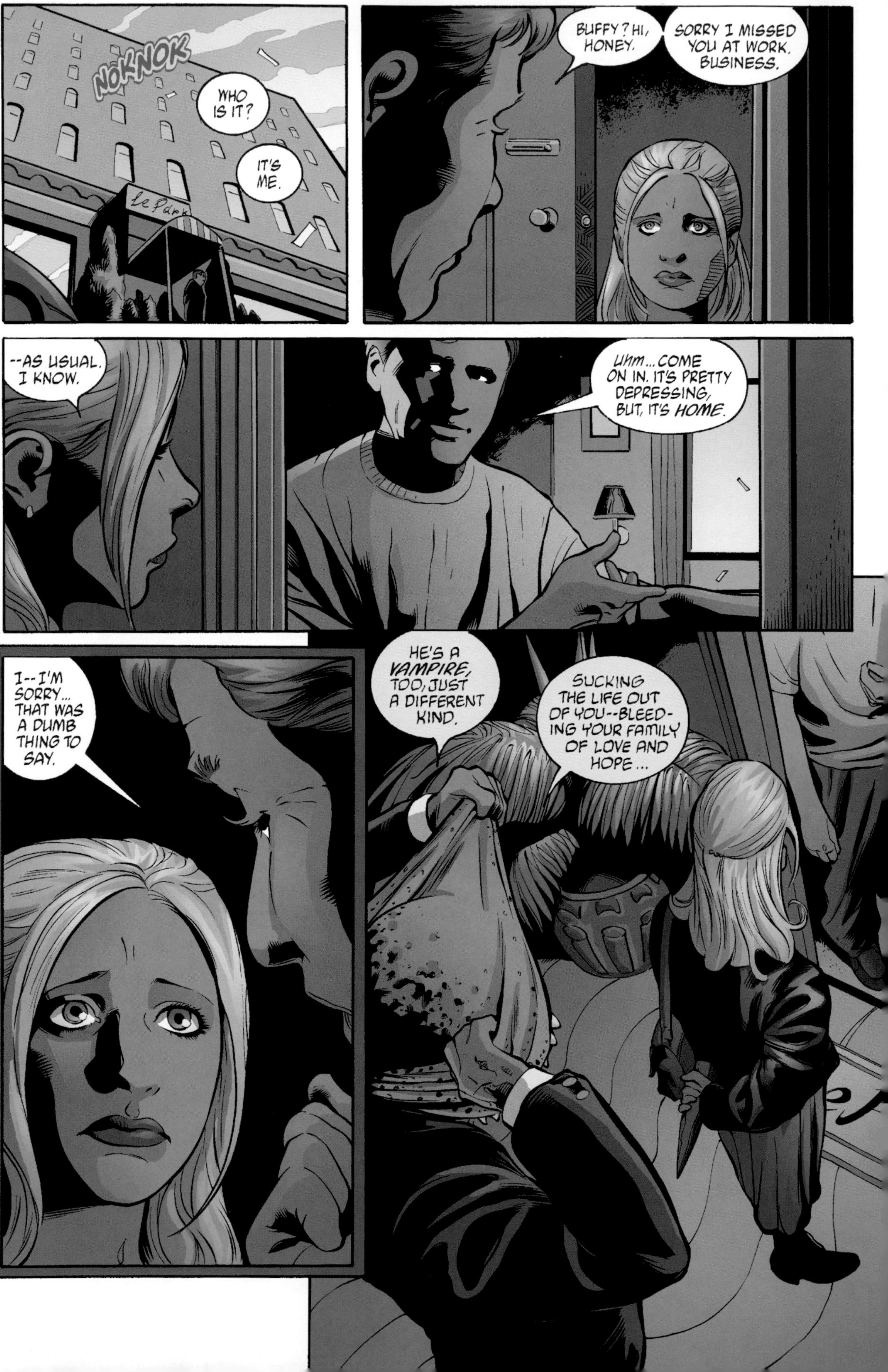
NOKNOK
WHO IS IT?
IT'S ME.
le Park
BUFFY? HI, HONEY.
SORRY I MISSED YOU AT WORK. BUSINESS.
--AS USUAL. I KNOW.
UHM... COME ON IN. IT'S PRETTY DEPRESSING, BUT, IT'S *HOME*.
I--I'M SORRY... THAT WAS A DUMB THING TO SAY.
HE'S A *VAMPIRE*, TOO, JUST A DIFFERENT KIND.
SUCKING THE LIFE OUT OF YOU--BLEEDING YOUR FAMILY OF LOVE AND HOPE...

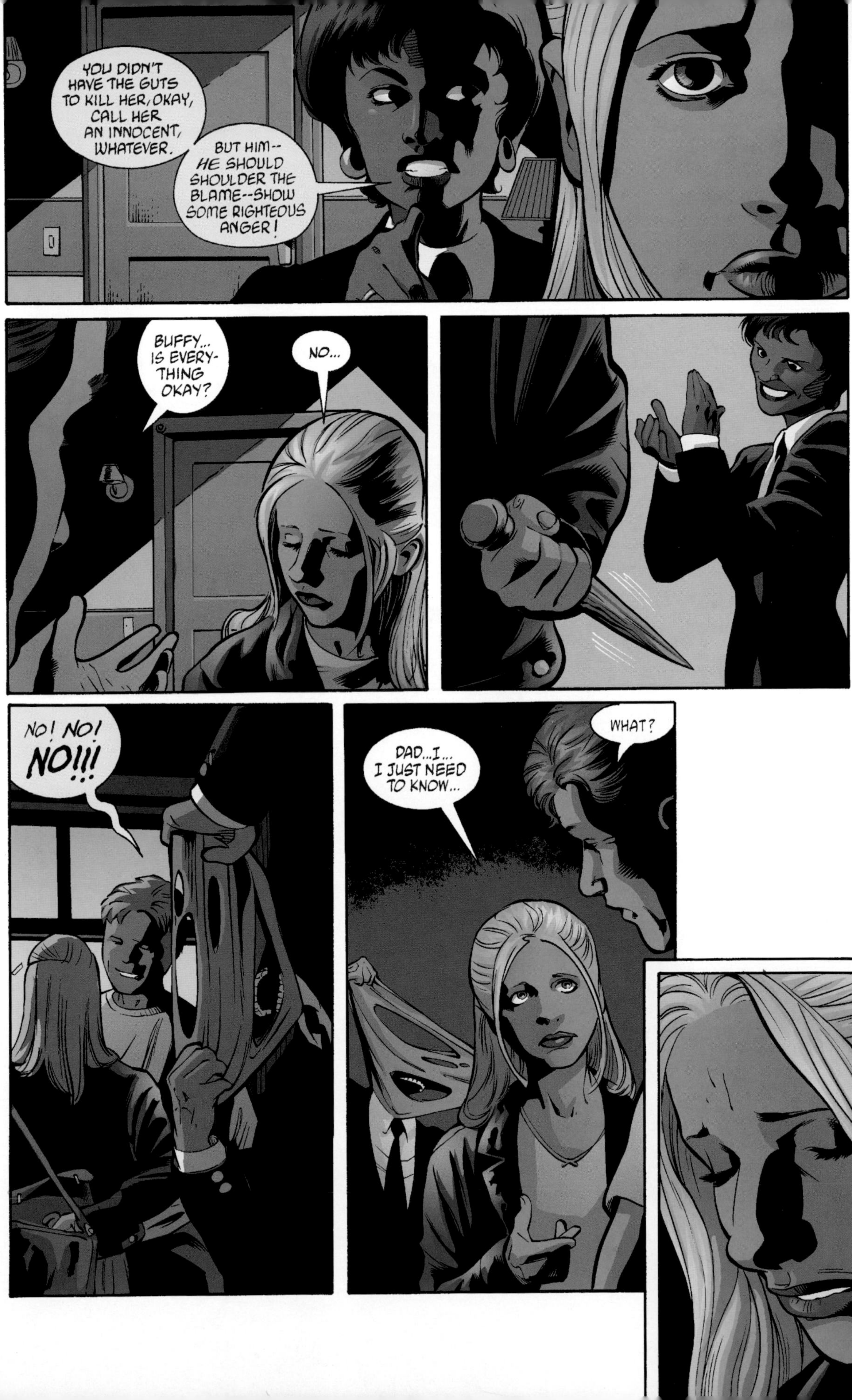
YOU DIDN'T HAVE THE GUTS TO KILL HER, OKAY, CALL HER AN INNOCENT, WHATEVER.
BUT HIM-- HE SHOULD SHOULDER THE BLAME--SHOW SOME RIGHTEOUS ANGER!
BUFFY... IS EVERY-THING OKAY?
NO...
NO! NO! NO!!!
DAD...I... I JUST NEED TO KNOW...
WHAT?

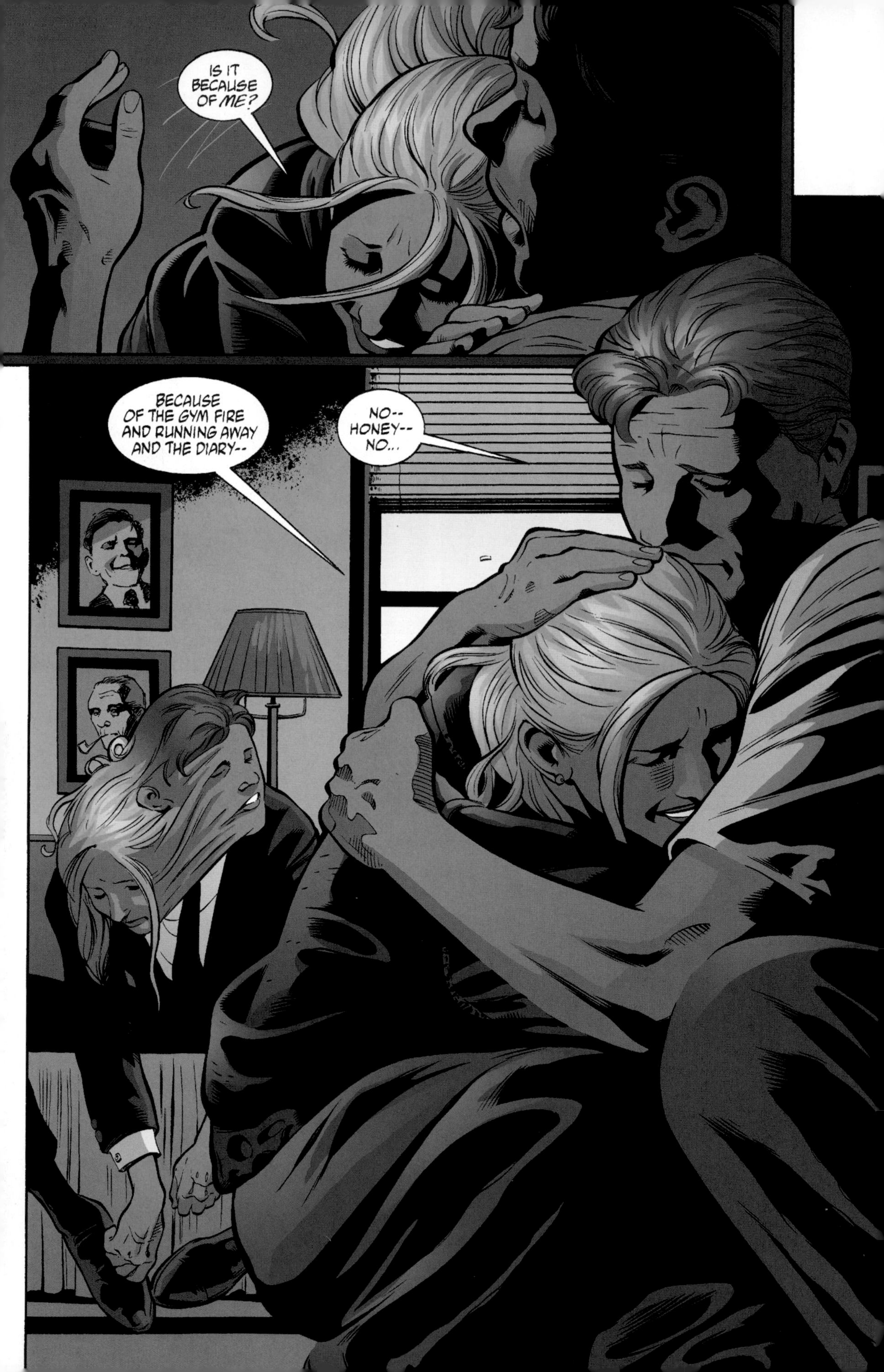
IS IT BECAUSE OF *ME*?
BECAUSE OF THE GYM FIRE AND RUNNING AWAY AND THE DIARY--
NO-- HONEY-- NO...

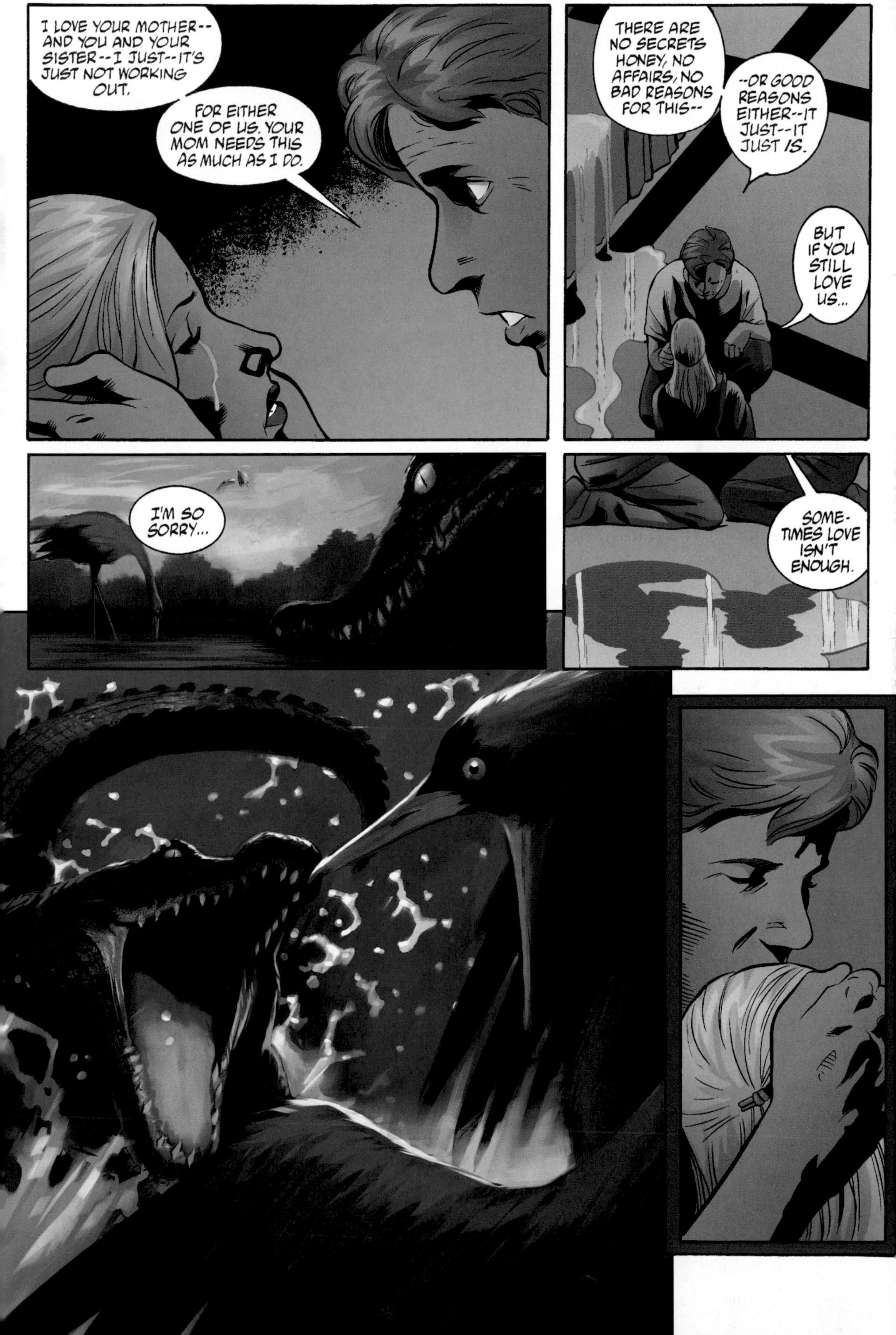
I LOVE YOUR MOTHER--AND YOU AND YOUR SISTER--I JUST--IT'S JUST NOT WORKING OUT.
FOR EITHER ONE OF US. YOUR MOM NEEDS THIS AS MUCH AS I DO.
THERE ARE NO SECRETS HONEY, NO AFFAIRS, NO BAD REASONS FOR THIS--
--OR GOOD REASONS EITHER--IT JUST--IT JUST *IS*.
BUT IF YOU STILL LOVE US...
I'M SO SORRY...
SOME-TIMES LOVE ISN'T ENOUGH.

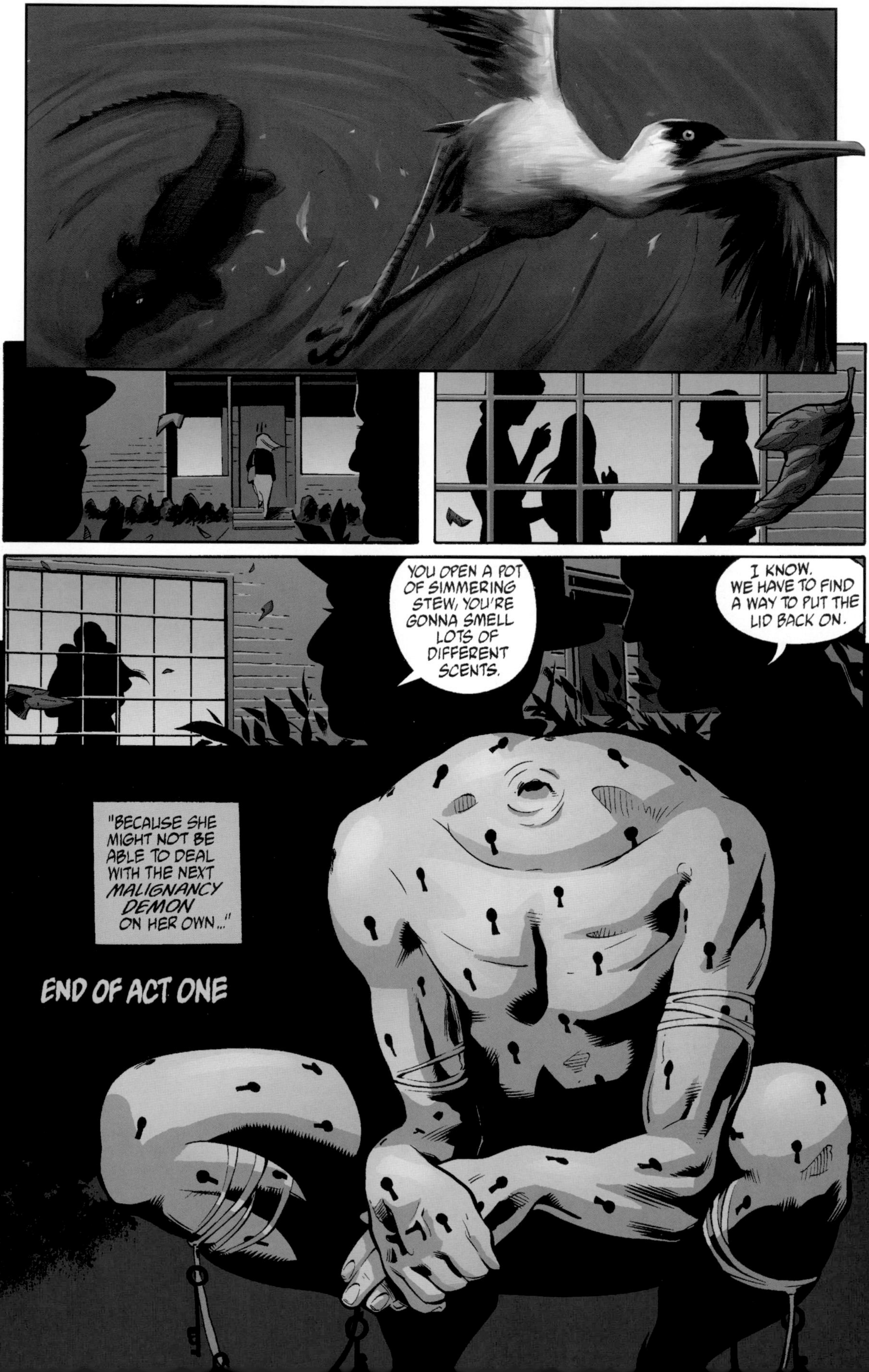
YOU OPEN A POT OF SIMMERING STEW, YOU'RE GONNA SMELL LOTS OF DIFFERENT SCENTS.
I KNOW. WE HAVE TO FIND A WAY TO PUT THE LID BACK ON.
"BECAUSE SHE MIGHT NOT BE ABLE TO DEAL WITH THE NEXT *MALIGNANCY DEMON* ON HER OWN..."
END OF ACT ONE

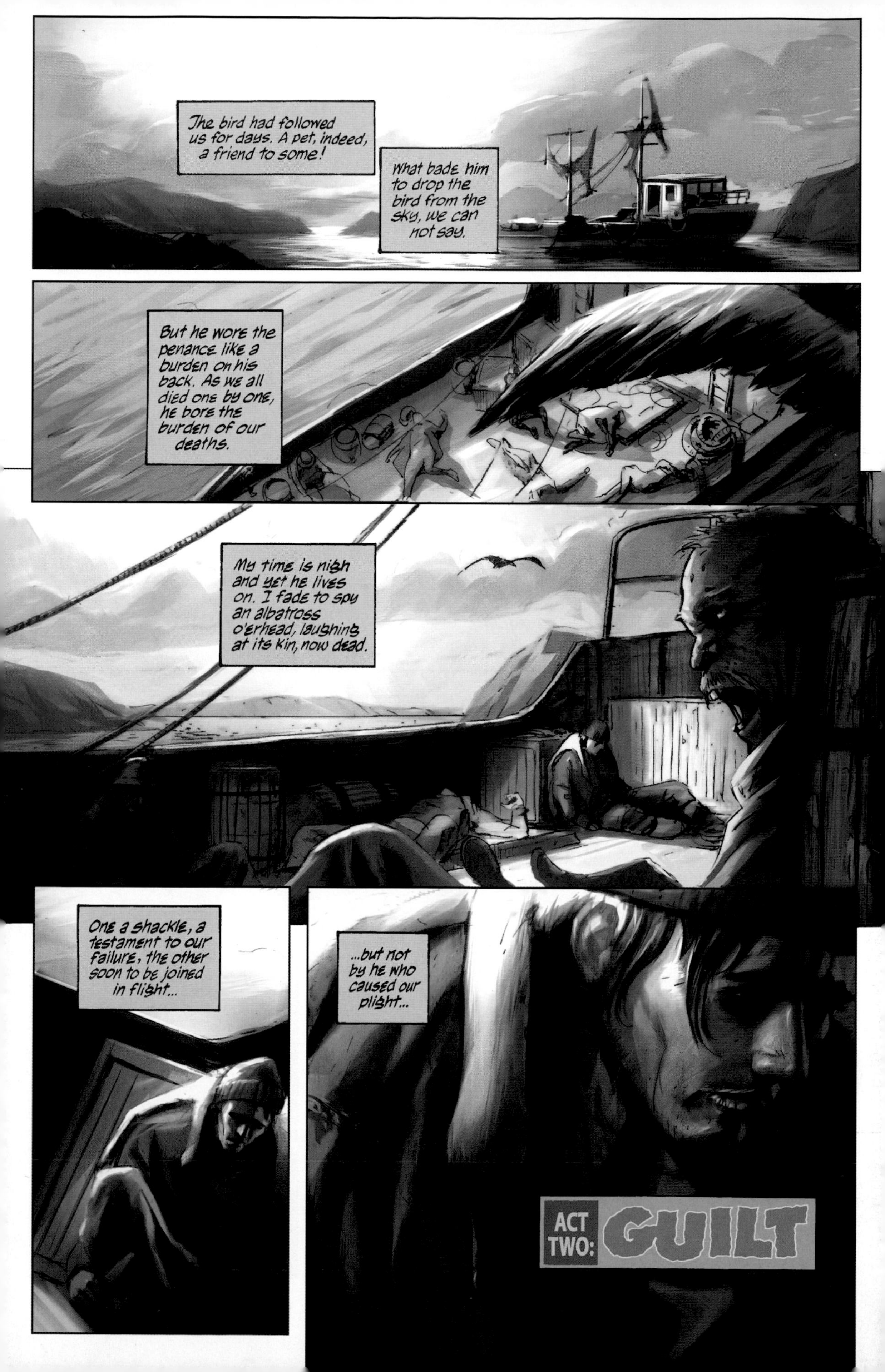
The bird had followed us for days. A pet, indeed, a friend to some!
What bade him to drop the bird from the sky, we can not say.
But he wore the penance like a burden on his back. As we all died one by one, he bore the burden of our deaths.
My time is nigh and yet he lives on. I fade to spy an albatross o'erhead, laughing at its kin, now dead.
One a shackle, a testament to our failure, the other soon to be joined in flight...
...but not by he who caused our plight...
ACT TWO: GUILT

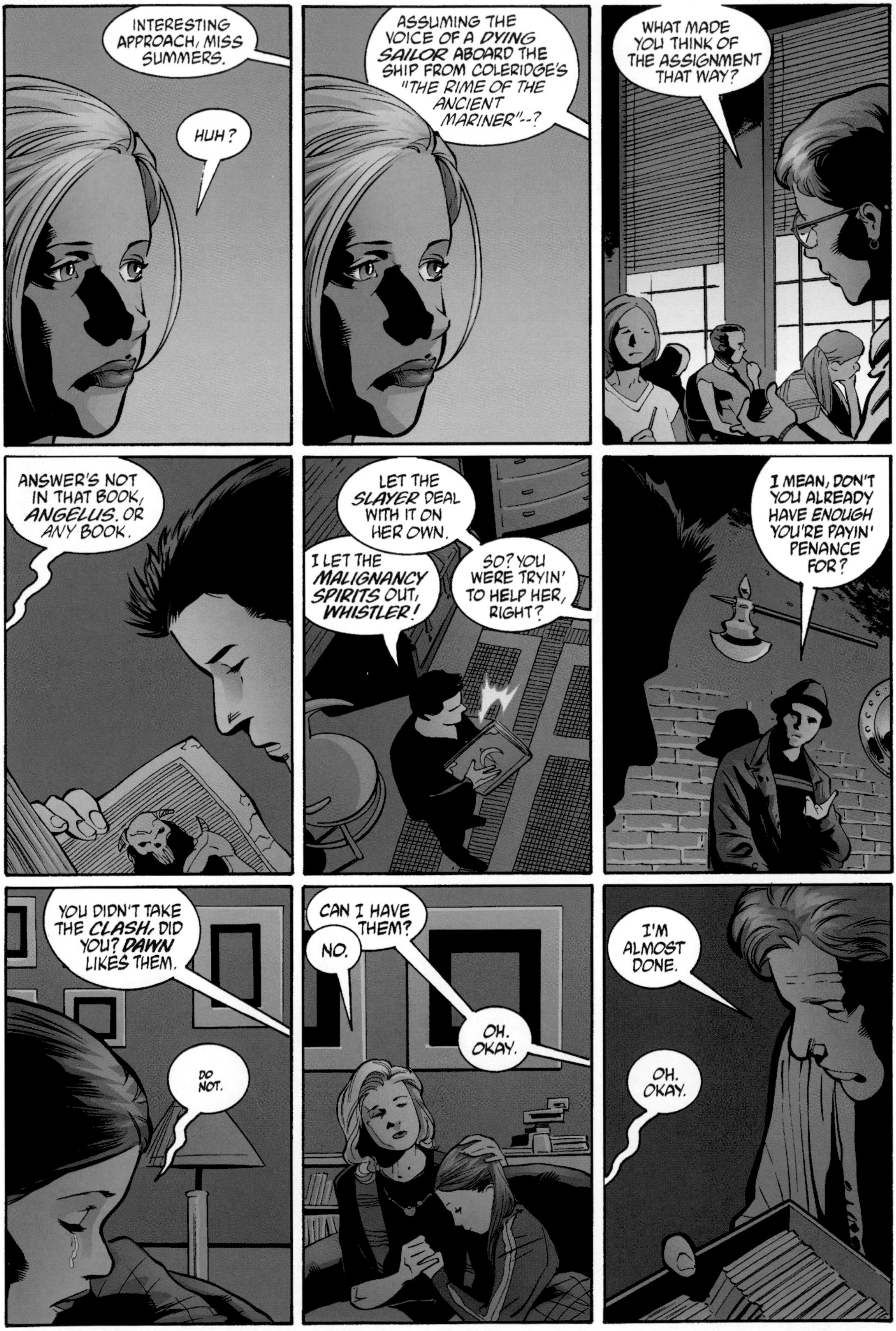
INTERESTING APPROACH, MISS SUMMERS.
HUH?
ASSUMING THE VOICE OF A DYING SAILOR ABOARD THE SHIP FROM COLERIDGE'S "THE RIME OF THE ANCIENT MARINER"--?
WHAT MADE YOU THINK OF THE ASSIGNMENT THAT WAY?
ANSWER'S NOT IN THAT BOOK, ANGELUS. OR ANY BOOK.
LET THE SLAYER DEAL WITH IT ON HER OWN.
I LET THE MALIGNANCY SPIRITS OUT, WHISTLER!
SO? YOU WERE TRYIN' TO HELP HER, RIGHT?
I MEAN, DON'T YOU ALREADY HAVE ENOUGH YOU'RE PAYIN' PENANCE FOR?
YOU DIDN'T TAKE THE CLASH, DID YOU? DAWN LIKES THEM.
DO NOT.
CAN I HAVE THEM?
NO.
OH. OKAY.
I'M ALMOST DONE.
OH. OKAY.

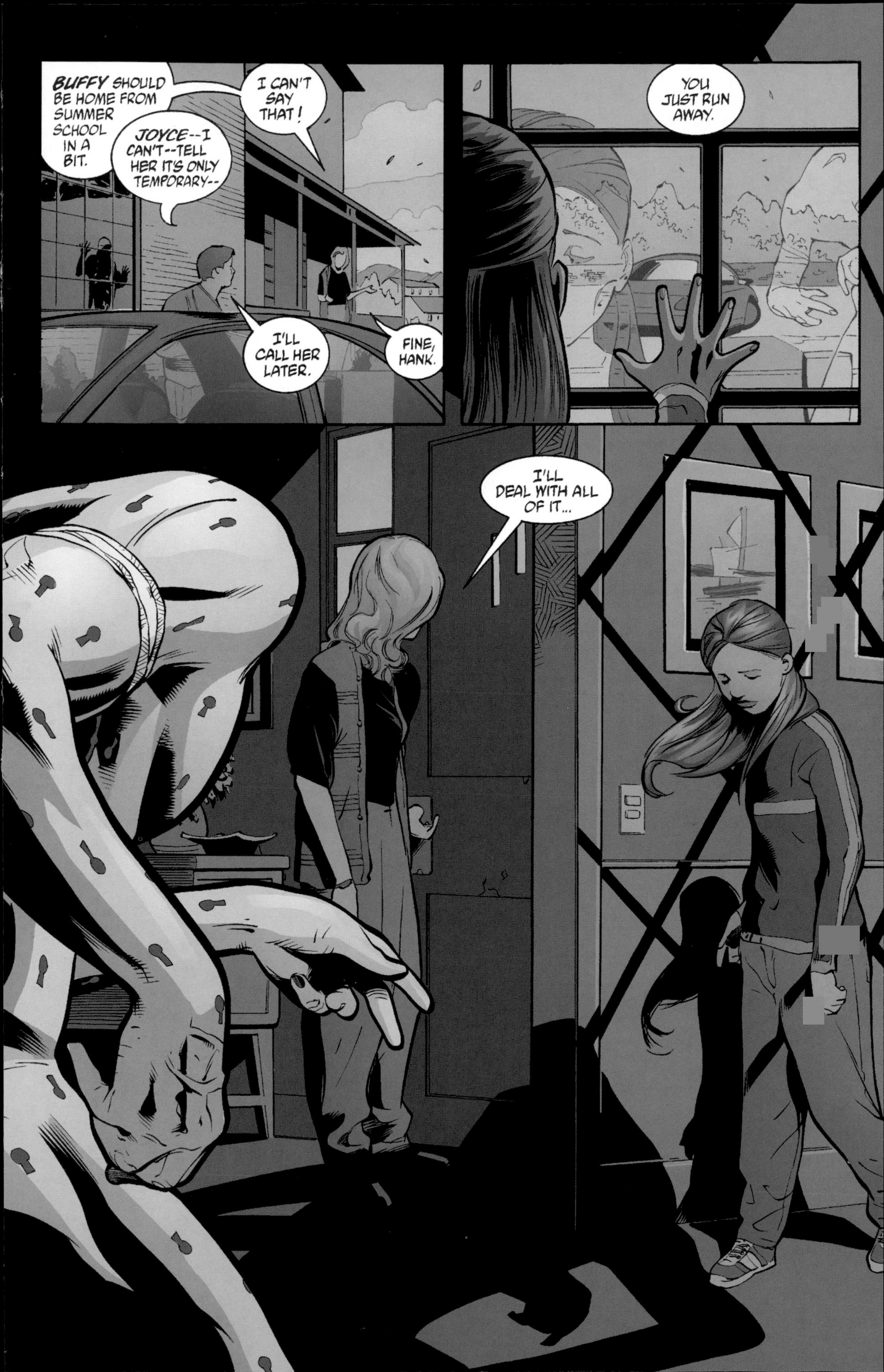
BUFFY SHOULD BE HOME FROM SUMMER SCHOOL IN A BIT.
I CAN'T SAY THAT!
JOYCE--I CAN'T--TELL HER IT'S ONLY TEMPORARY--
I'LL CALL HER LATER.
FINE, HANK.
YOU JUST RUN AWAY.
I'LL DEAL WITH ALL OF IT...

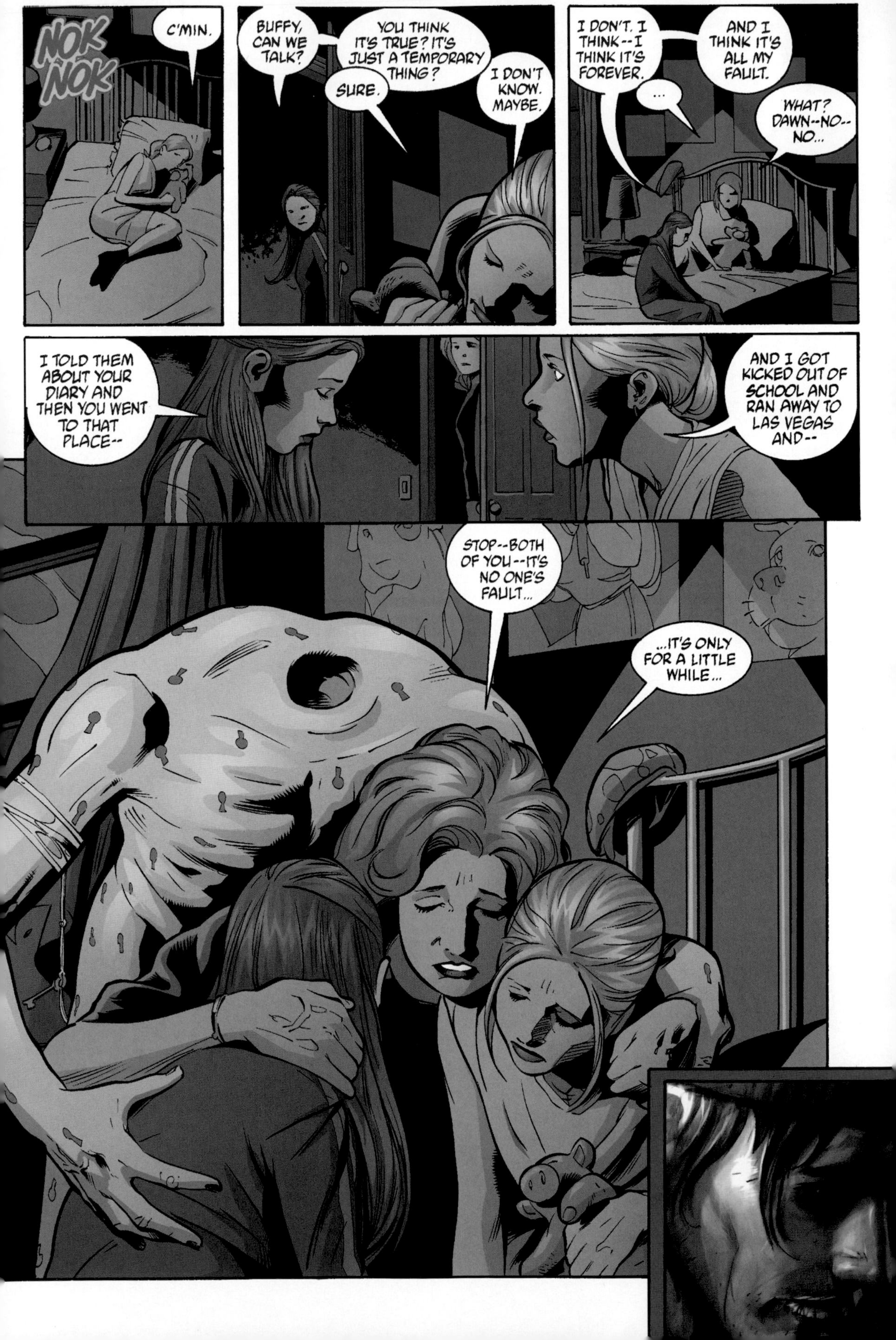
NOK NOK
C'MIN.
BUFFY, CAN WE TALK?
SURE.
YOU THINK IT'S TRUE? IT'S JUST A TEMPORARY THING?
I DON'T KNOW. MAYBE.
I DON'T. I THINK--I THINK IT'S FOREVER.
...
AND I THINK IT'S ALL MY FAULT.
WHAT? DAWN--NO--NO...
I TOLD THEM ABOUT YOUR DIARY AND THEN YOU WENT TO THAT PLACE--
AND I GOT KICKED OUT OF SCHOOL AND RAN AWAY TO LAS VEGAS AND--
STOP--BOTH OF YOU--IT'S NO ONE'S FAULT...
...IT'S ONLY FOR A LITTLE WHILE...

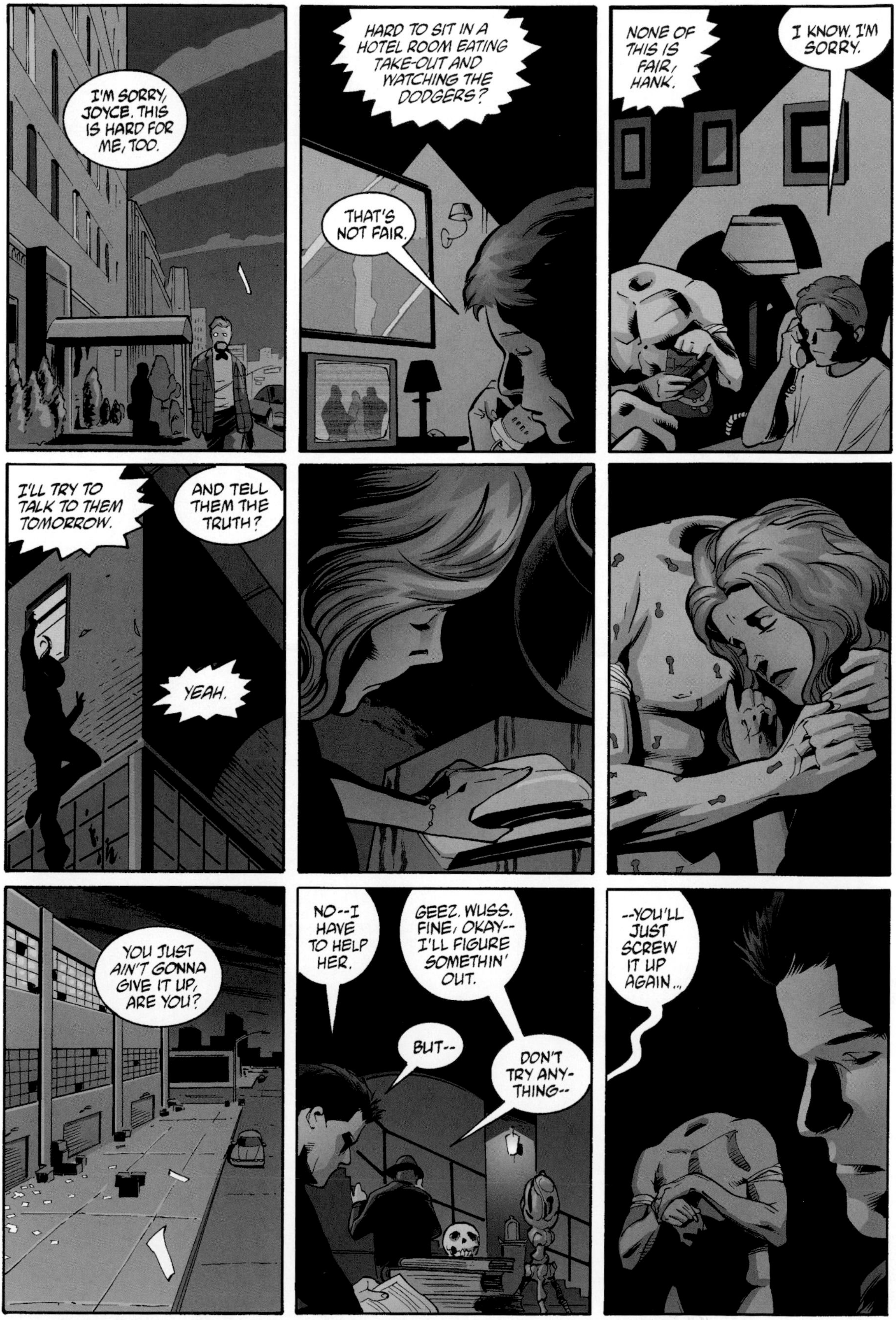
I'M SORRY, JOYCE. THIS IS HARD FOR ME, TOO.
HARD TO SIT IN A HOTEL ROOM EATING TAKE-OUT AND WATCHING THE DODGERS?
THAT'S NOT FAIR.
NONE OF THIS IS FAIR, HANK.
I KNOW. I'M SORRY.
I'LL TRY TO TALK TO THEM TOMORROW.
AND TELL THEM THE TRUTH?
YEAH.
YOU JUST AIN'T GONNA GIVE IT UP, ARE YOU?
NO--I HAVE TO HELP HER.
GEEZ. WUSS. FINE, OKAY--I'LL FIGURE SOMETHIN' OUT.
BUT--
DON'T TRY ANY-THING--
--YOU'LL JUST SCREW IT UP AGAIN...

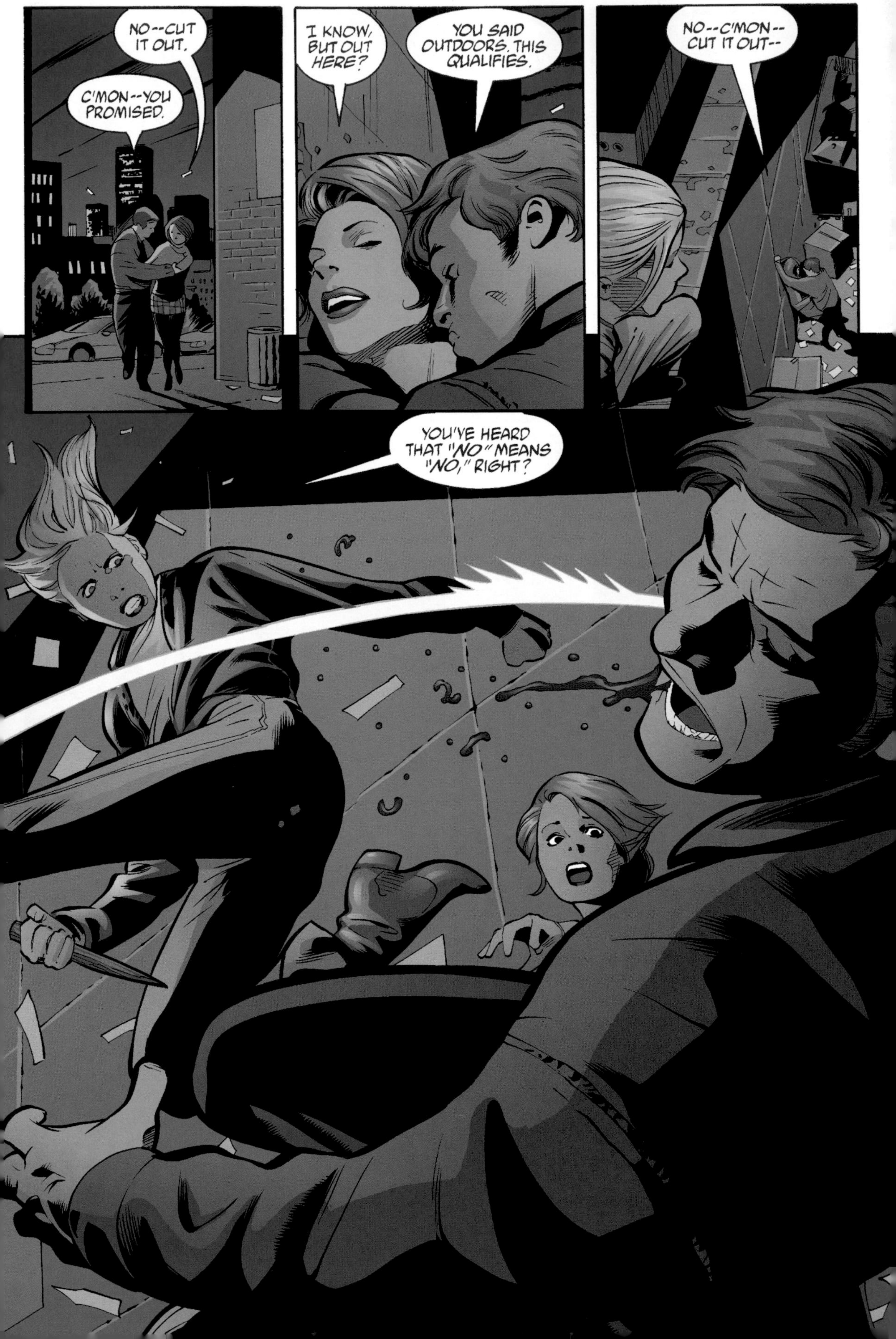
NO--CUT IT OUT.
C'MON--YOU PROMISED.
I KNOW, BUT OUT HERE?
YOU SAID OUTDOORS. THIS QUALIFIES.
NO--C'MON--CUT IT OUT--
YOU'VE HEARD THAT "NO" MEANS "NO," RIGHT?

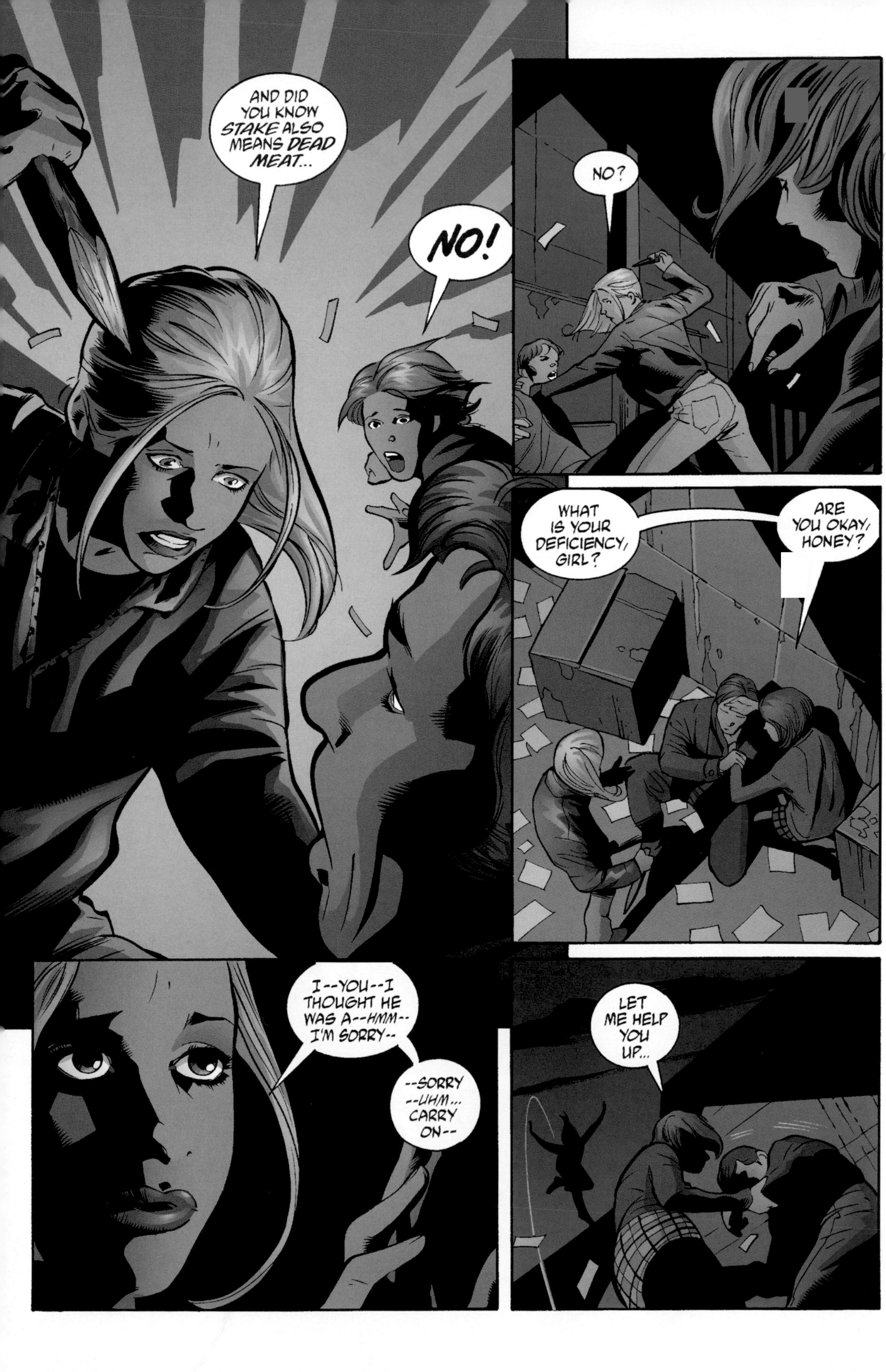
AND DID YOU KNOW STAKE ALSO MEANS DEAD MEAT...
NO!
NO?
WHAT IS YOUR DEFICIENCY, GIRL?
ARE YOU OKAY, HONEY?
I--YOU--I THOUGHT HE WAS A--HMM--I'M SORRY--
--SORRY --UHM... CARRY ON--
LET ME HELP YOU UP...

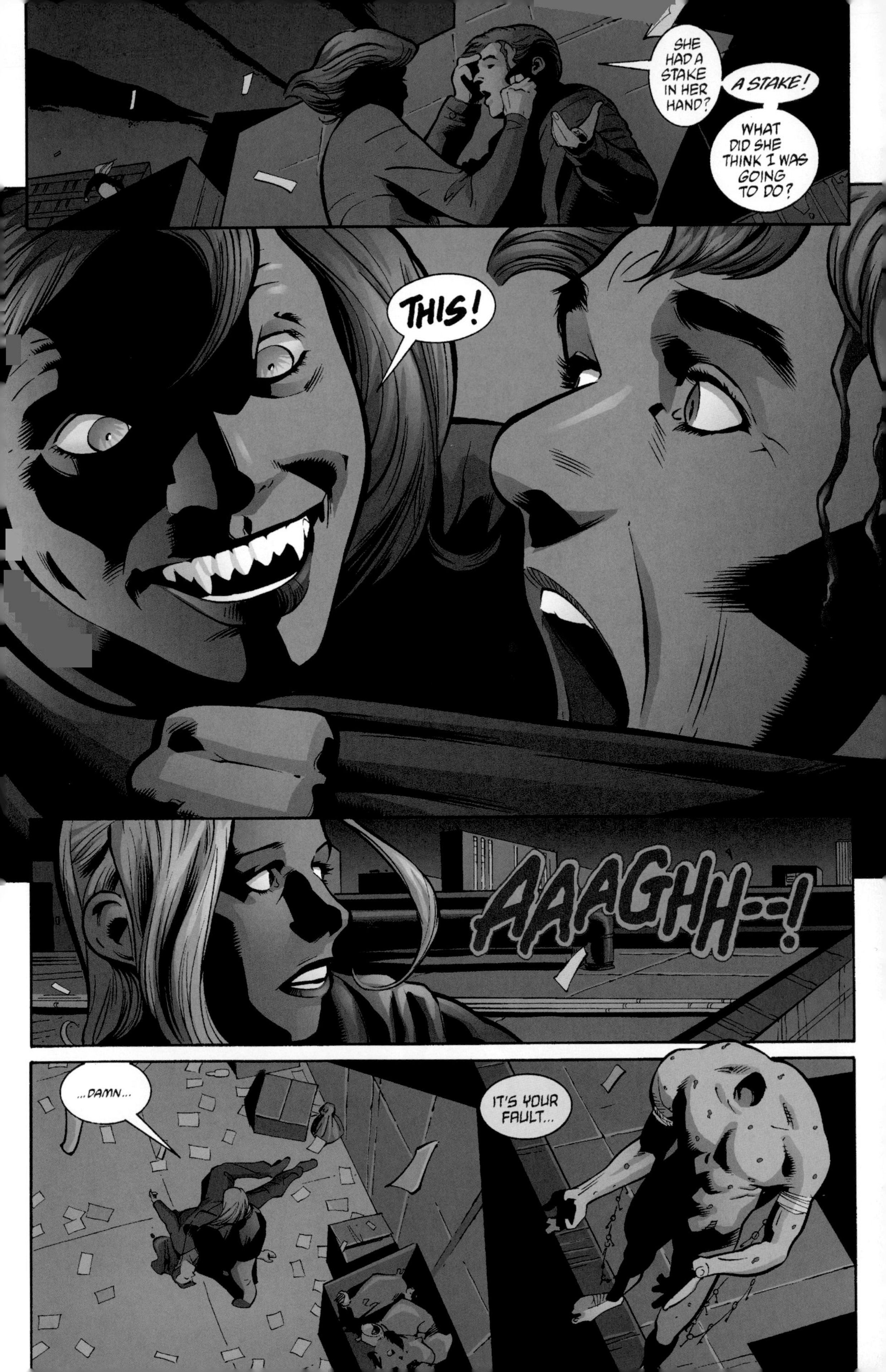
SHE HAD A STAKE IN HER HAND?
A STAKE!
WHAT DID SHE THINK I WAS GOING TO DO?
THIS!
AAAGHH--!
...DAMN...
IT'S YOUR FAULT...

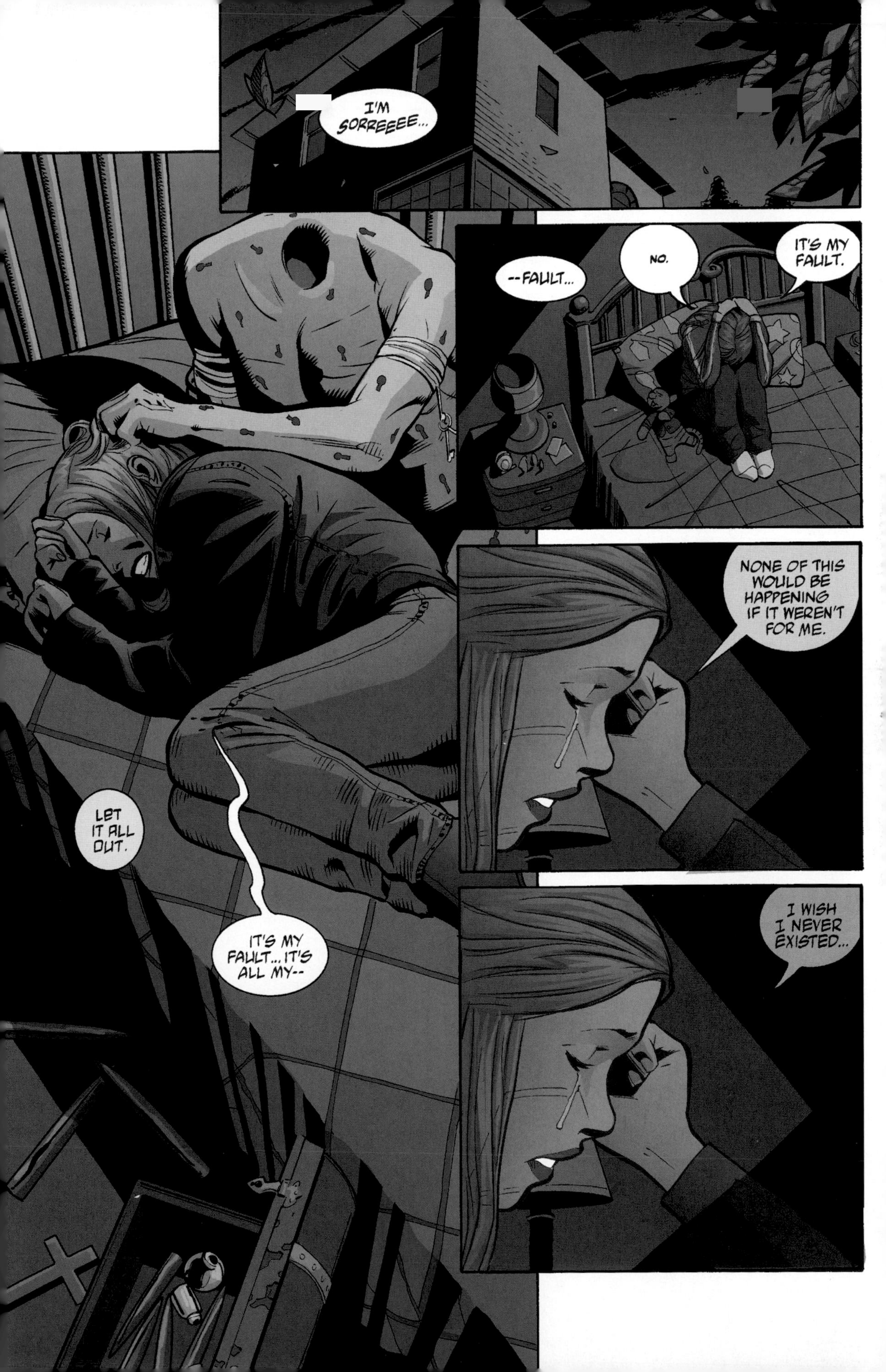
I'M SORREEEE...
LET IT ALL OUT.
IT'S MY FAULT... IT'S ALL MY--
--FAULT...
NO.
IT'S MY FAULT.
NONE OF THIS WOULD BE HAPPENING IF IT WEREN'T FOR ME.
I WISH I NEVER EXISTED...

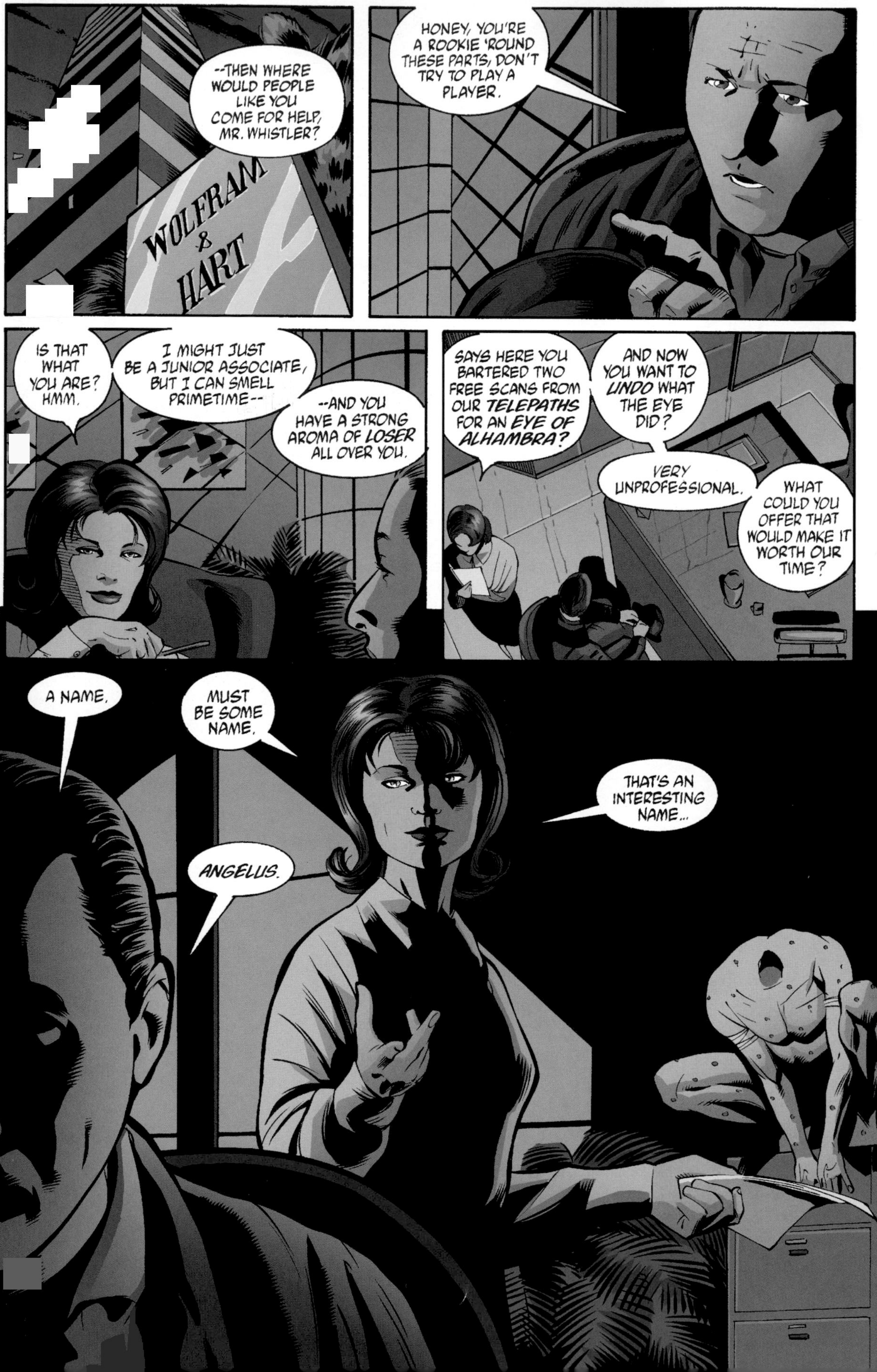
--THEN WHERE WOULD PEOPLE LIKE YOU COME FOR HELP, MR. WHISTLER?
WOLFRAM & HART
HONEY, YOU'RE A ROOKIE 'ROUND THESE PARTS, DON'T TRY TO PLAY A PLAYER.
IS THAT WHAT YOU ARE? HMM.
I MIGHT JUST BE A JUNIOR ASSOCIATE, BUT I CAN SMELL PRIMETIME--
--AND YOU HAVE A STRONG AROMA OF LOSER ALL OVER YOU.
SAYS HERE YOU BARTERED TWO FREE SCANS FROM OUR TELEPATHS FOR AN EYE OF ALHAMBRA?
AND NOW YOU WANT TO UNDO WHAT THE EYE DID?
VERY UNPROFESSIONAL.
WHAT COULD YOU OFFER THAT WOULD MAKE IT WORTH OUR TIME?
A NAME.
MUST BE SOME NAME.
ANGELUS.
THAT'S AN INTERESTING NAME...

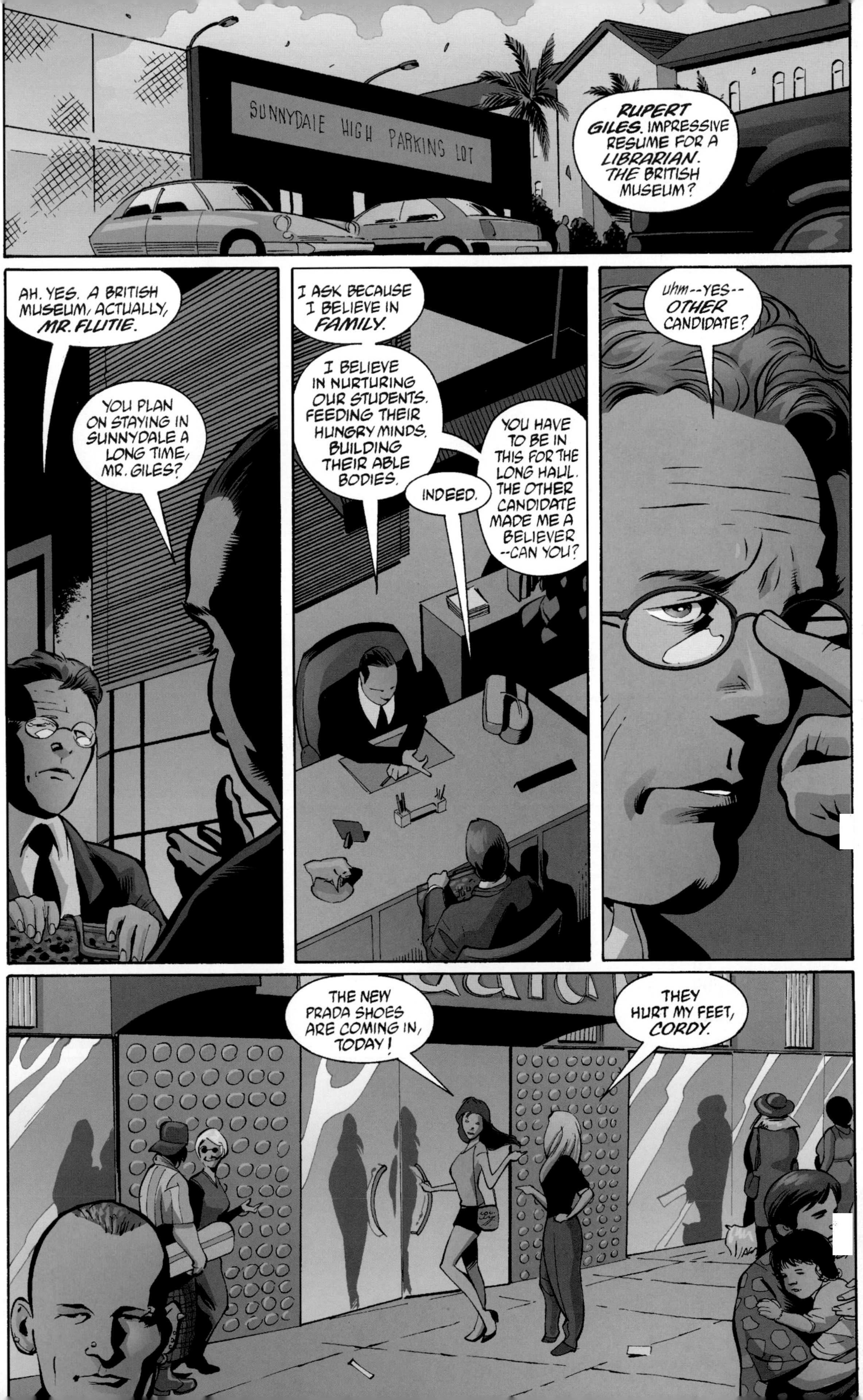
SUNNYDALE HIGH PARKING LOT
RUPERT GILES. IMPRESSIVE RESUME FOR A LIBRARIAN. THE BRITISH MUSEUM?
AH. YES. A BRITISH MUSEUM, ACTUALLY, MR. FLUTIE.
YOU PLAN ON STAYING IN SUNNYDALE A LONG TIME, MR. GILES?
I ASK BECAUSE I BELIEVE IN FAMILY.
I BELIEVE IN NURTURING OUR STUDENTS. FEEDING THEIR HUNGRY MINDS. BUILDING THEIR ABLE BODIES.
INDEED.
YOU HAVE TO BE IN THIS FOR THE LONG HAUL. THE OTHER CANDIDATE MADE ME A BELIEVER --CAN YOU?
uhm--YES-- OTHER CANDIDATE?
THE NEW PRADA SHOES ARE COMING IN, TODAY!
THEY HURT MY FEET, CORDY.

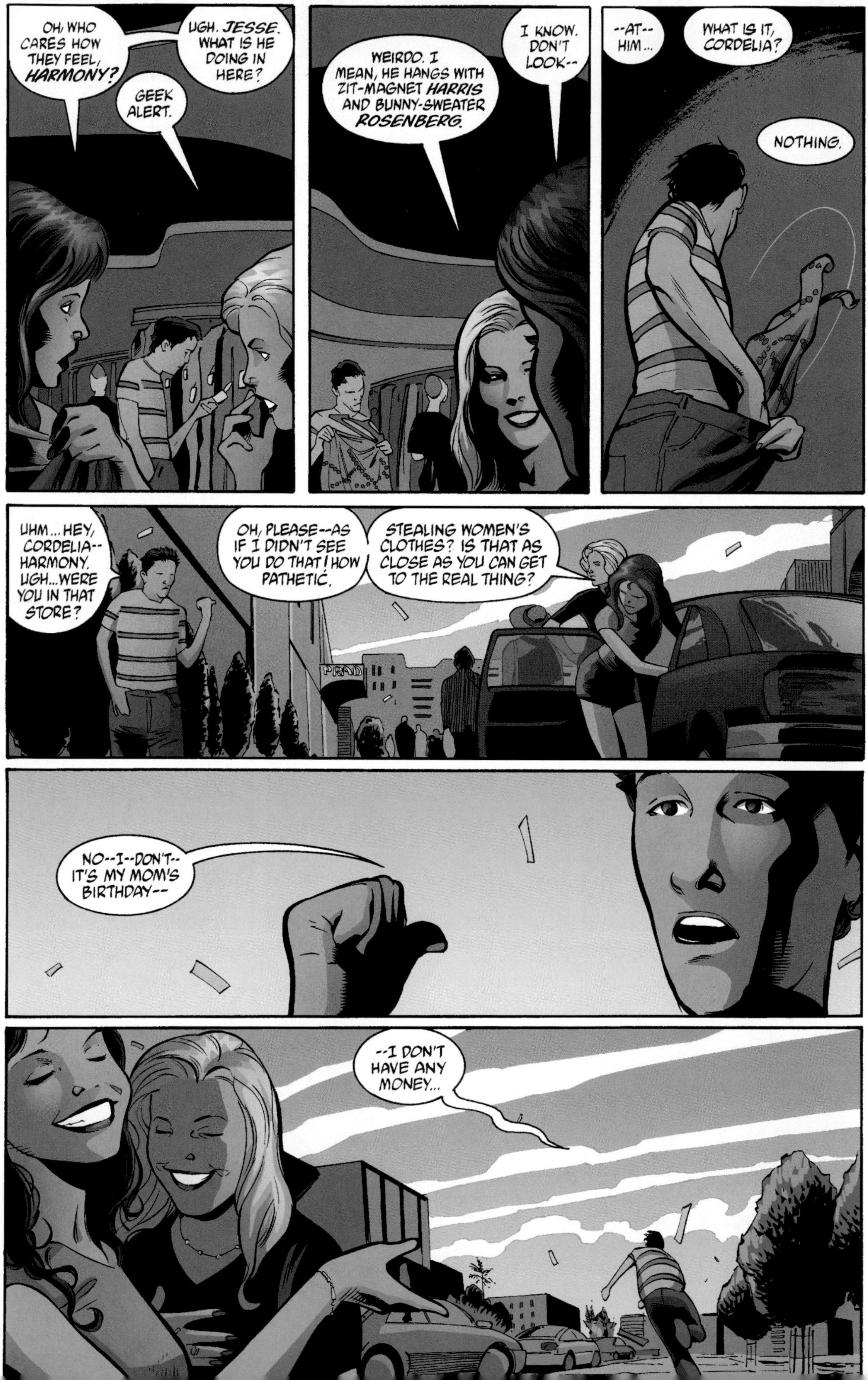
OH, WHO CARES HOW THEY FEEL, *HARMONY?*
UGH. *JESSE.* WHAT IS HE DOING IN HERE?
GEEK ALERT.
WEIRDO. I MEAN, HE HANGS WITH ZIT-MAGNET *HARRIS* AND BUNNY-SWEATER *ROSENBERG.*
I KNOW. DON'T LOOK--
--AT-- HIM...
WHAT IS IT, CORDELIA?
NOTHING.
UHM... HEY, CORDELIA-- HARMONY. UGH...WERE YOU IN THAT STORE?
OH, PLEASE--AS IF I DIDN'T SEE YOU DO THAT! HOW PATHETIC.
STEALING WOMEN'S CLOTHES? IS THAT AS CLOSE AS YOU CAN GET TO THE REAL THING?
NO--I--DON'T-- IT'S MY MOM'S BIRTHDAY--
--I DON'T HAVE ANY MONEY...

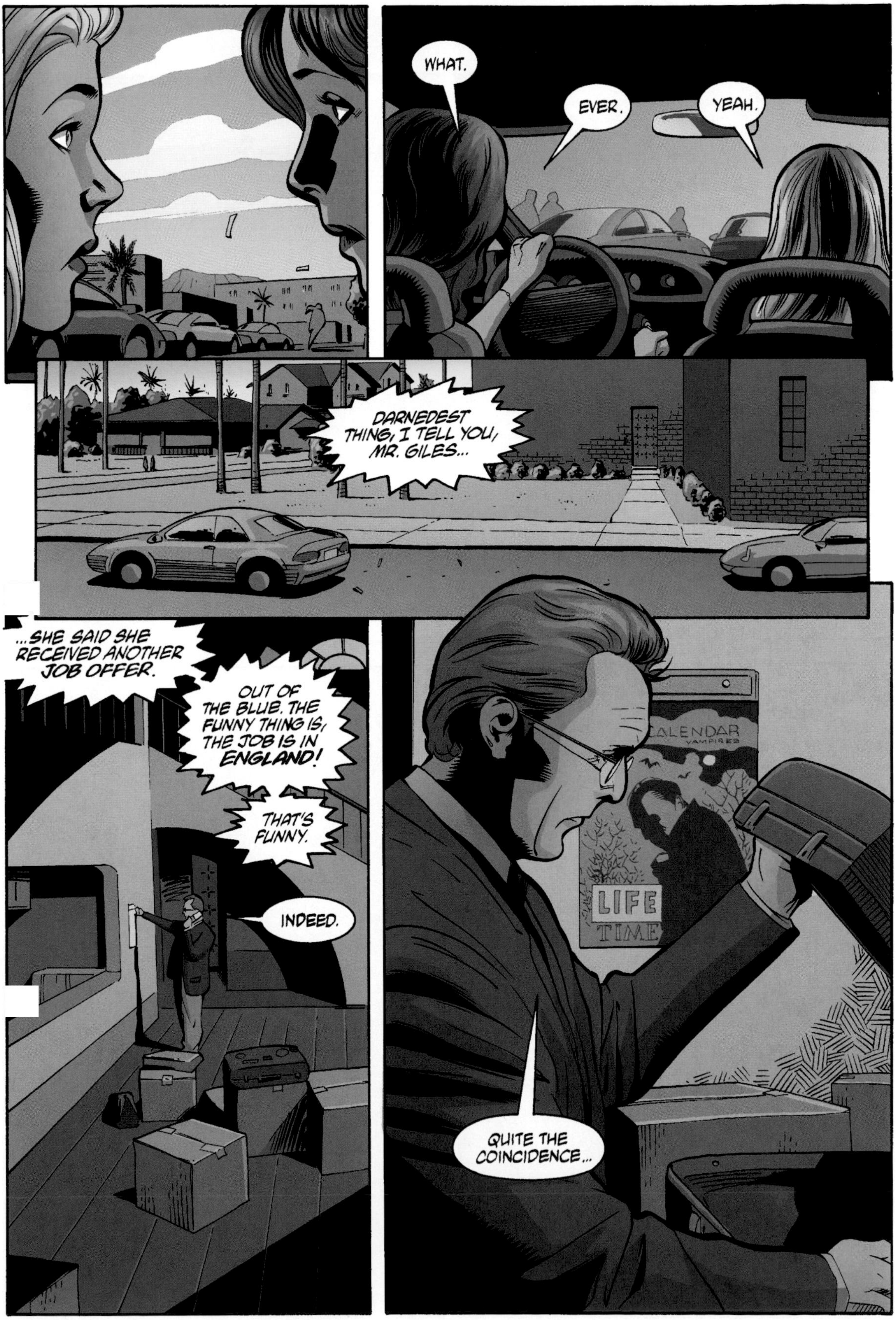
WHAT.
EVER.
YEAH.
DARNEDEST THING, I TELL YOU, MR. GILES...
...SHE SAID SHE RECEIVED ANOTHER JOB OFFER.
OUT OF THE BLUE. THE FUNNY THING IS, THE JOB IS IN ENGLAND!
THAT'S FUNNY.
INDEED.
CALENDAR
VAMPIRES
LIFE
TIME
QUITE THE COINCIDENCE...

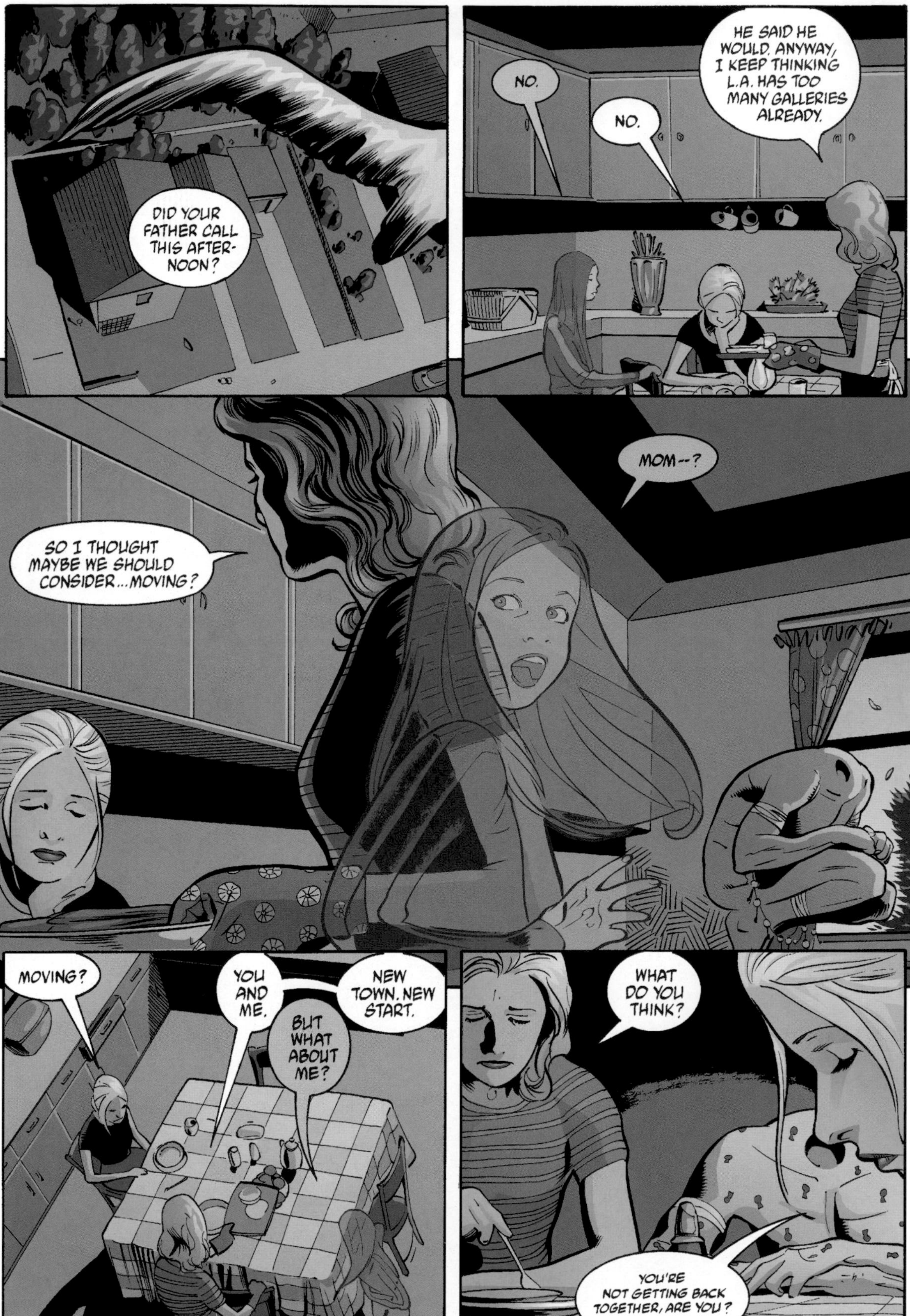
DID YOUR FATHER CALL THIS AFTER-NOON?
NO.
NO.
HE SAID HE WOULD. ANYWAY, I KEEP THINKING L.A. HAS TOO MANY GALLERIES ALREADY.
MOM--?
SO I THOUGHT MAYBE WE SHOULD CONSIDER...MOVING?
MOVING?
YOU AND ME.
NEW TOWN. NEW START.
BUT WHAT ABOUT ME?
WHAT DO YOU THINK?
YOU'RE NOT GETTING BACK TOGETHER, ARE YOU?

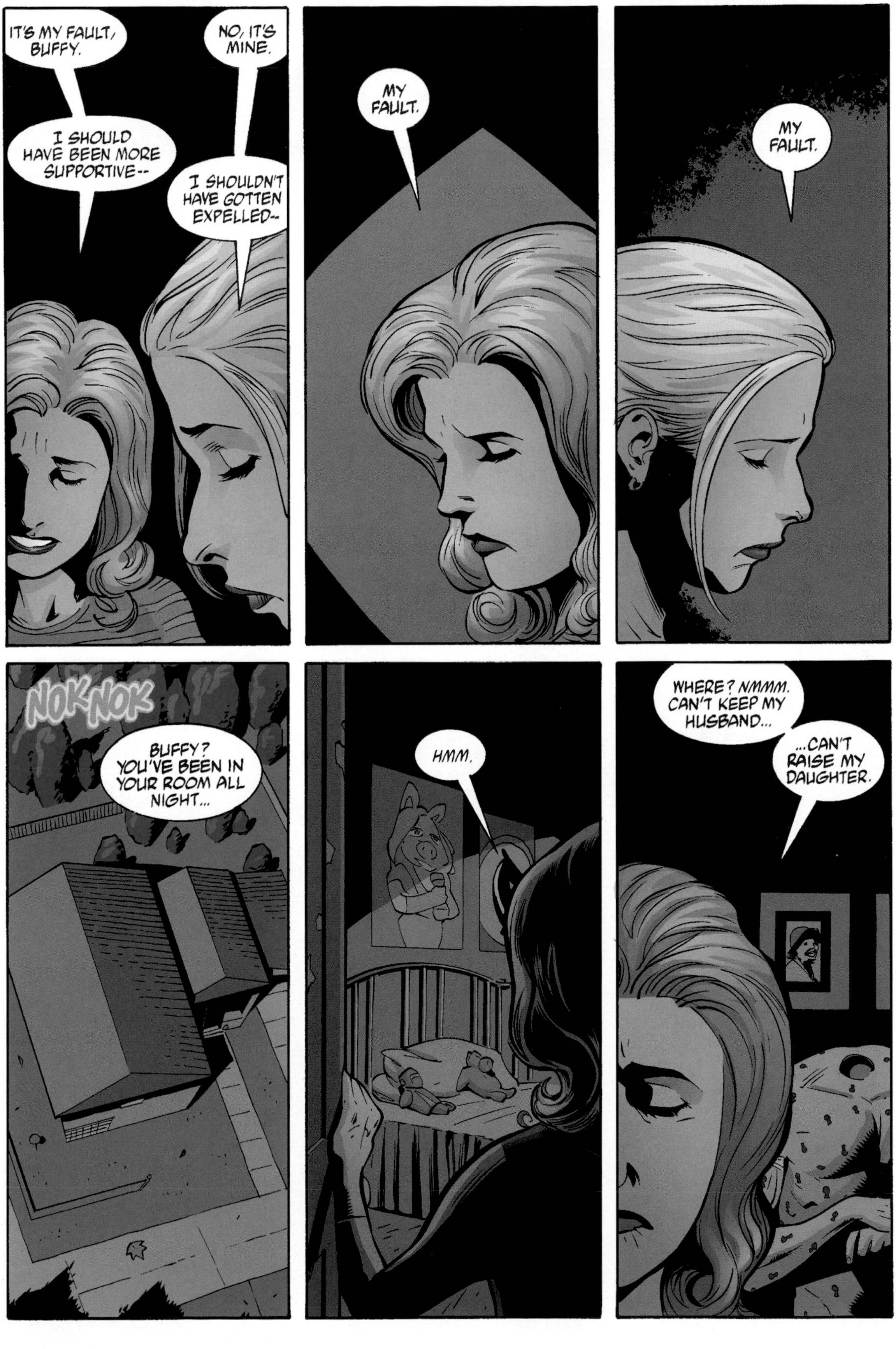

IT'S MY FAULT, BUFFY.
NO, IT'S MINE.
I SHOULD HAVE BEEN MORE SUPPORTIVE--
I SHOULDN'T HAVE GOTTEN EXPELLED--
MY FAULT.
MY FAULT.
NOK NOK
BUFFY? YOU'VE BEEN IN YOUR ROOM ALL NIGHT...
HMM.
WHERE? NMMM. CAN'T KEEP MY HUSBAND...
...CAN'T RAISE MY DAUGHTER.

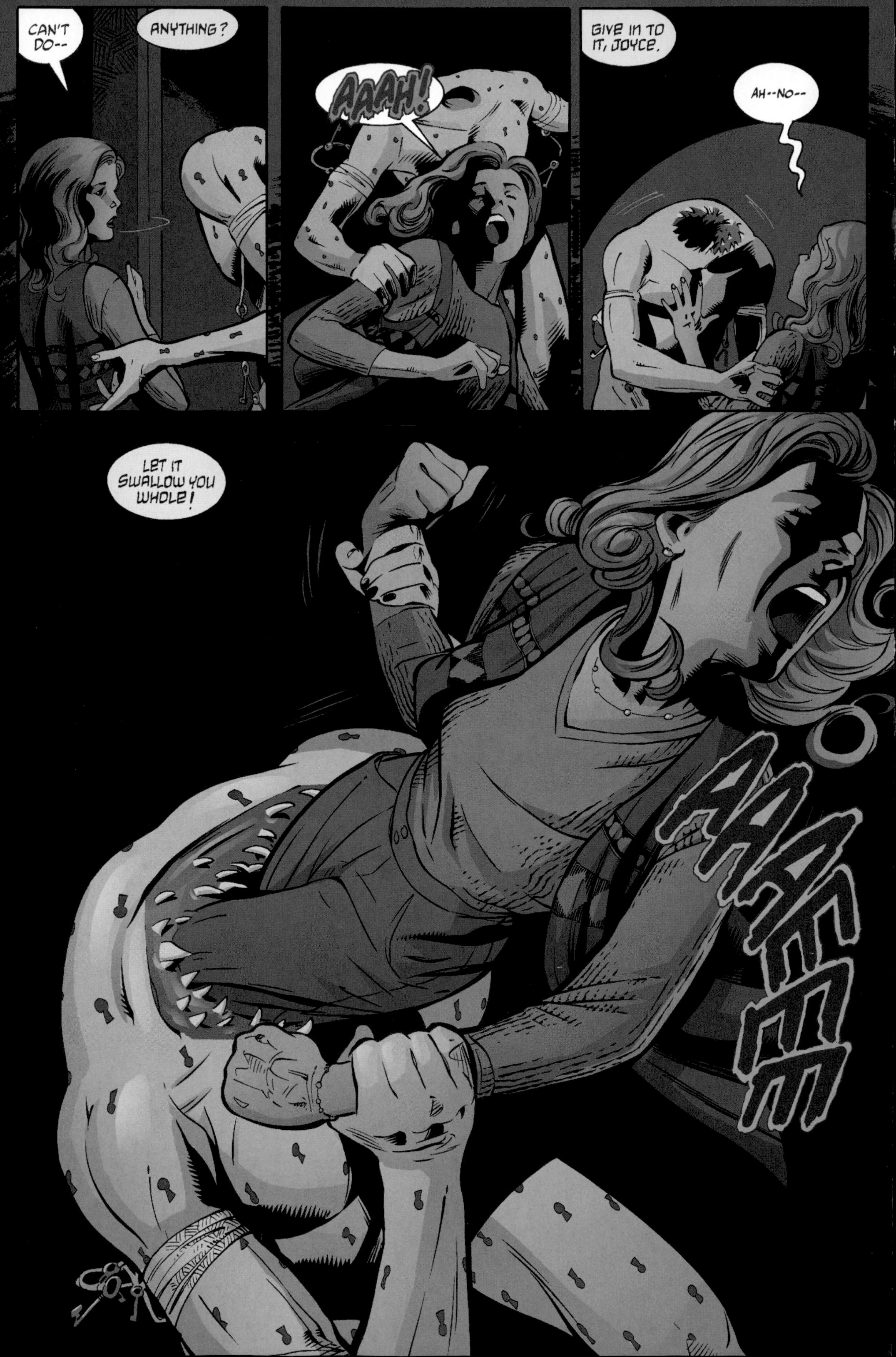
CAN'T DO--
ANYTHING?
AAAH!
GIVE IN TO IT, JOYCE.
AH--NO--
LET IT SWALLOW YOU WHOLE!
AAAEEEE

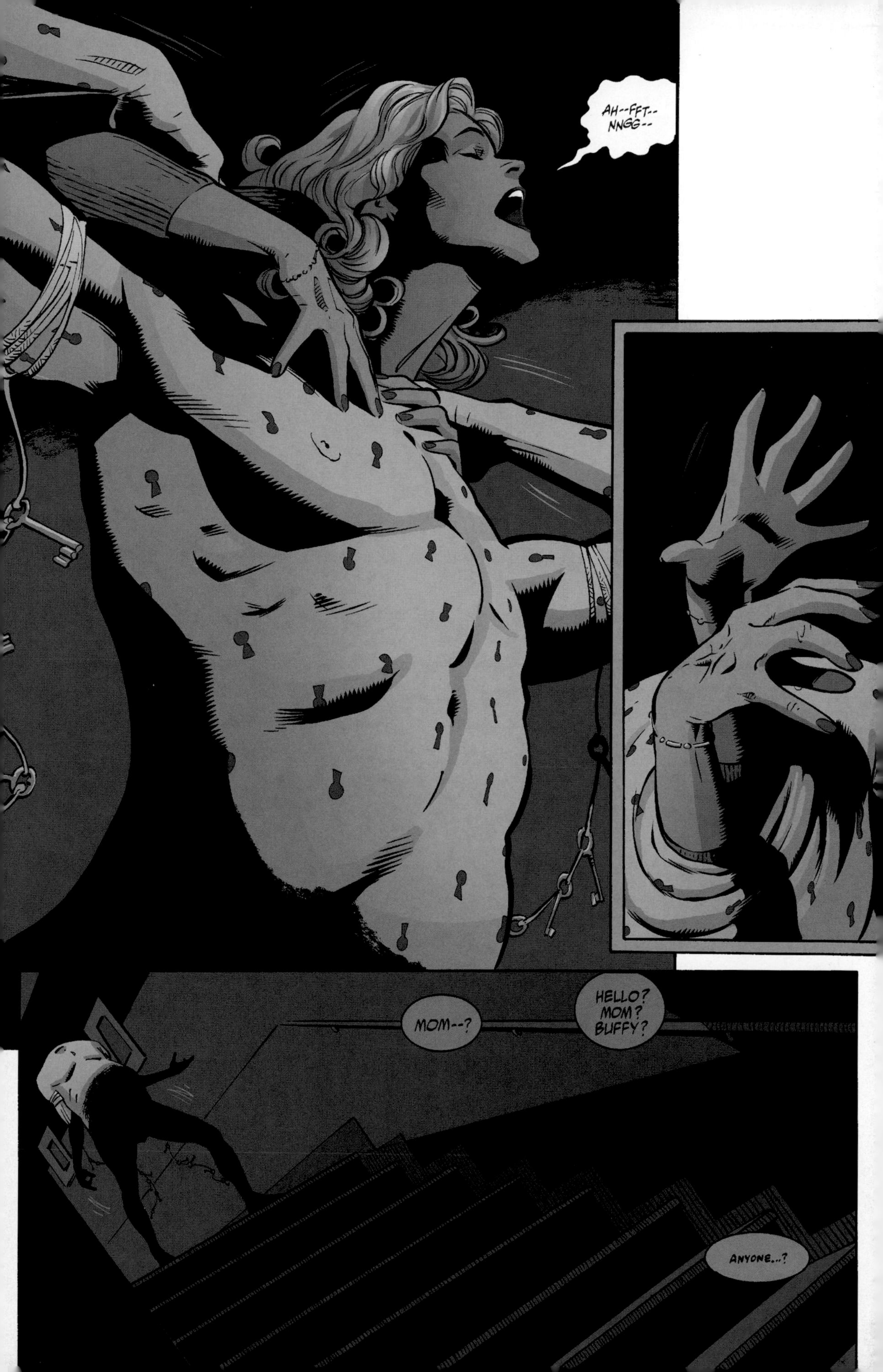
AH--FFT--
NNGG--
MOM--?
HELLO?
MOM?
BUFFY?
ANYONE...?

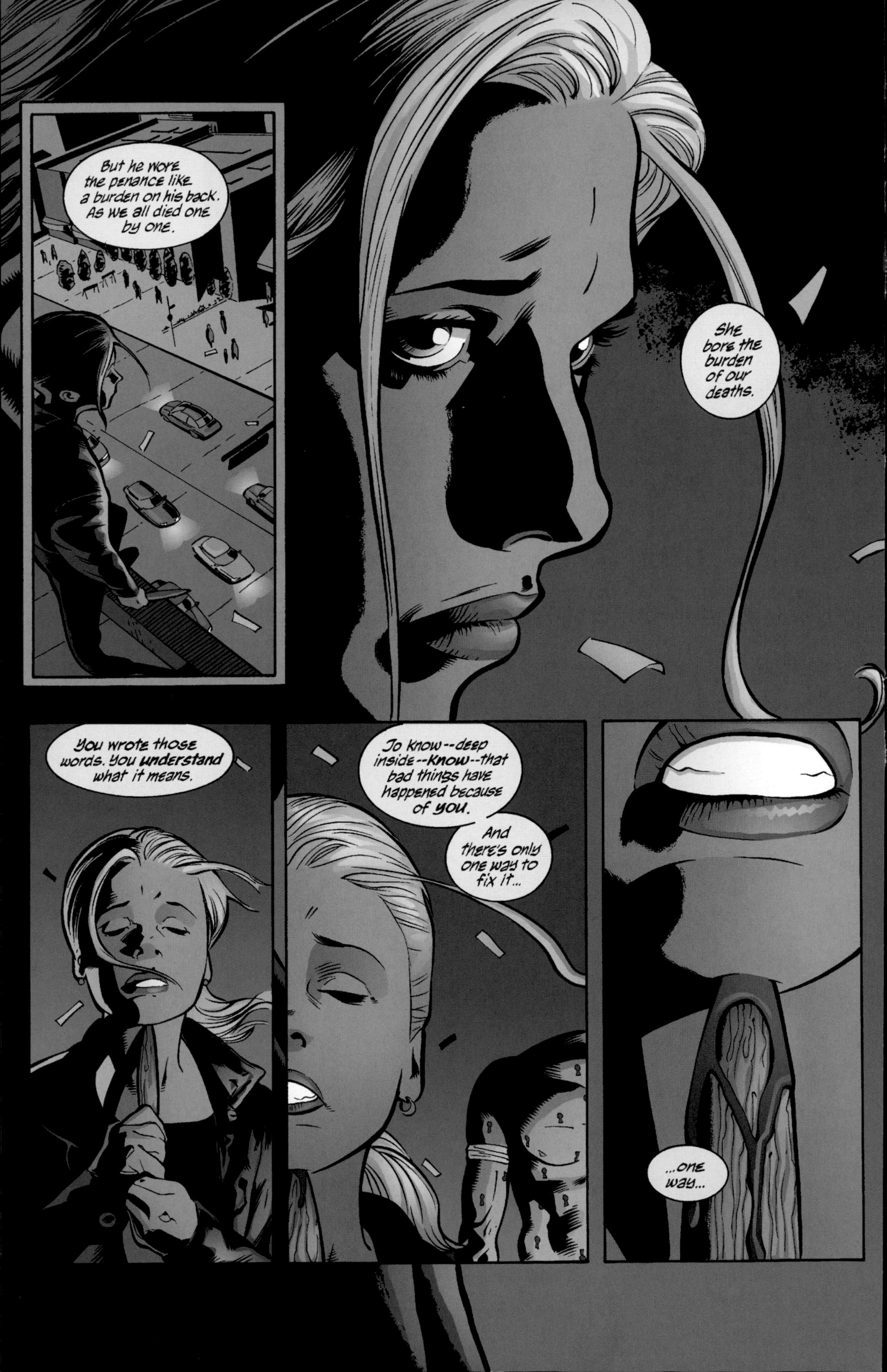
But he wore the penance like a burden on his back. As we all died one by one.
She bore the burden of our deaths.
You wrote those words. You understand what it means.
To know--deep inside--know--that bad things have happened because of you.
And there's only one way to fix it...
...one way...

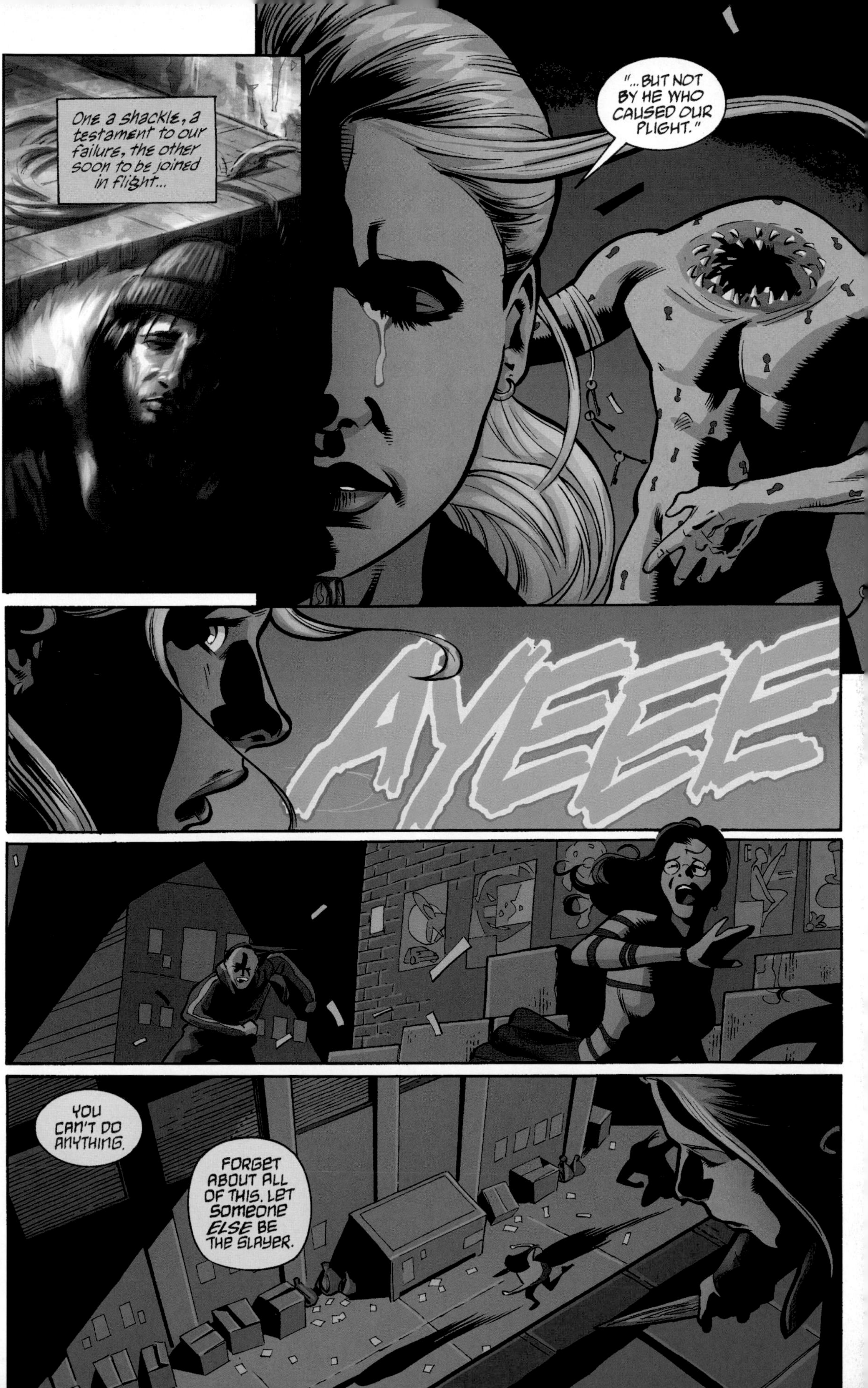

One a shackle, a testament to our failure, the other soon to be joined in flight...
"...BUT NOT BY HE WHO CAUSED OUR PLIGHT."
AYEEE
YOU CAN'T DO ANYTHING.
FORGET ABOUT ALL OF THIS. LET SOMEONE ELSE BE THE SLAYER.

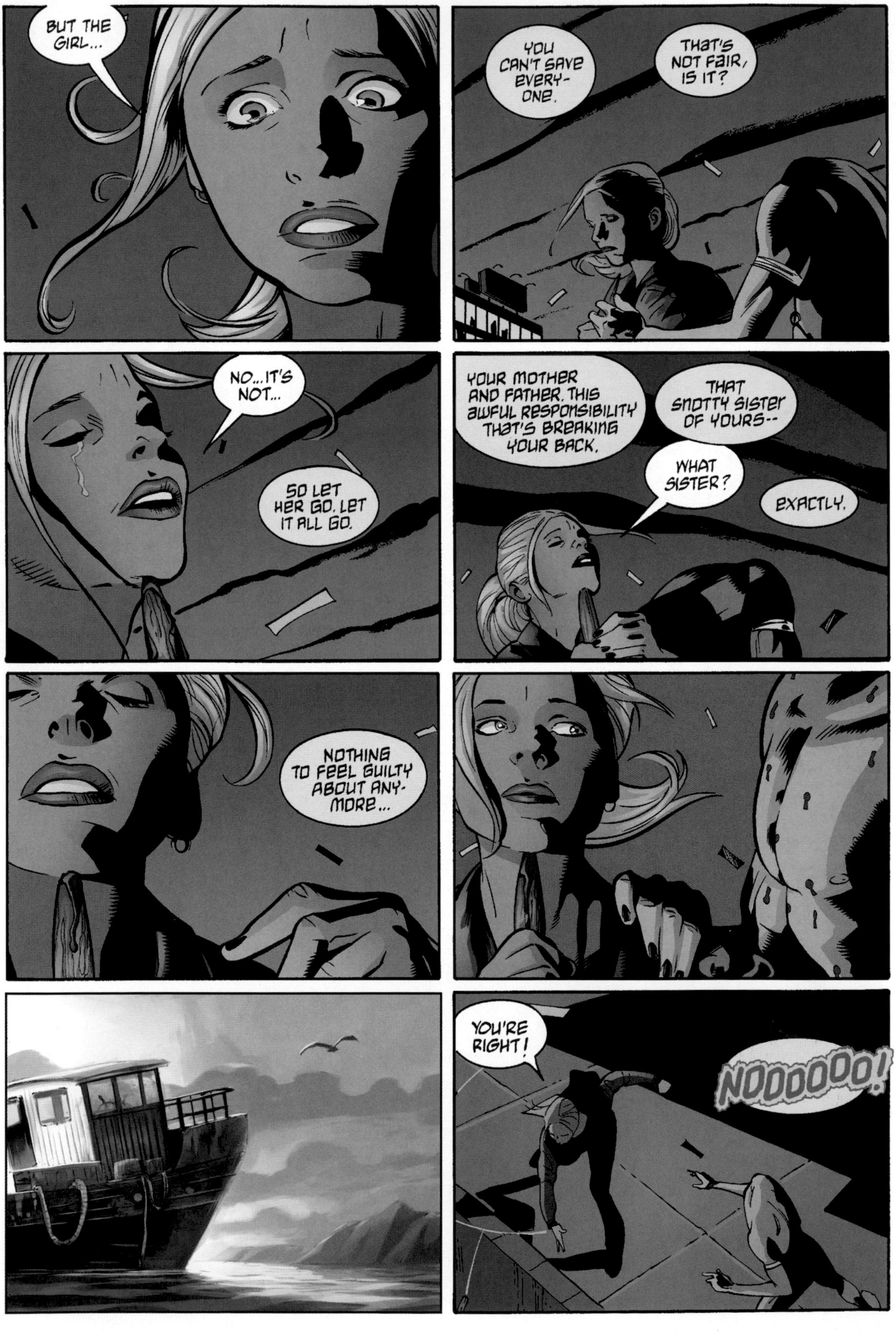
BUT THE GIRL...
YOU CAN'T SAVE EVERY-ONE.
THAT'S NOT FAIR, IS IT?
NO...IT'S NOT...
SO LET HER GO. LET IT ALL GO.
YOUR MOTHER AND FATHER. THIS AWFUL RESPONSIBILITY THAT'S BREAKING YOUR BACK.
THAT SNOTTY SISTER OF YOURS--
WHAT SISTER?
EXACTLY.
NOTHING TO FEEL GUILTY ABOUT ANY-MORE...
YOU'RE RIGHT!
NOOOOOO!

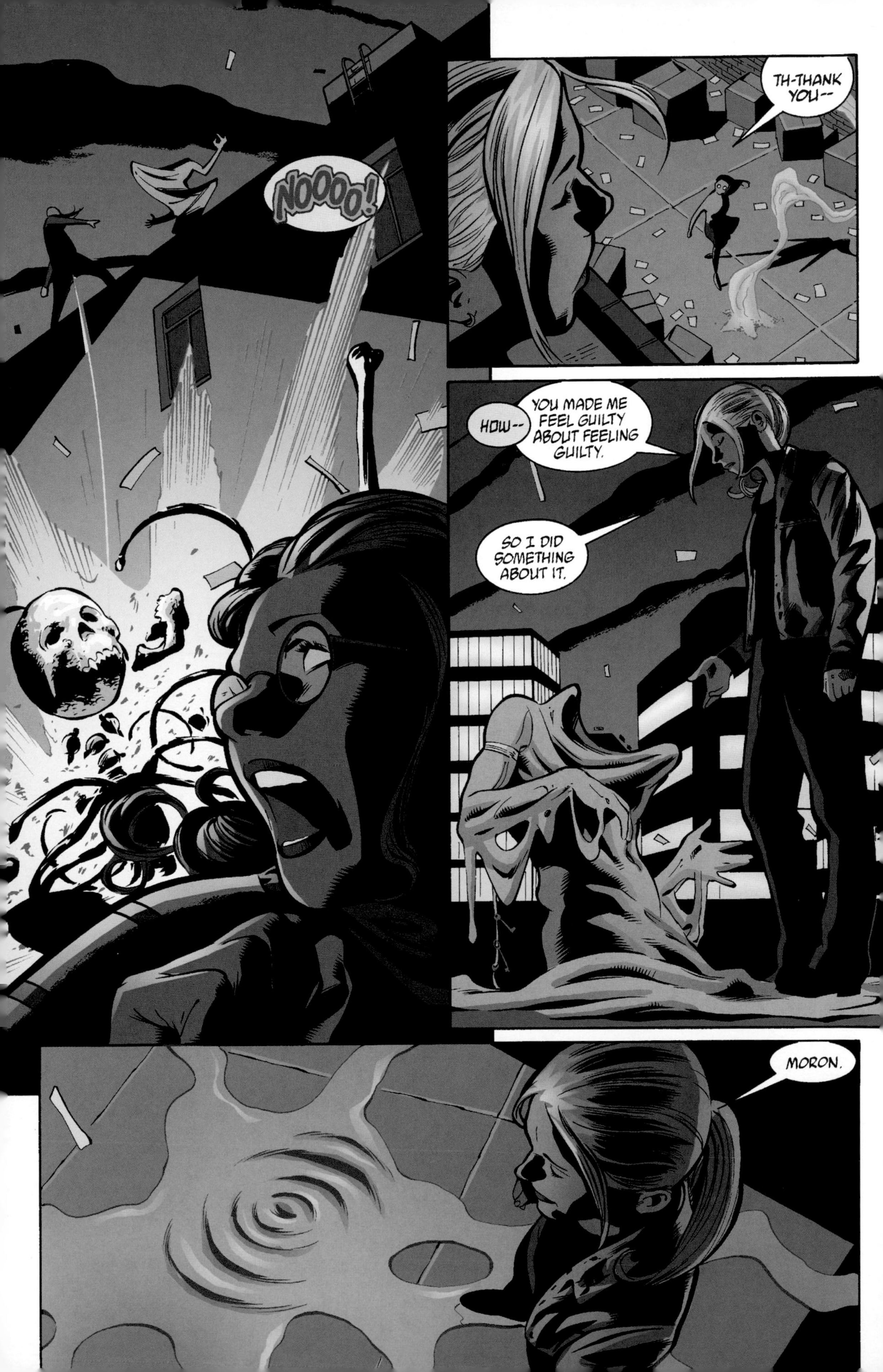
NOOOO!
TH-THANK YOU--
HOW--
YOU MADE ME FEEL GUILTY ABOUT FEELING GUILTY.
SO I DID SOMETHING ABOUT IT.
MORON.

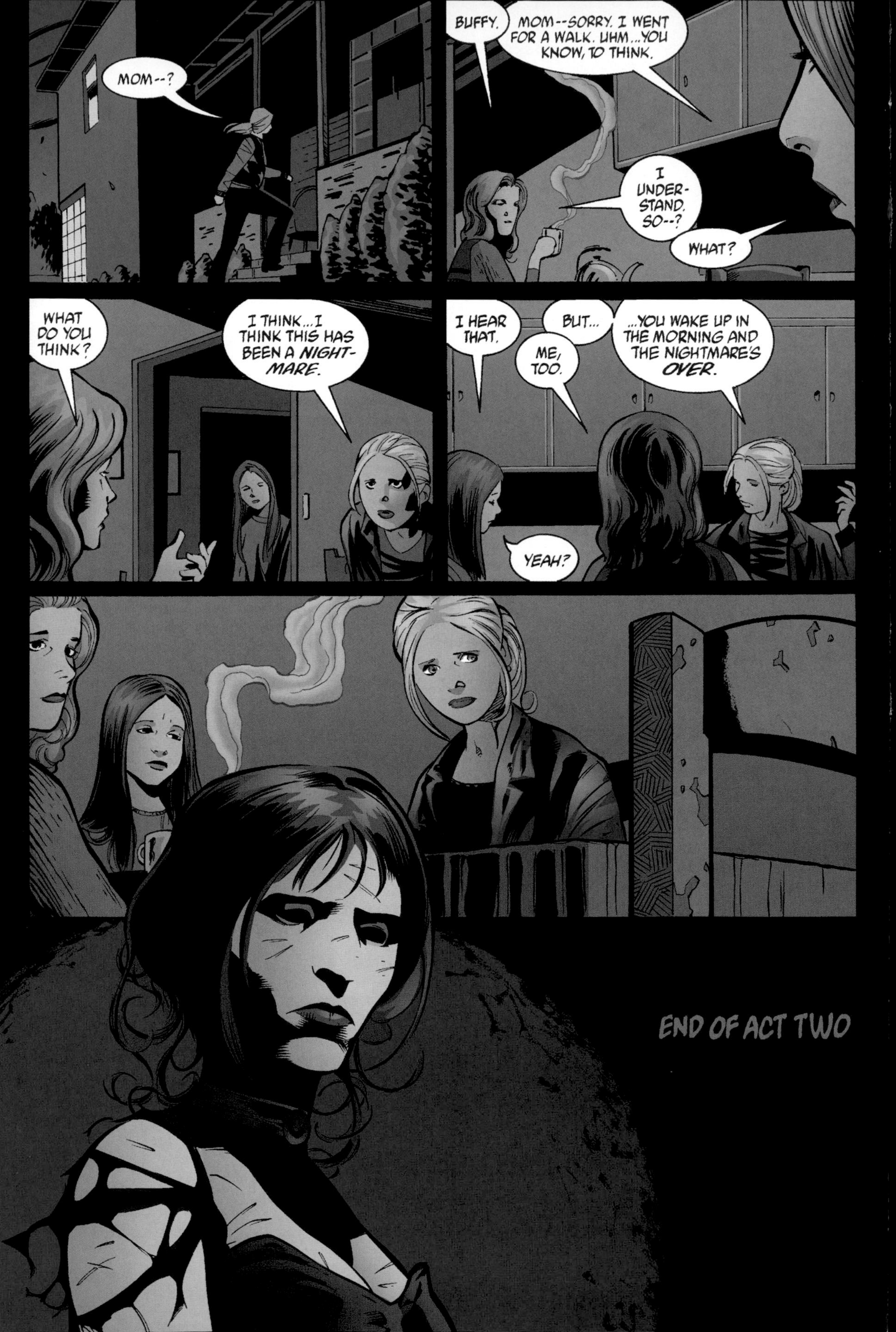
MOM--?
BUFFY.
MOM--SORRY. I WENT FOR A WALK. UHM...YOU KNOW, TO THINK.
I UNDER-STAND. SO--?
WHAT?
WHAT DO YOU THINK?
I THINK...I THINK THIS HAS BEEN A NIGHT-MARE.
I HEAR THAT.
BUT...
ME, TOO.
...YOU WAKE UP IN THE MORNING AND THE NIGHTMARE'S OVER.
YEAH?
END OF ACT TWO

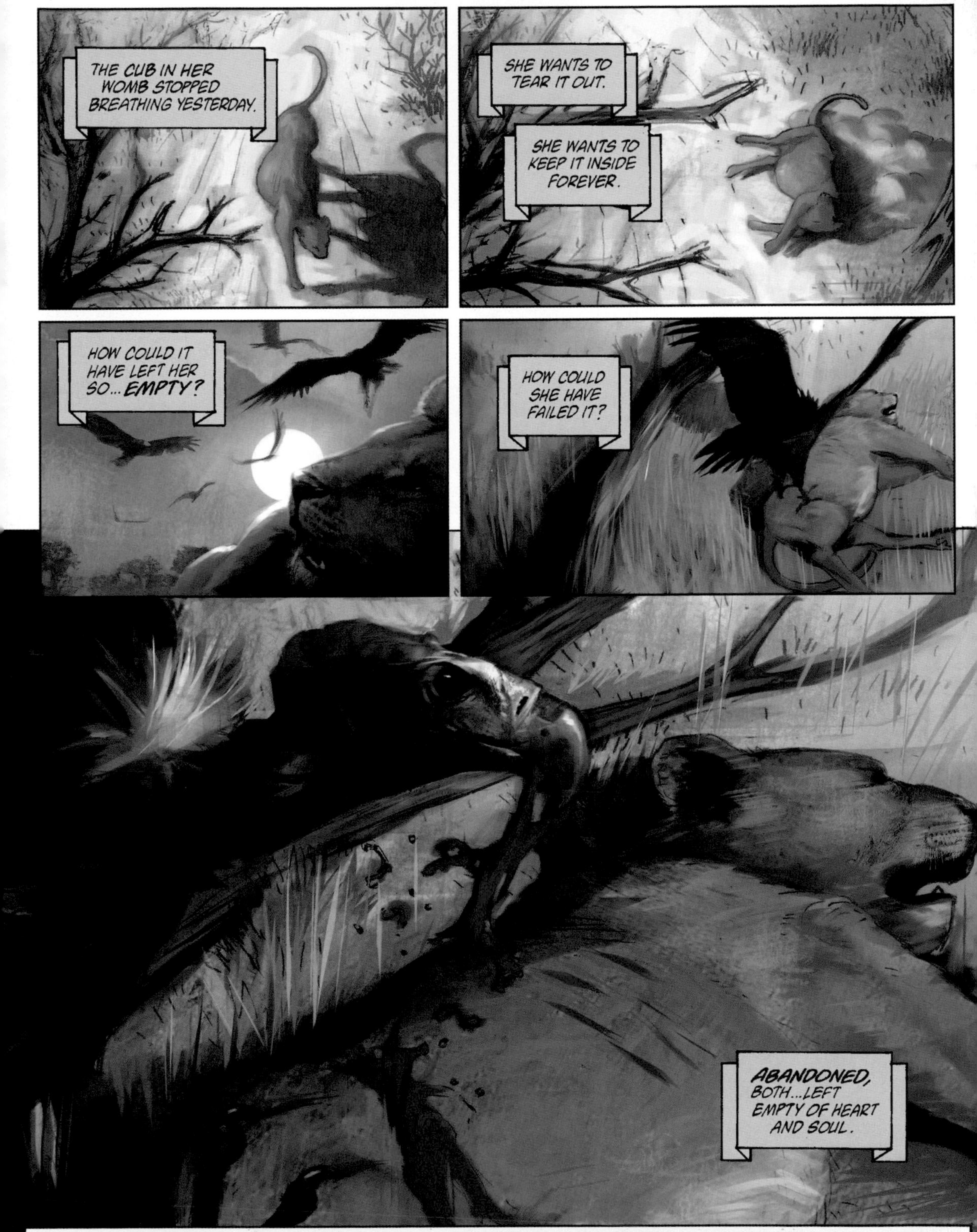
THE CUB IN HER WOMB STOPPED BREATHING YESTERDAY.
SHE WANTS TO TEAR IT OUT.
SHE WANTS TO KEEP IT INSIDE FOREVER.
HOW COULD IT HAVE LEFT HER SO... EMPTY?
HOW COULD SHE HAVE FAILED IT?
ABANDONED, BOTH...LEFT EMPTY OF HEART AND SOUL.

# act three: ABANDONMENT

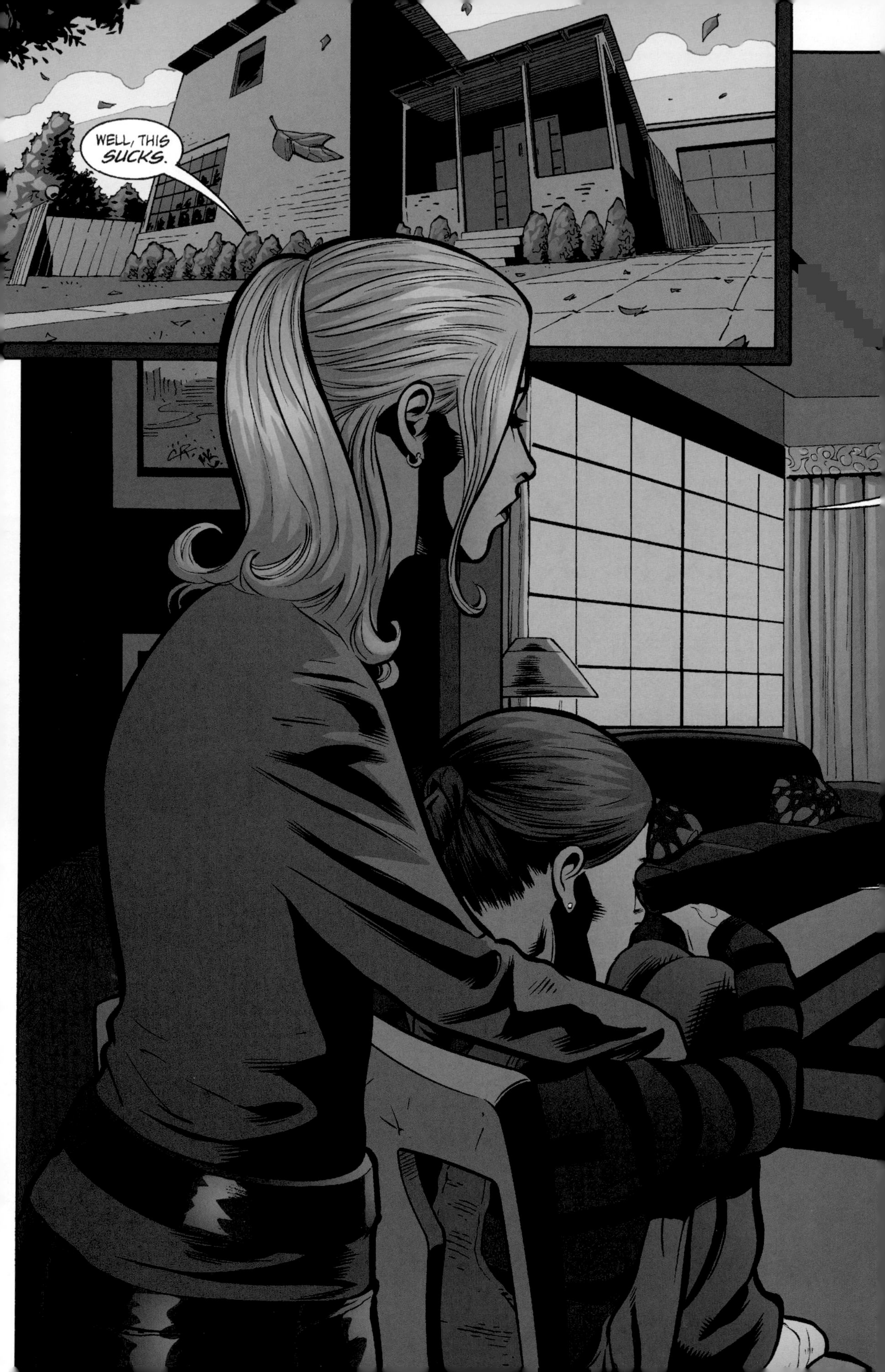
WELL, THIS SUCKS.

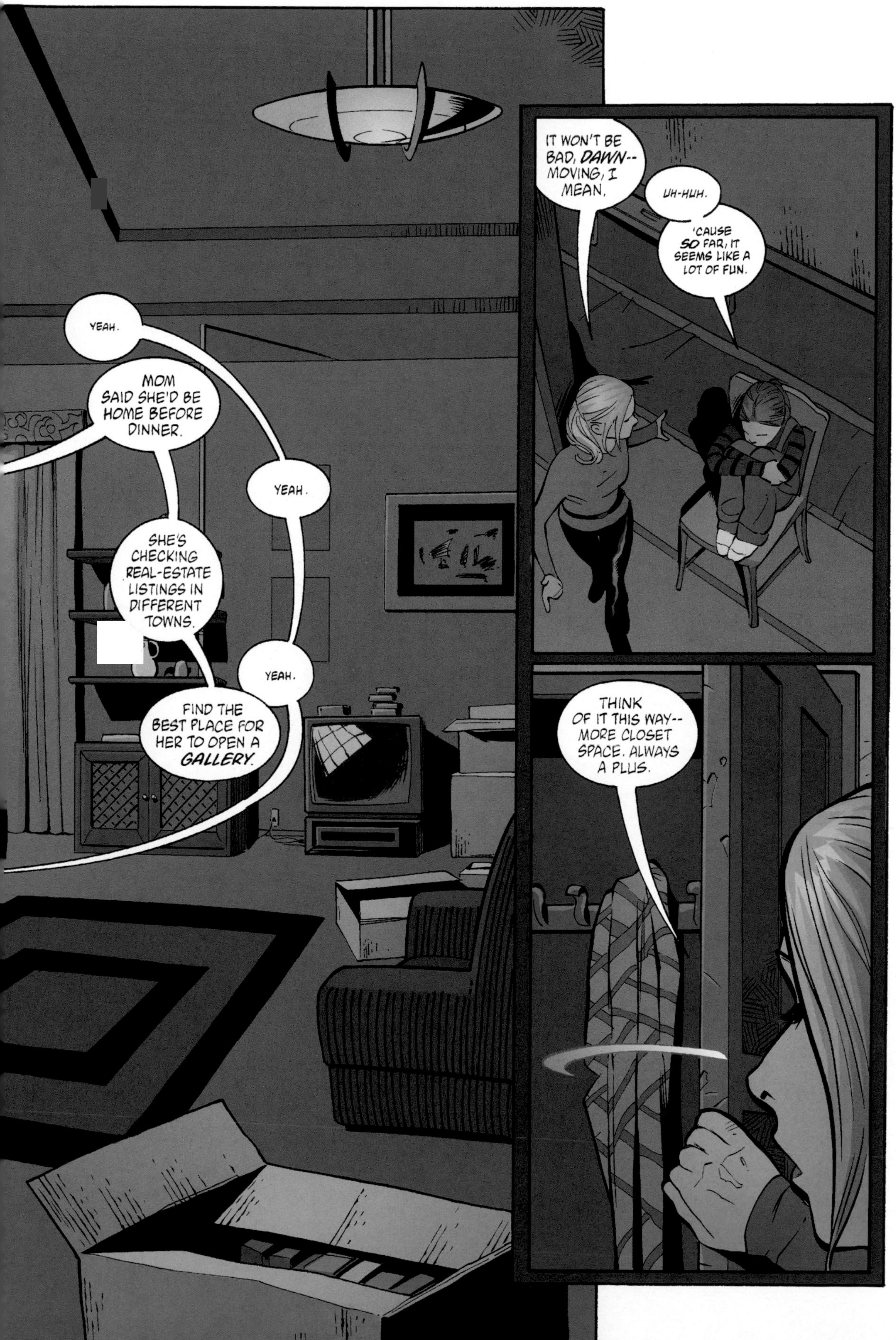
MOM SAID SHE'D BE HOME BEFORE DINNER.
YEAH.
SHE'S CHECKING REAL-ESTATE LISTINGS IN DIFFERENT TOWNS.
YEAH.
FIND THE BEST PLACE FOR HER TO OPEN A *GALLERY*.
YEAH.
IT WON'T BE BAD, *DAWN*-- MOVING, I MEAN.
UH-HUH.
'CAUSE *SO* FAR, IT SEEMS LIKE A LOT OF FUN.
THINK OF IT THIS WAY-- MORE CLOSET SPACE. ALWAYS A PLUS.

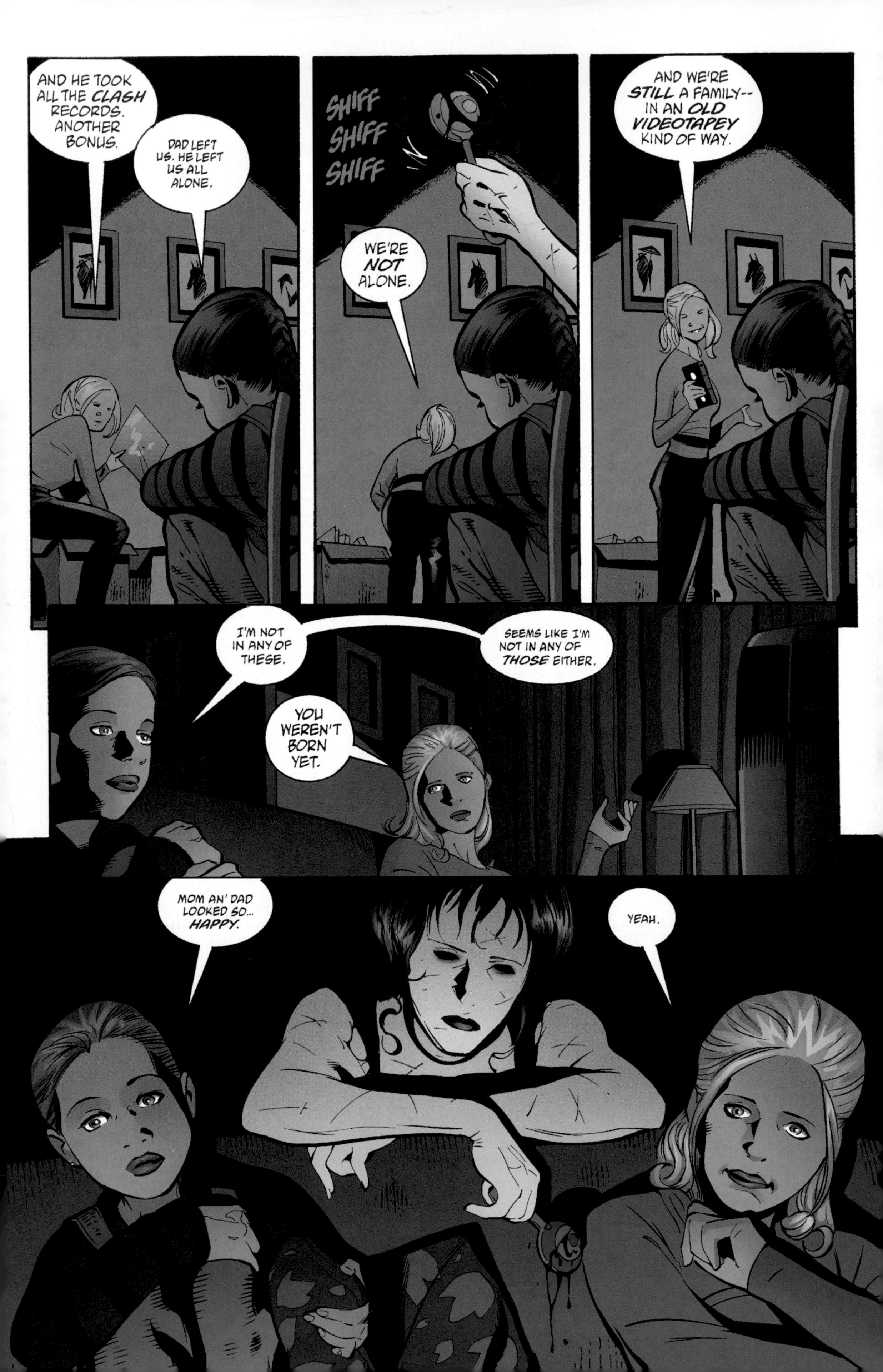
AND HE TOOK ALL THE *CLASH* RECORDS. ANOTHER BONUS.
DAD LEFT US. HE LEFT US ALL ALONE.
SHIFF SHIFF SHIFF
WE'RE *NOT* ALONE.
AND WE'RE *STILL* A FAMILY-- IN AN *OLD VIDEOTAPEY* KIND OF WAY.
I'M NOT IN ANY OF THESE.
SEEMS LIKE I'M NOT IN ANY OF *THOSE* EITHER.
YOU WEREN'T BORN YET.
MOM AN' DAD LOOKED SO... *HAPPY*.
YEAH.

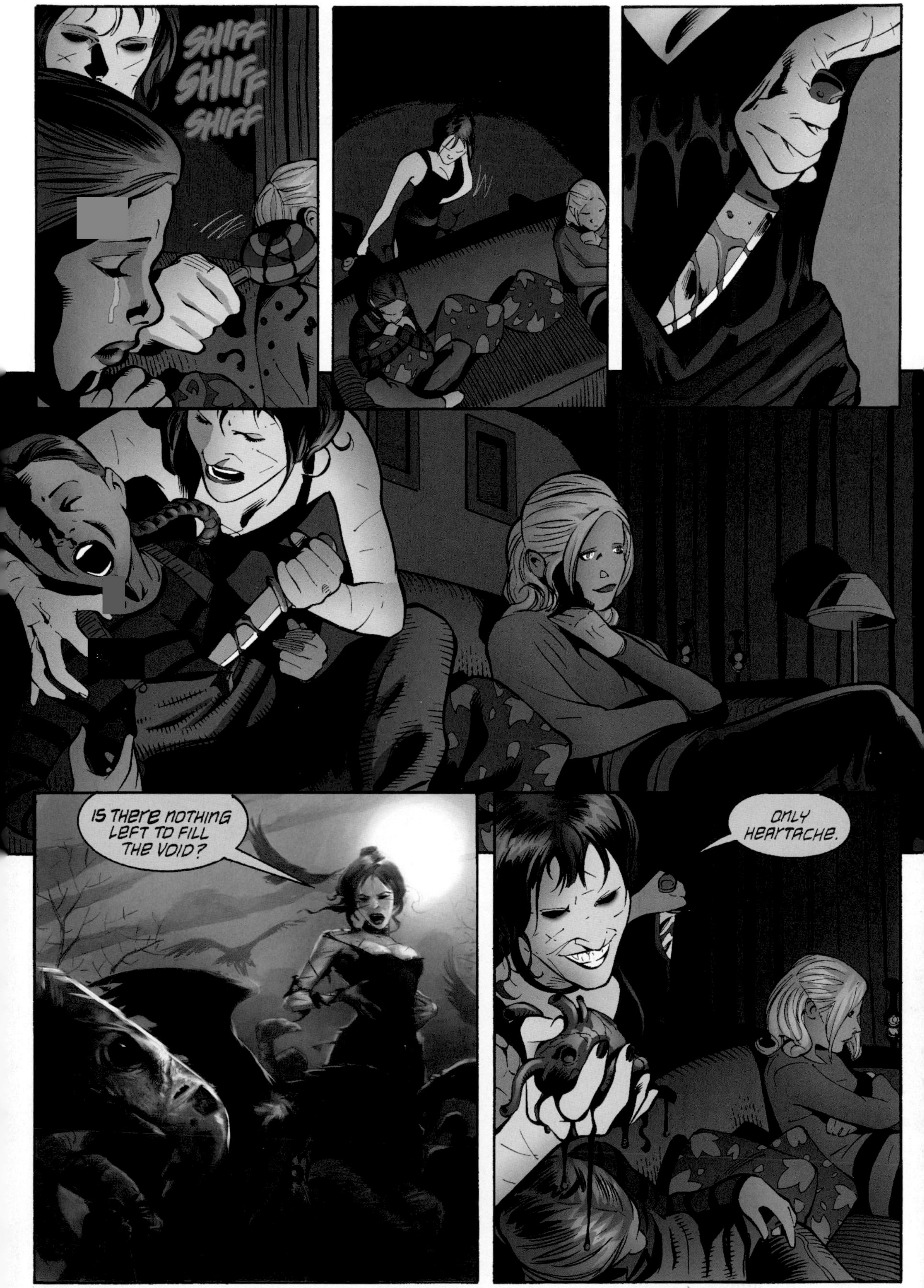
SHIFF
SHIFF
SHIFF
IS THERE NOTHING LEFT TO FILL THE VOID?
ONLY HEARTACHE.

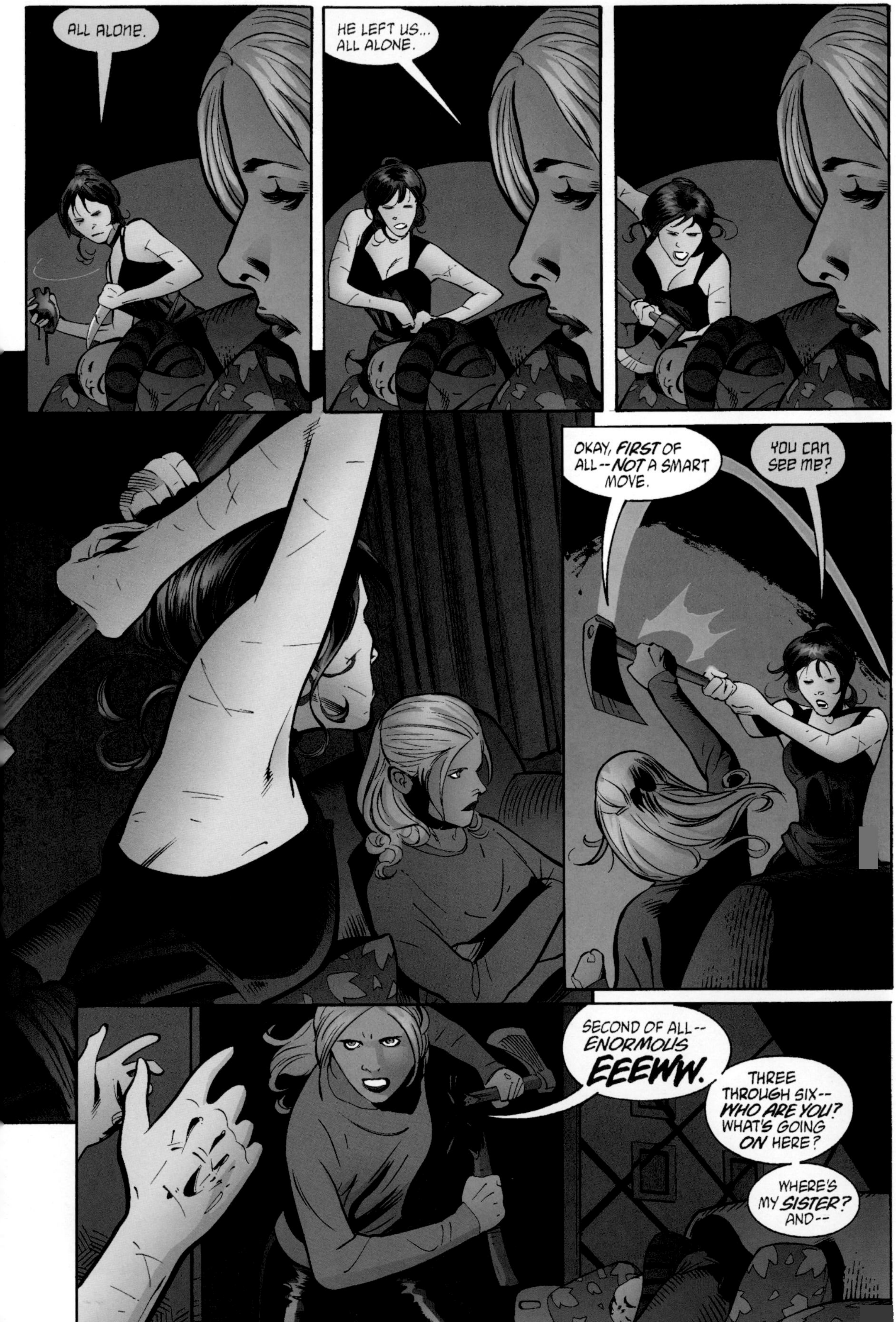
ALL ALONE.
HE LEFT US... ALL ALONE.
OKAY, FIRST OF ALL -- NOT A SMART MOVE.
YOU CAN SEE ME?
SECOND OF ALL -- ENORMOUS EEEWW.
THREE THROUGH SIX -- WHO ARE YOU? WHAT'S GOING ON HERE?
WHERE'S MY SISTER? AND --

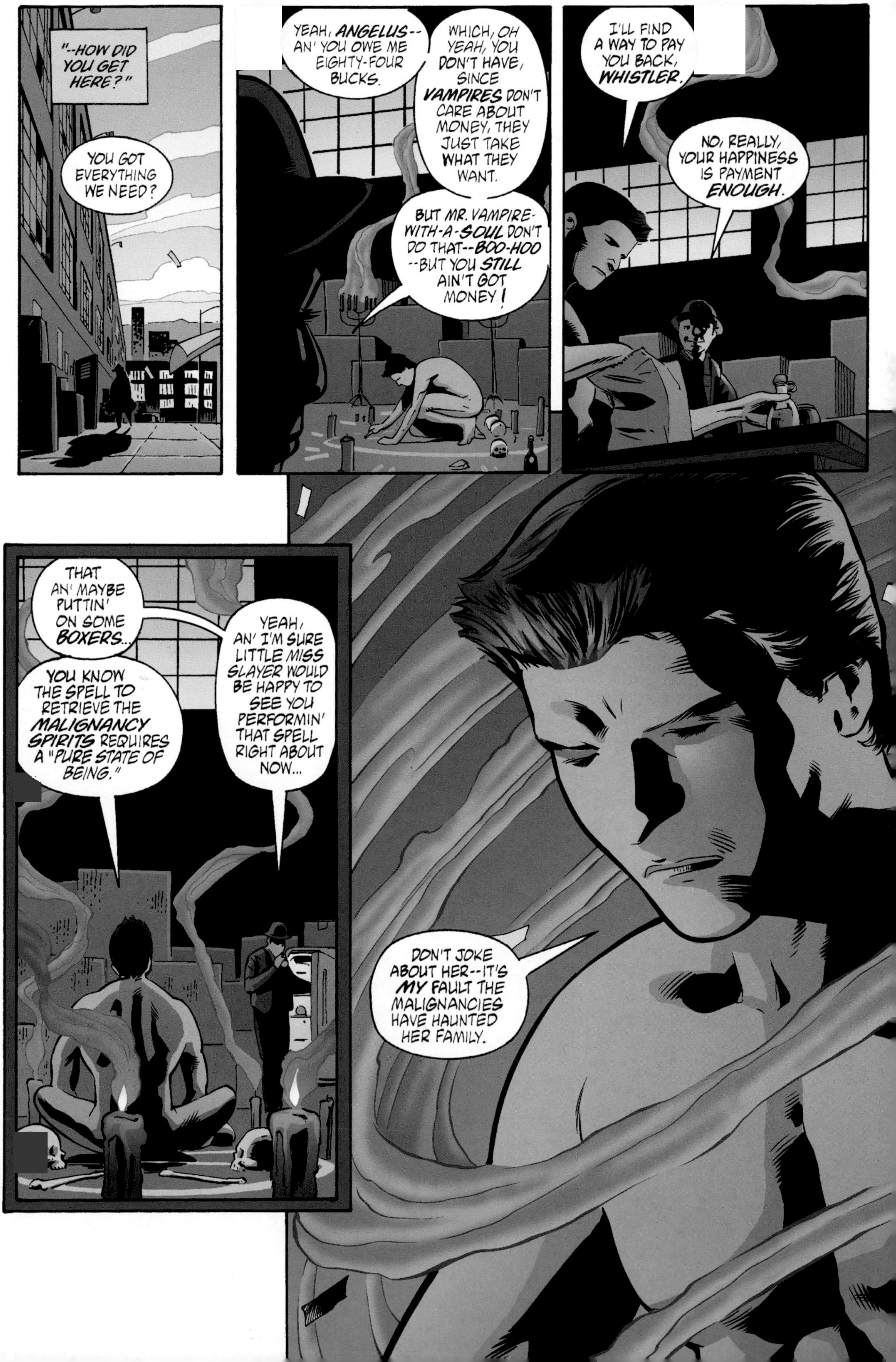
"--HOW DID YOU GET HERE?"
YOU GOT EVERYTHING WE NEED?
YEAH, ANGELUS-- AN' YOU OWE ME EIGHTY-FOUR BUCKS.
WHICH, OH YEAH, YOU DON'T HAVE, SINCE VAMPIRES DON'T CARE ABOUT MONEY, THEY JUST TAKE WHAT THEY WANT.
BUT MR. VAMPIRE-WITH-A-SOUL DON'T DO THAT--BOO-HOO--BUT YOU STILL AIN'T GOT MONEY!
I'LL FIND A WAY TO PAY YOU BACK, WHISTLER.
NO, REALLY, YOUR HAPPINESS IS PAYMENT ENOUGH.
THAT AN' MAYBE PUTTIN' ON SOME BOXERS...
YOU KNOW THE SPELL TO RETRIEVE THE MALIGNANCY SPIRITS REQUIRES A "PURE STATE OF BEING."
YEAH, AN' I'M SURE LITTLE MISS SLAYER WOULD BE HAPPY TO SEE YOU PERFORMIN' THAT SPELL RIGHT ABOUT NOW...
DON'T JOKE ABOUT HER--IT'S MY FAULT THE MALIGNANCIES HAVE HAUNTED HER FAMILY.

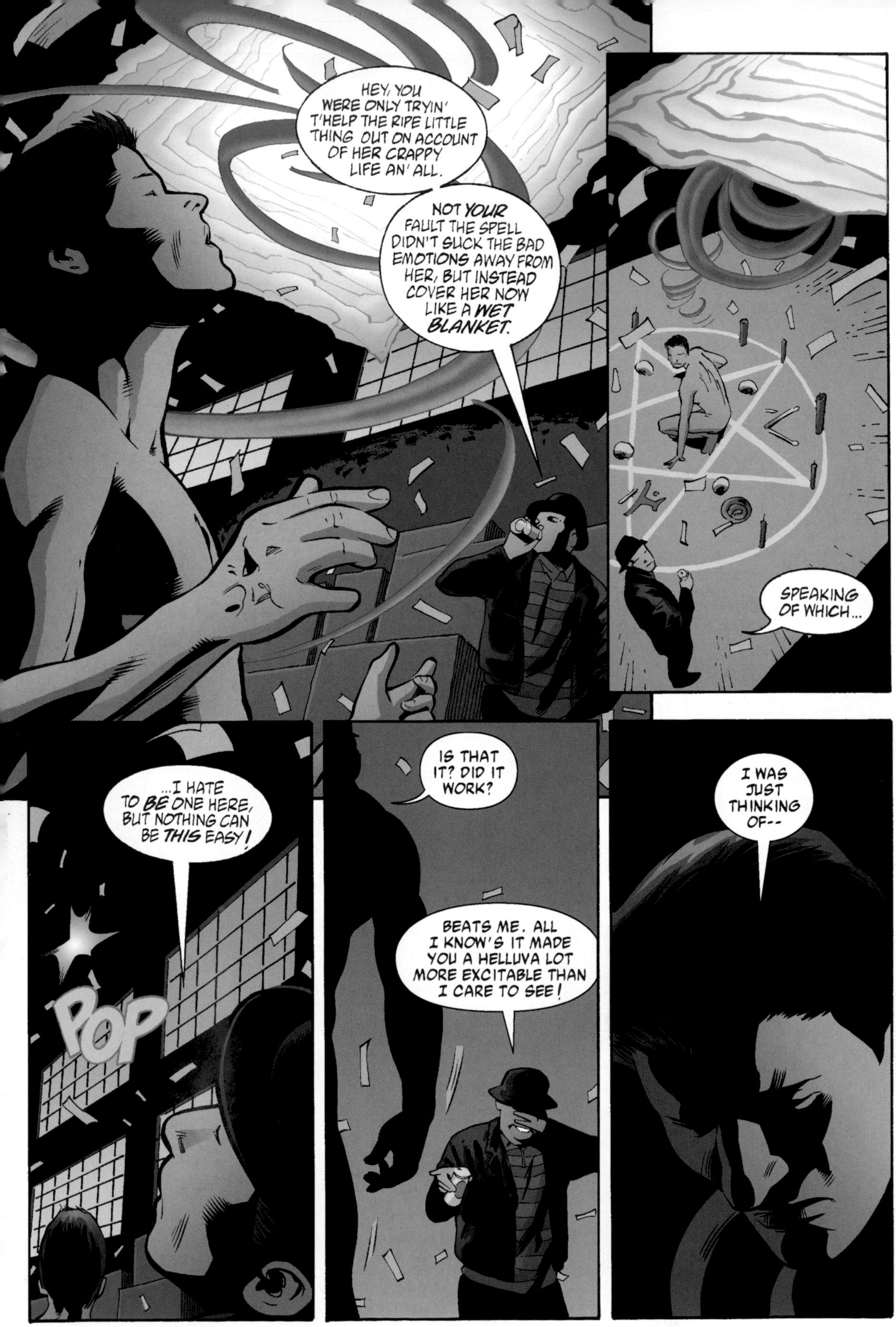
HEY, YOU WERE ONLY TRYIN' T'HELP THE RIPE LITTLE THING OUT ON ACCOUNT OF HER CRAPPY LIFE AN' ALL.
NOT YOUR FAULT THE SPELL DIDN'T SUCK THE BAD EMOTIONS AWAY FROM HER, BUT INSTEAD COVER HER NOW LIKE A WET BLANKET.
SPEAKING OF WHICH...
...I HATE TO BE ONE HERE, BUT NOTHING CAN BE THIS EASY!
POP
IS THAT IT? DID IT WORK?
BEATS ME. ALL I KNOW'S IT MADE YOU A HELLUVA LOT MORE EXCITABLE THAN I CARE TO SEE!
I WAS JUST THINKING OF--

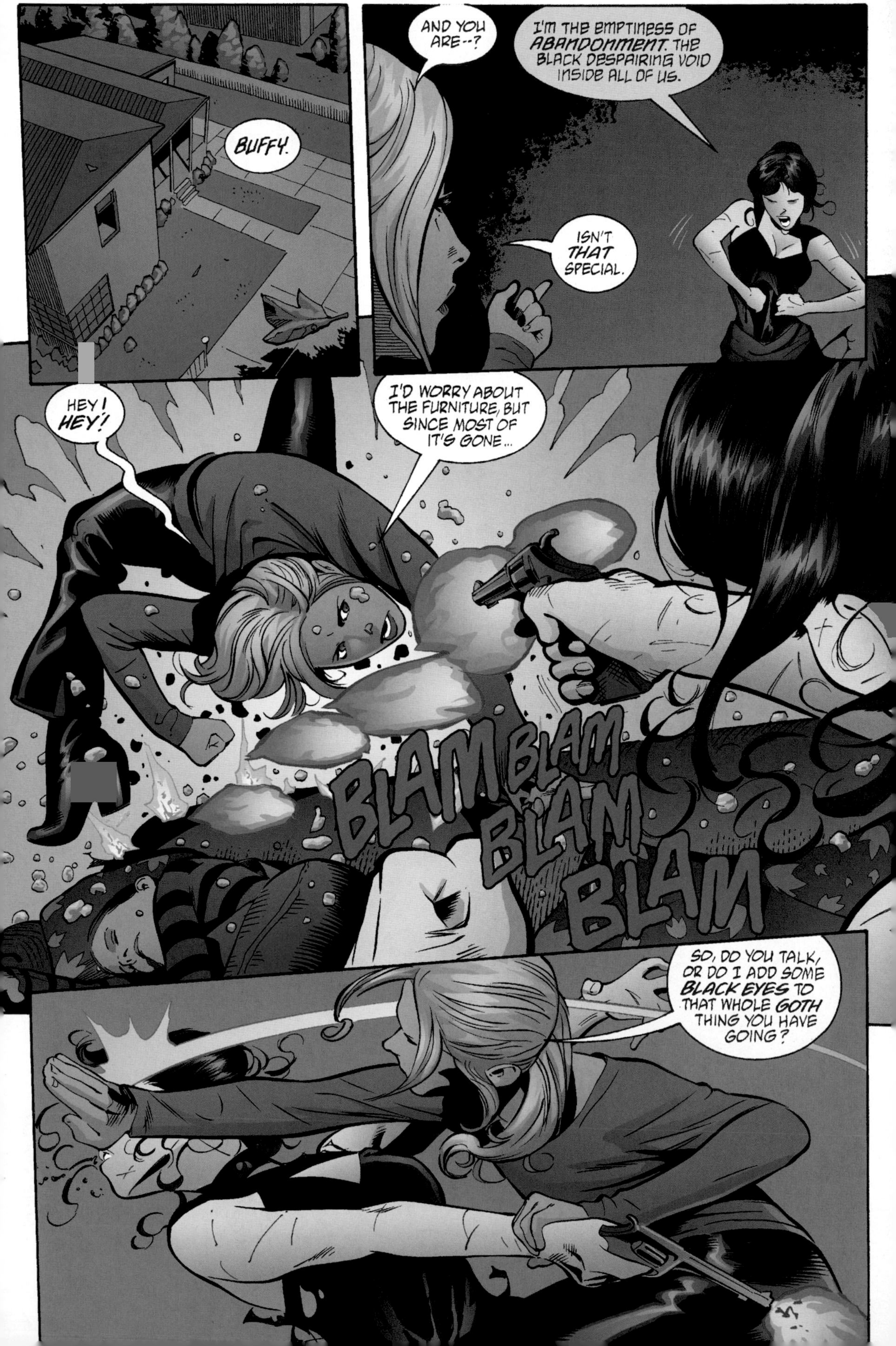
BUFFY.
AND YOU ARE--?
I'M THE EMPTINESS OF ABANDONMENT. THE BLACK DESPAIRING VOID INSIDE ALL OF US.
ISN'T THAT SPECIAL.
HEY! HEY!
I'D WORRY ABOUT THE FURNITURE, BUT SINCE MOST OF IT'S GONE...
BLAM BLAM BLAM BLAM BLAM
SO, DO YOU TALK, OR DO I ADD SOME BLACK EYES TO THAT WHOLE GOTH THING YOU HAVE GOING?

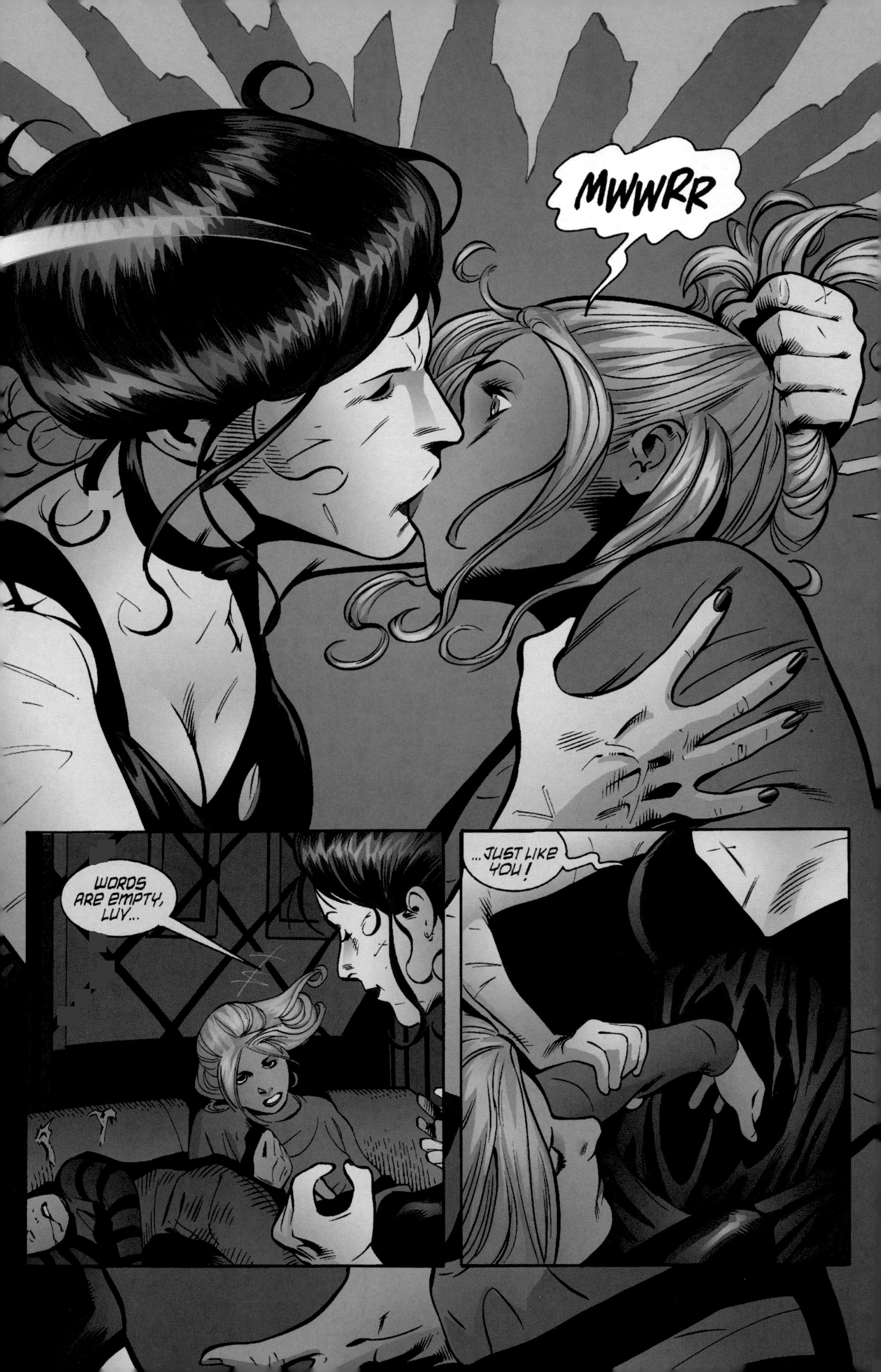
MWWRR
WORDS ARE EMPTY, LUV...
...JUST LIKE YOU!

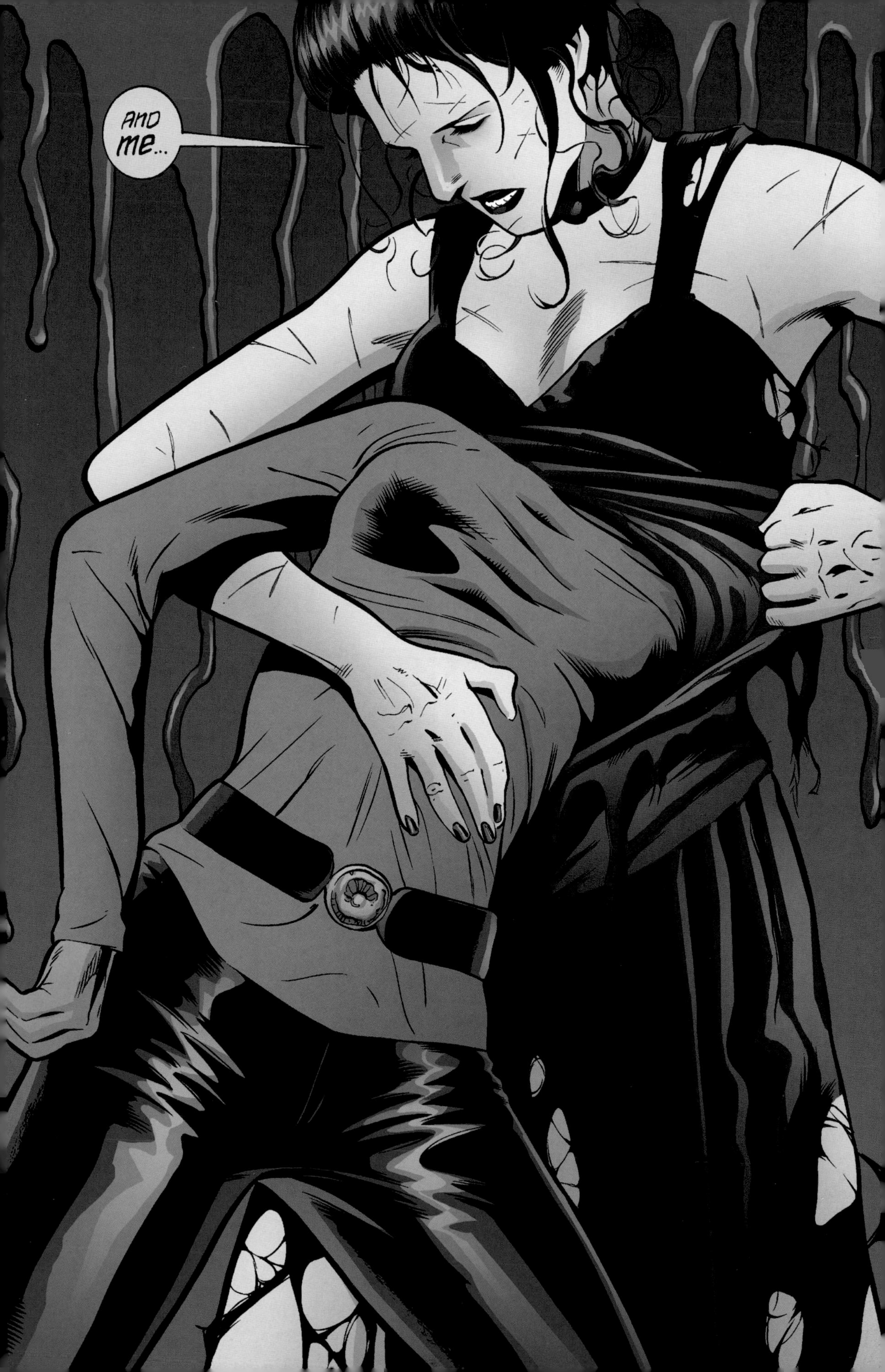
AND ME...

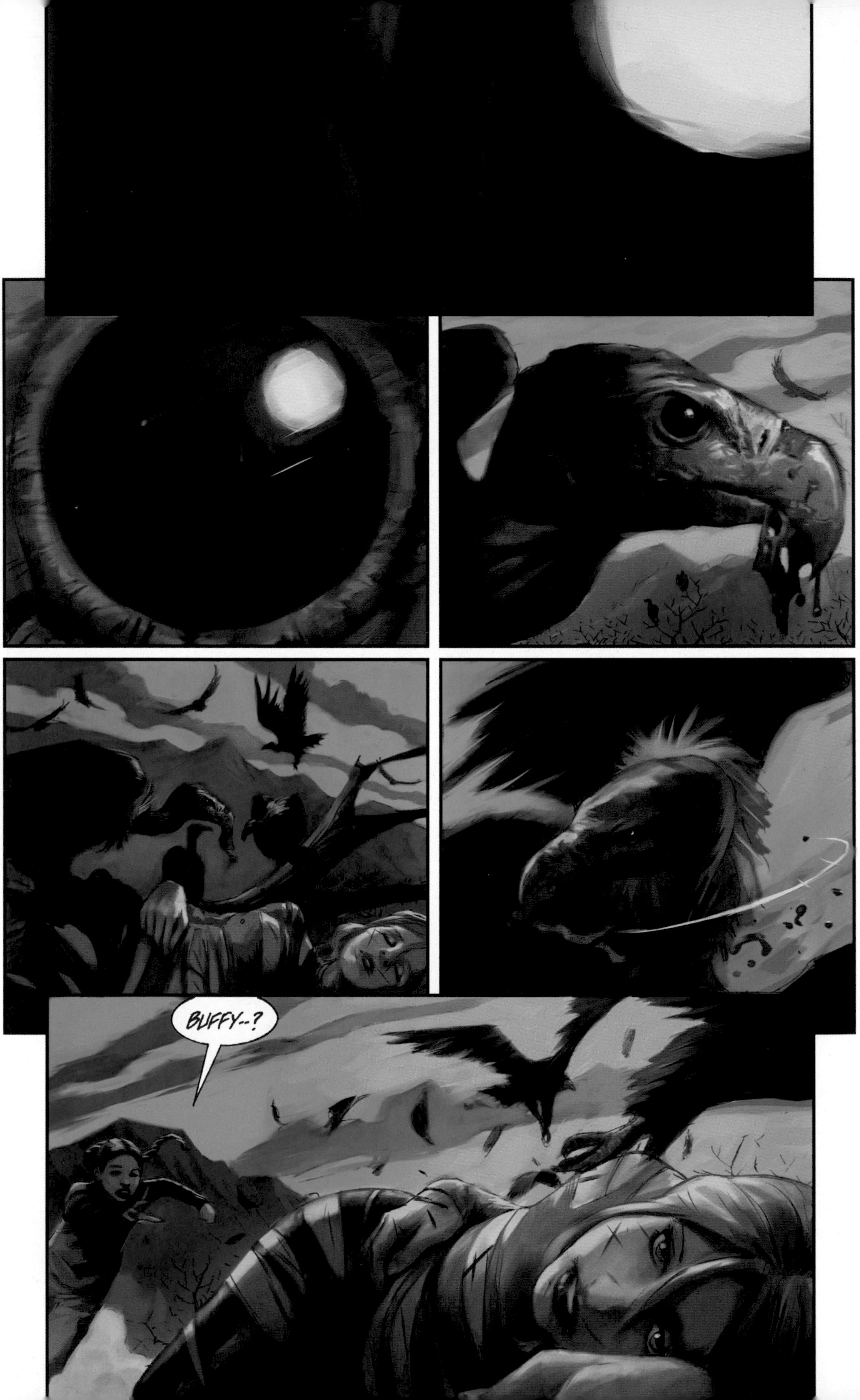
BUFFY--?

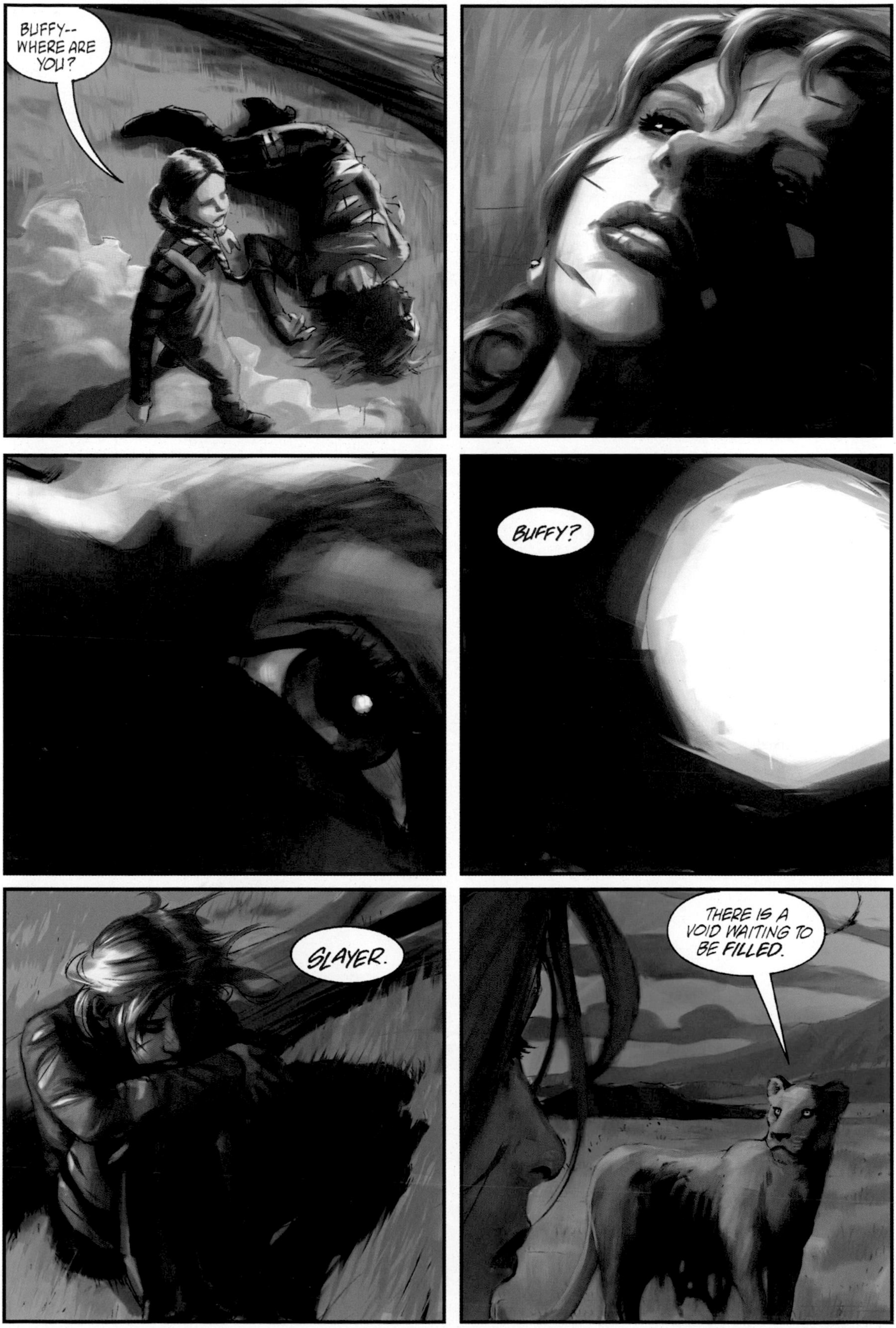
BUFFY-- WHERE ARE YOU?
BUFFY?
SLAYER.
THERE IS A VOID WAITING TO BE FILLED.

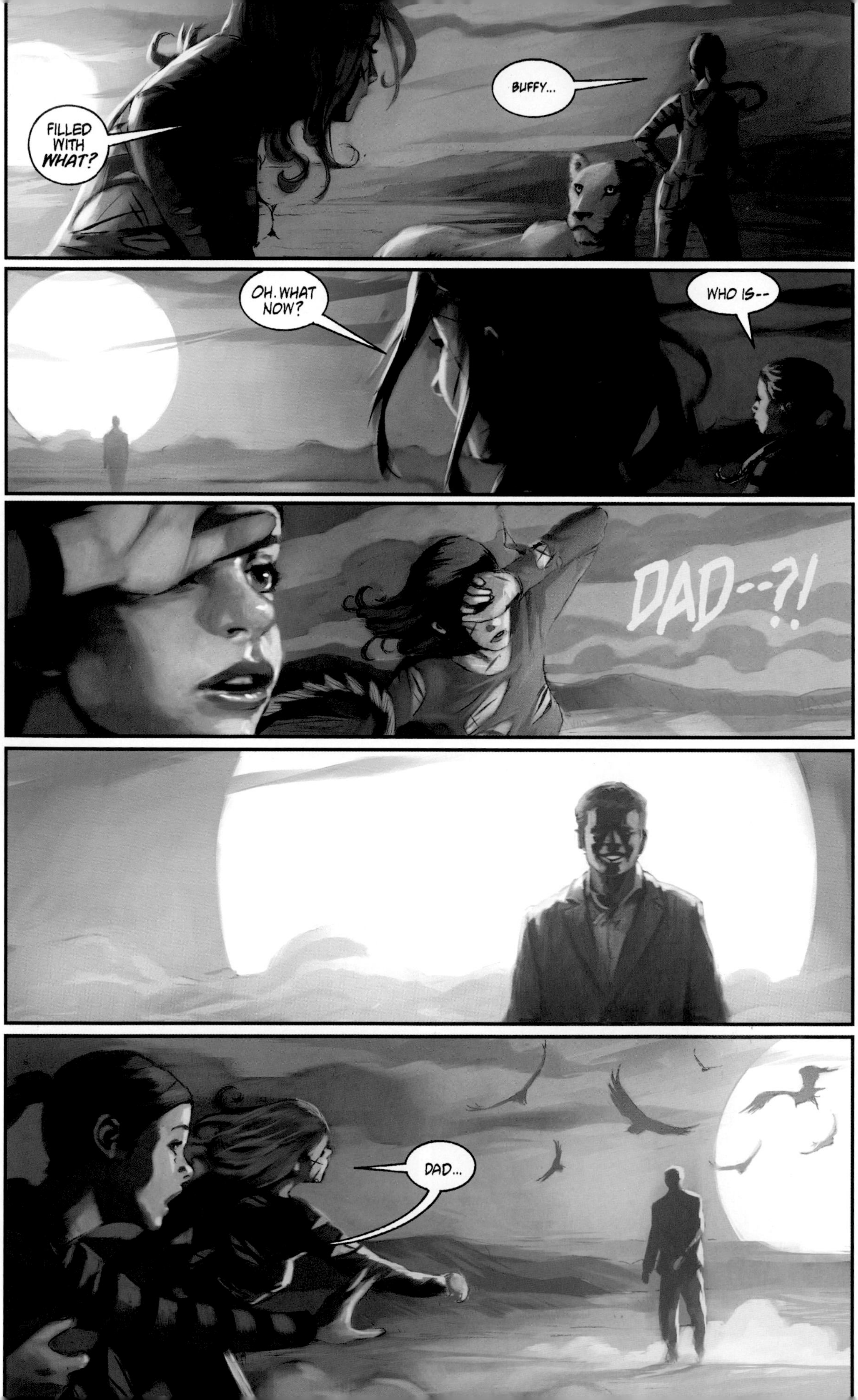
FILLED WITH WHAT?
BUFFY...
OH. WHAT NOW?
WHO IS--
DAD--?!
DAD...

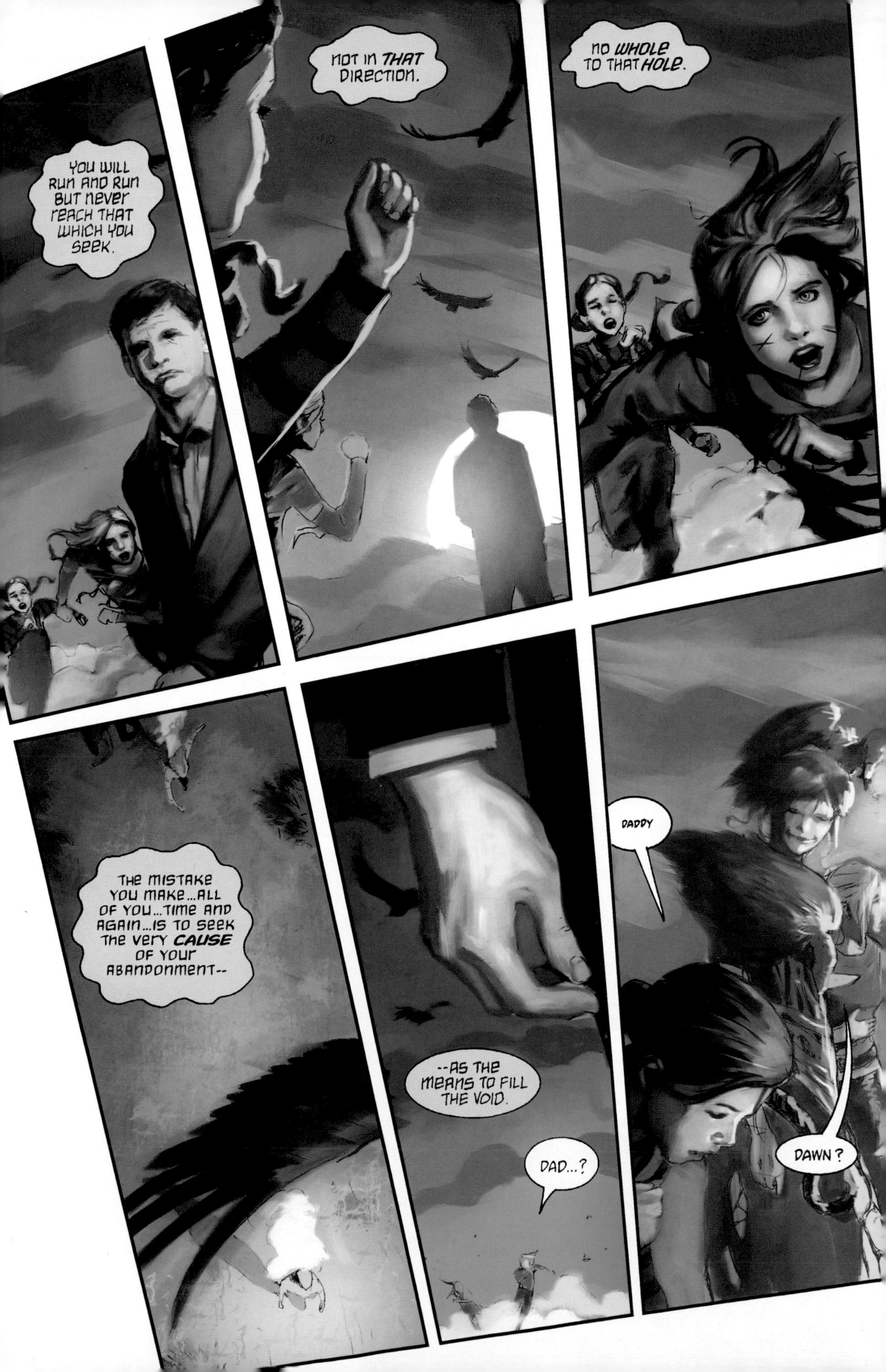
You will Run and Run But never reach that which you seek.
not in THAT Direction.
no WHOLE to that HOLE.
The mistake you make...all of you...time and again...is to seek the very CAUSE of your abandonment--
--As the means to fill the void.
DAD...?
DADDY
DAWN?

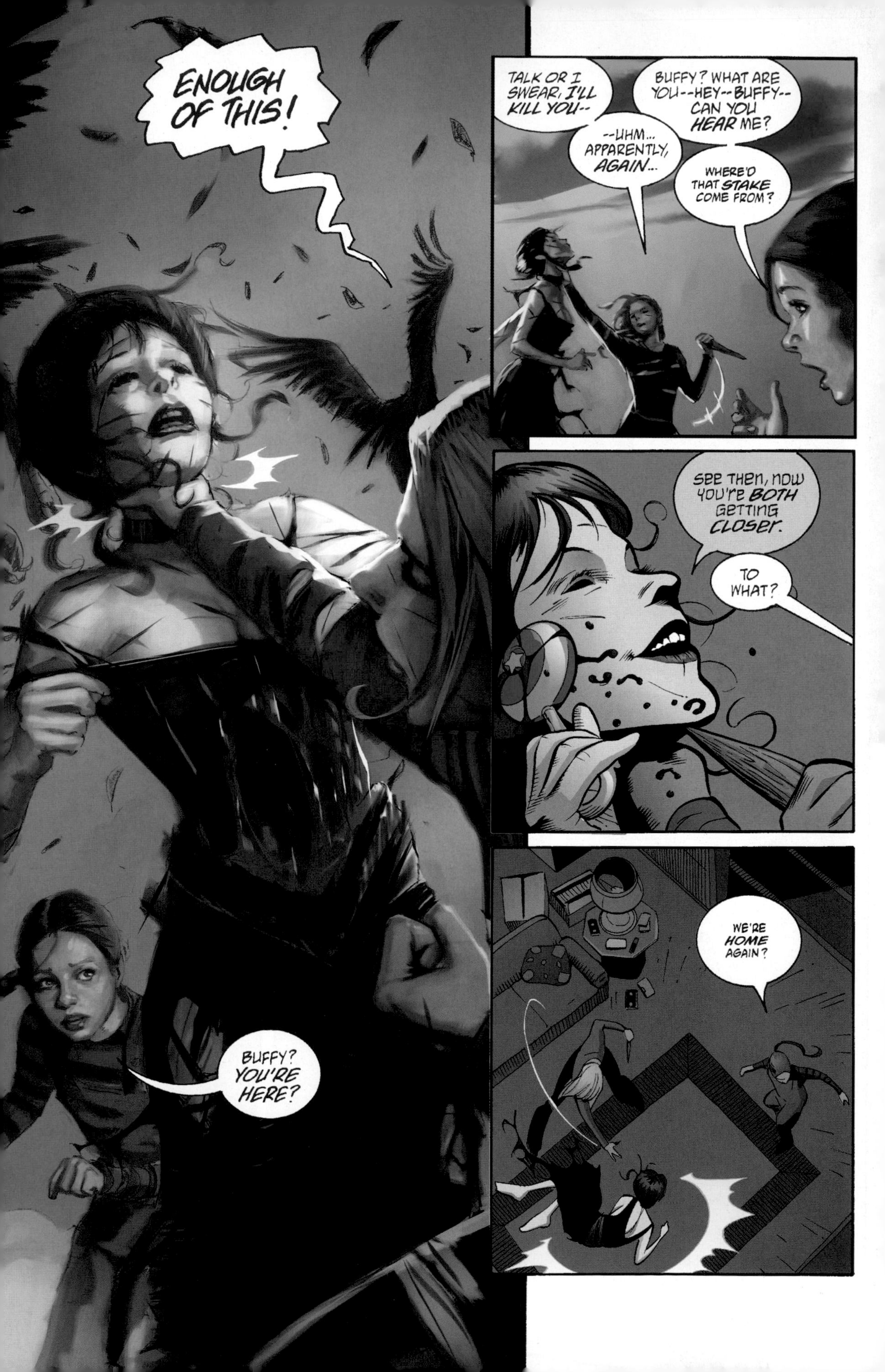
ENOUGH OF THIS!
BUFFY? YOU'RE HERE?
TALK OR I SWEAR, I'LL KILL YOU--
--UHM... APPARENTLY, AGAIN...
BUFFY? WHAT ARE YOU--HEY--BUFFY--CAN YOU HEAR ME?
WHERE'D THAT STAKE COME FROM?
SEE THEN, NOW YOU'RE BOTH GETTING CLOSER.
TO WHAT?
WE'RE HOME AGAIN?

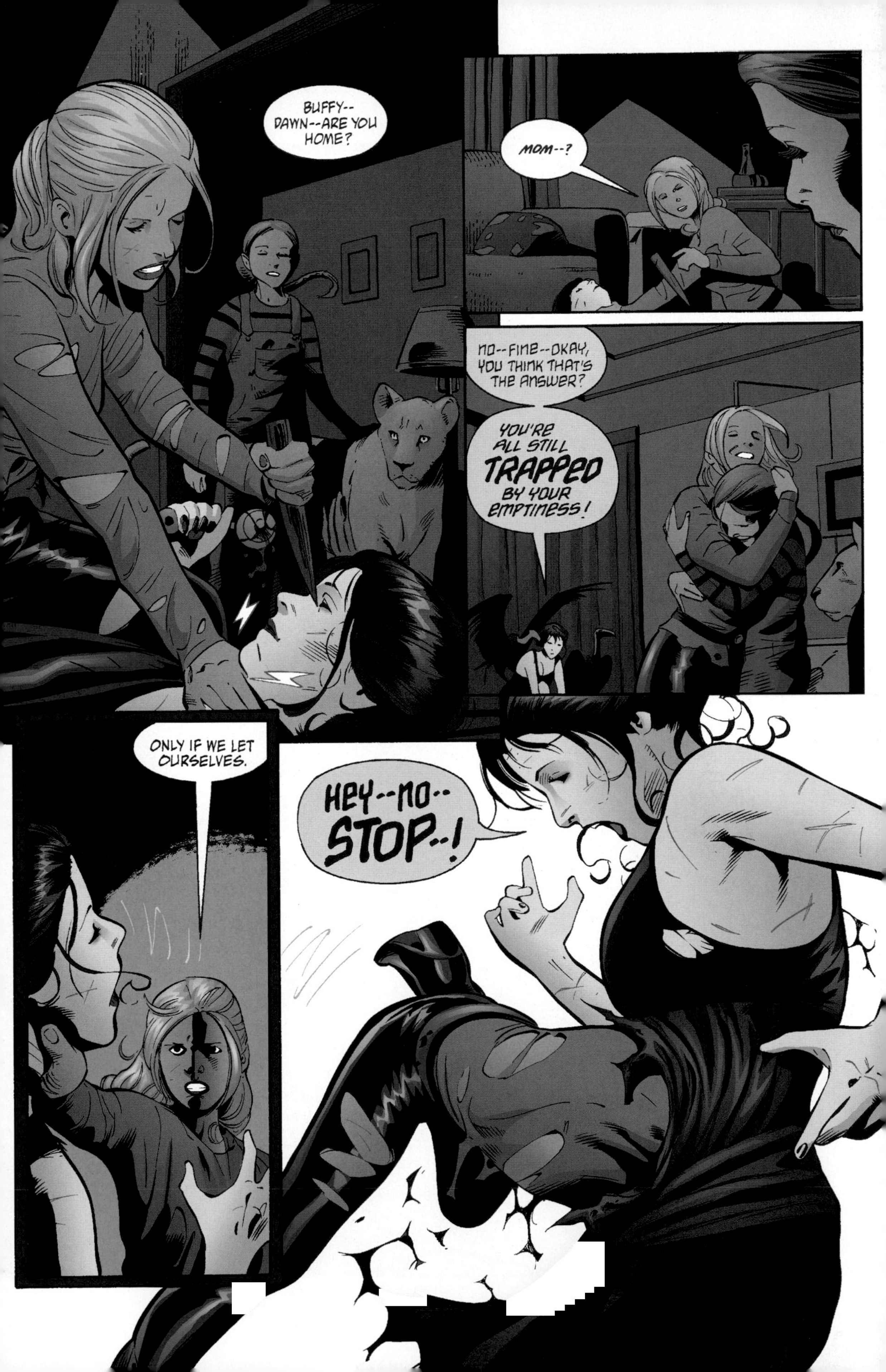
BUFFY--
DAWN--ARE YOU
HOME?
MOM--?
NO--FINE--OKAY,
YOU THINK THAT'S
THE ANSWER?
YOU'RE
ALL STILL
TRAPPED
BY YOUR
EMPTINESS!
ONLY IF WE LET
OURSELVES.
HEY--NO--
STOP--!

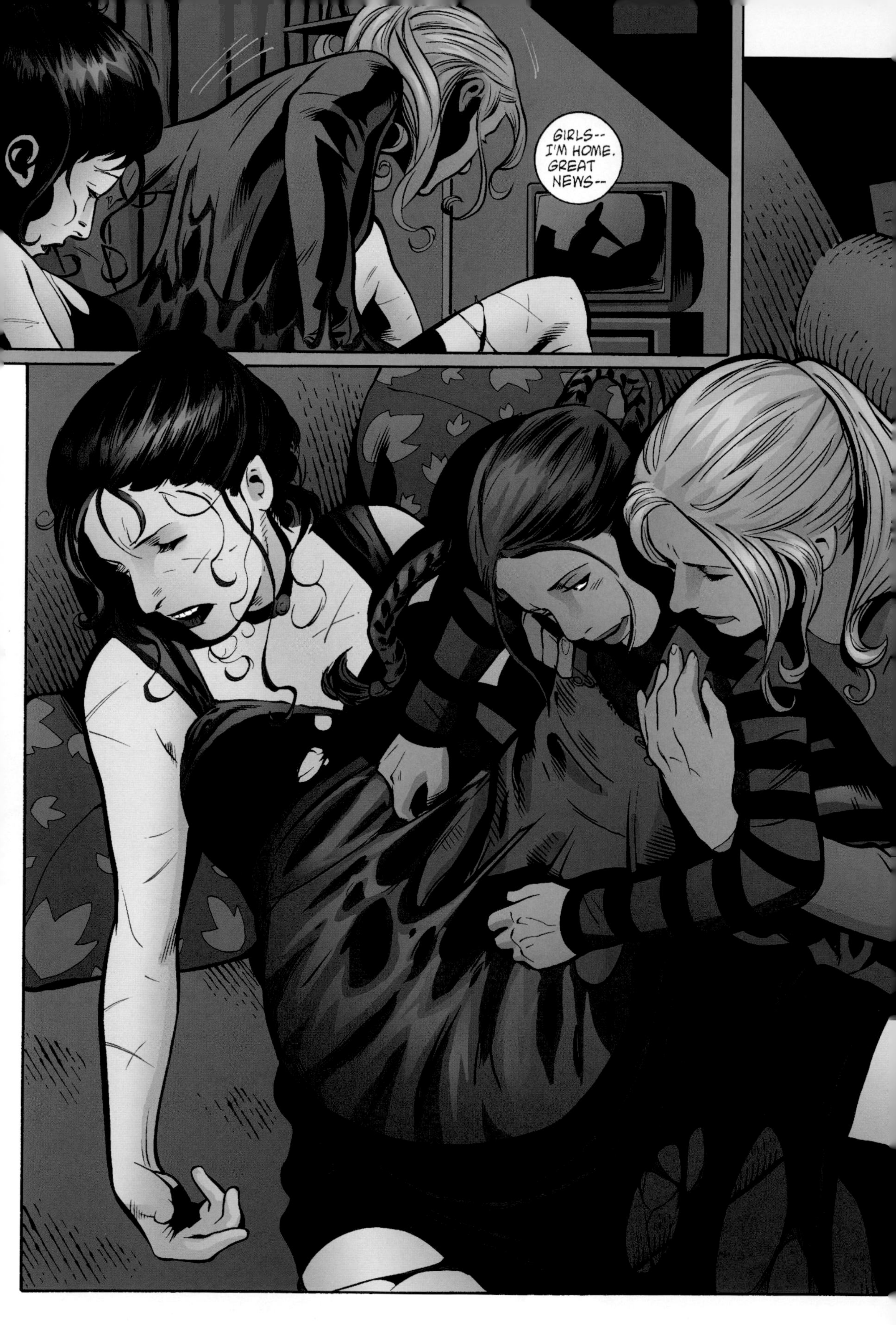
GIRLS-- I'M HOME. GREAT NEWS--

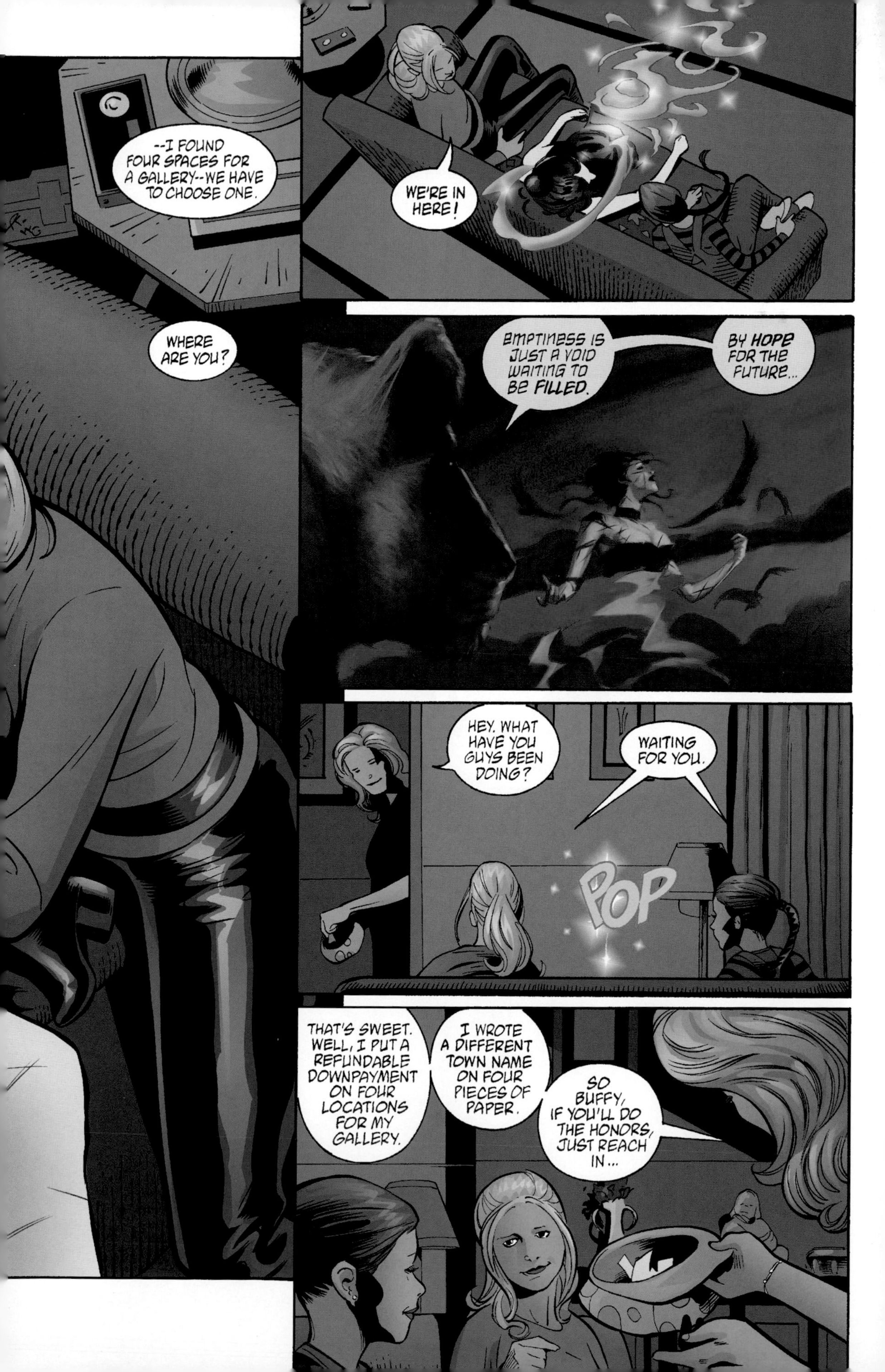
--I FOUND FOUR SPACES FOR A GALLERY--WE HAVE TO CHOOSE ONE.
WHERE ARE YOU?
WE'RE IN HERE!
EMPTINESS IS JUST A VOID WAITING TO BE FILLED.
BY HOPE FOR THE FUTURE...
HEY. WHAT HAVE YOU GUYS BEEN DOING?
WAITING FOR YOU.
POP
THAT'S SWEET. WELL, I PUT A REFUNDABLE DOWNPAYMENT ON FOUR LOCATIONS FOR MY GALLERY.
I WROTE A DIFFERENT TOWN NAME ON FOUR PIECES OF PAPER.
SO BUFFY, IF YOU'LL DO THE HONORS, JUST REACH IN...

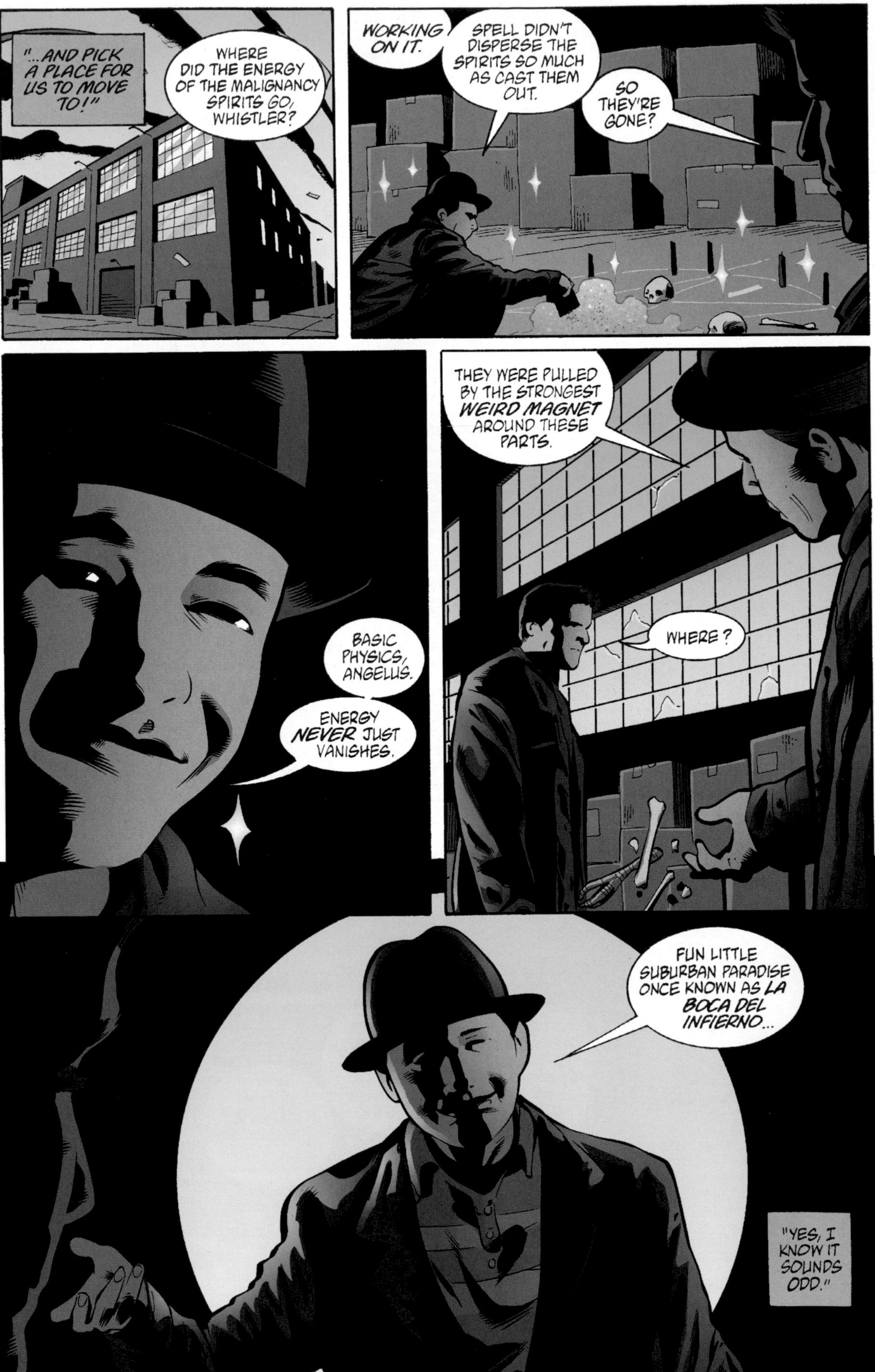
"...AND PICK A PLACE FOR US TO MOVE TO!"
WHERE DID THE ENERGY OF THE MALIGNANCY SPIRITS GO, WHISTLER?
WORKING ON IT.
SPELL DIDN'T DISPERSE THE SPIRITS SO MUCH AS CAST THEM OUT.
SO THEY'RE GONE?
BASIC PHYSICS, ANGELUS.
ENERGY NEVER JUST VANISHES.
THEY WERE PULLED BY THE STRONGEST WEIRD MAGNET AROUND THESE PARTS.
WHERE ?
FUN LITTLE SUBURBAN PARADISE ONCE KNOWN AS LA BOCA DEL INFIERNO...
"YES, I KNOW IT SOUNDS ODD."

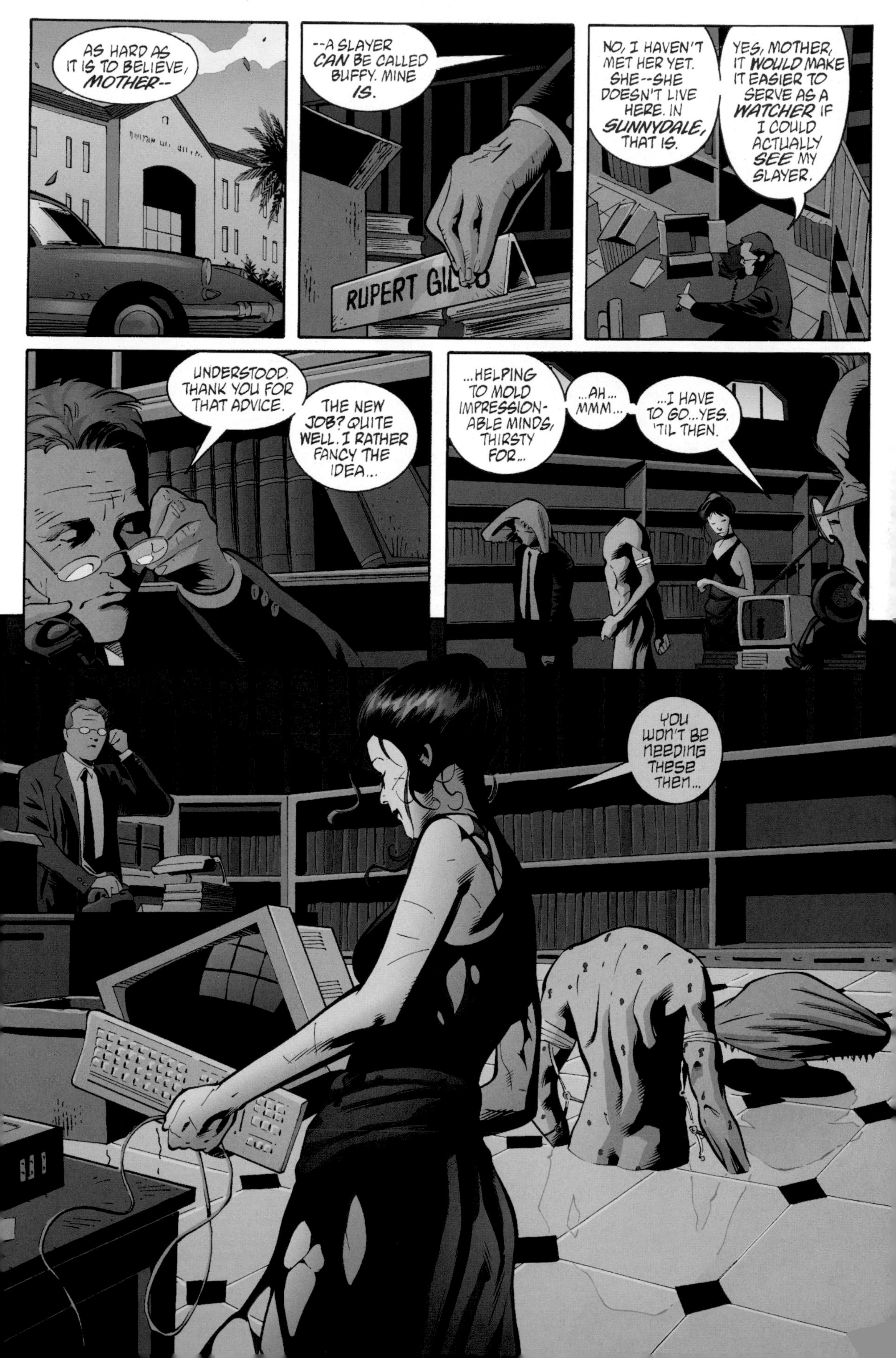
AS HARD AS IT IS TO BELIEVE, MOTHER--
--A SLAYER CAN BE CALLED BUFFY. MINE IS.
RUPERT GILES
NO, I HAVEN'T MET HER YET. SHE--SHE DOESN'T LIVE HERE. IN SUNNYDALE, THAT IS.
YES, MOTHER, IT WOULD MAKE IT EASIER TO SERVE AS A WATCHER IF I COULD ACTUALLY SEE MY SLAYER.
UNDERSTOOD. THANK YOU FOR THAT ADVICE.
THE NEW JOB? QUITE WELL. I RATHER FANCY THE IDEA...
...HELPING TO MOLD IMPRESSION-ABLE MINDS, THIRSTY FOR...
...AH... MMM...
...I HAVE TO GO...YES. 'TIL THEN.
YOU WON'T BE NEEDING THESE THEN...

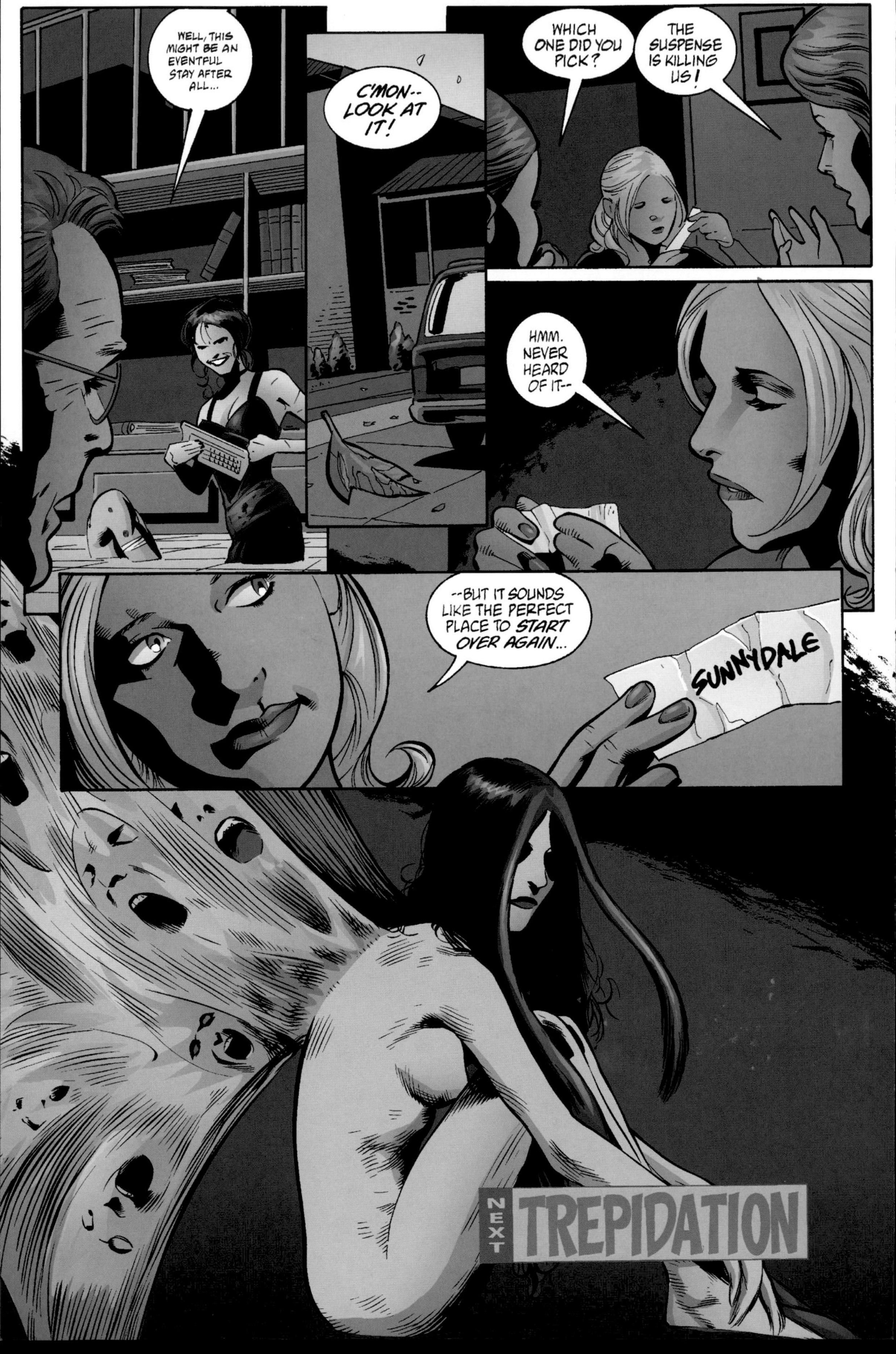

WELL, THIS MIGHT BE AN EVENTFUL STAY AFTER ALL...
C'MON-- LOOK AT IT!
WHICH ONE DID YOU PICK?
THE SUSPENSE IS KILLING US!
HMM. NEVER HEARD OF IT--
--BUT IT SOUNDS LIKE THE PERFECT PLACE TO START OVER AGAIN...
SUNNYDALE
NEXT TREPIDATION

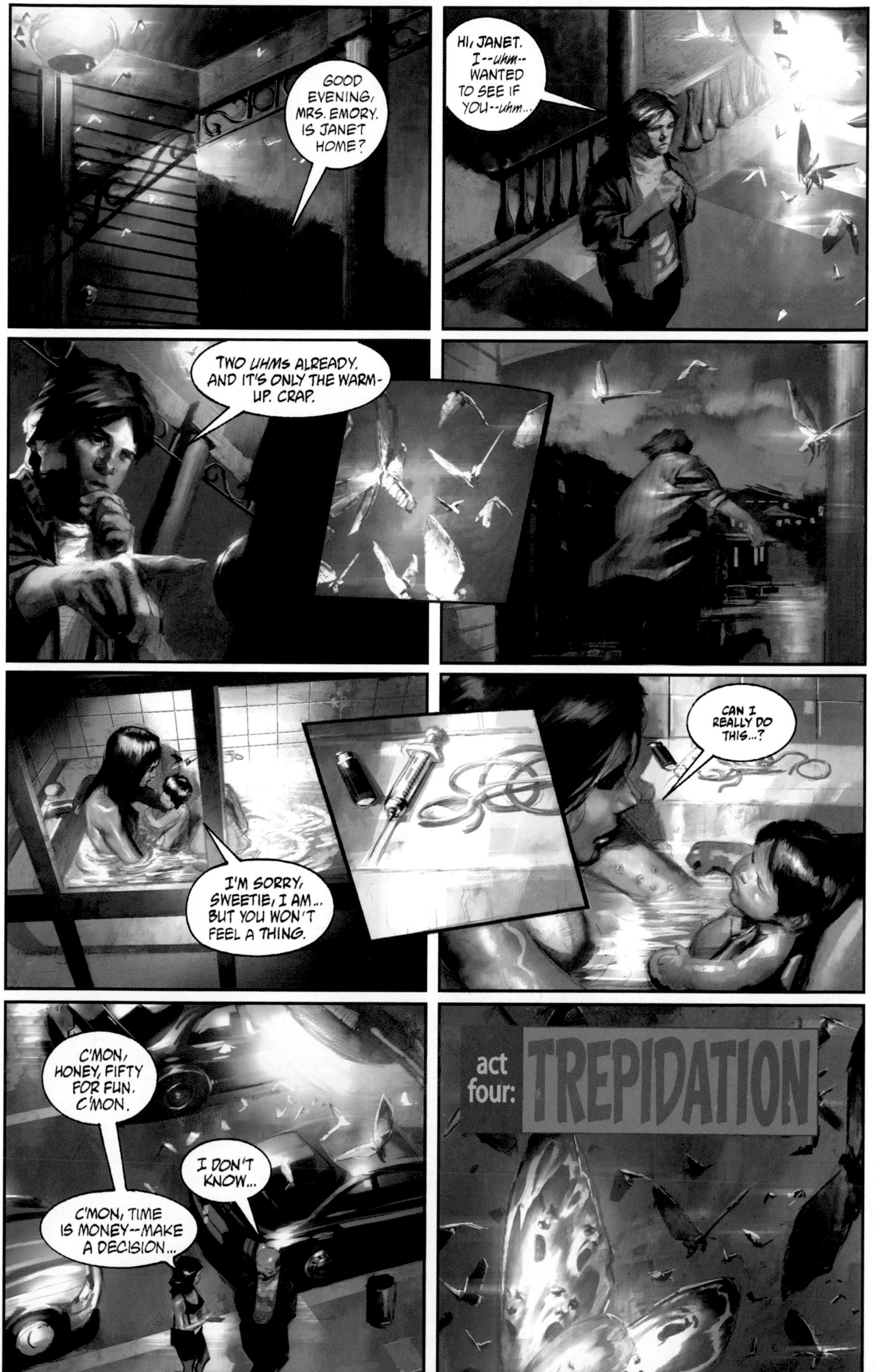
GOOD EVENING, MRS. EMORY. IS JANET HOME?
HI, JANET. I--uhm--WANTED TO SEE IF YOU--uhm...
TWO UHMS ALREADY. AND IT'S ONLY THE WARM-UP. CRAP.
I'M SORRY, SWEETIE, I AM... BUT YOU WON'T FEEL A THING.
CAN I REALLY DO THIS...?
C'MON, HONEY, FIFTY FOR FUN. C'MON.
I DON'T KNOW...
C'MON, TIME IS MONEY--MAKE A DECISION...
act four: TREPIDATION

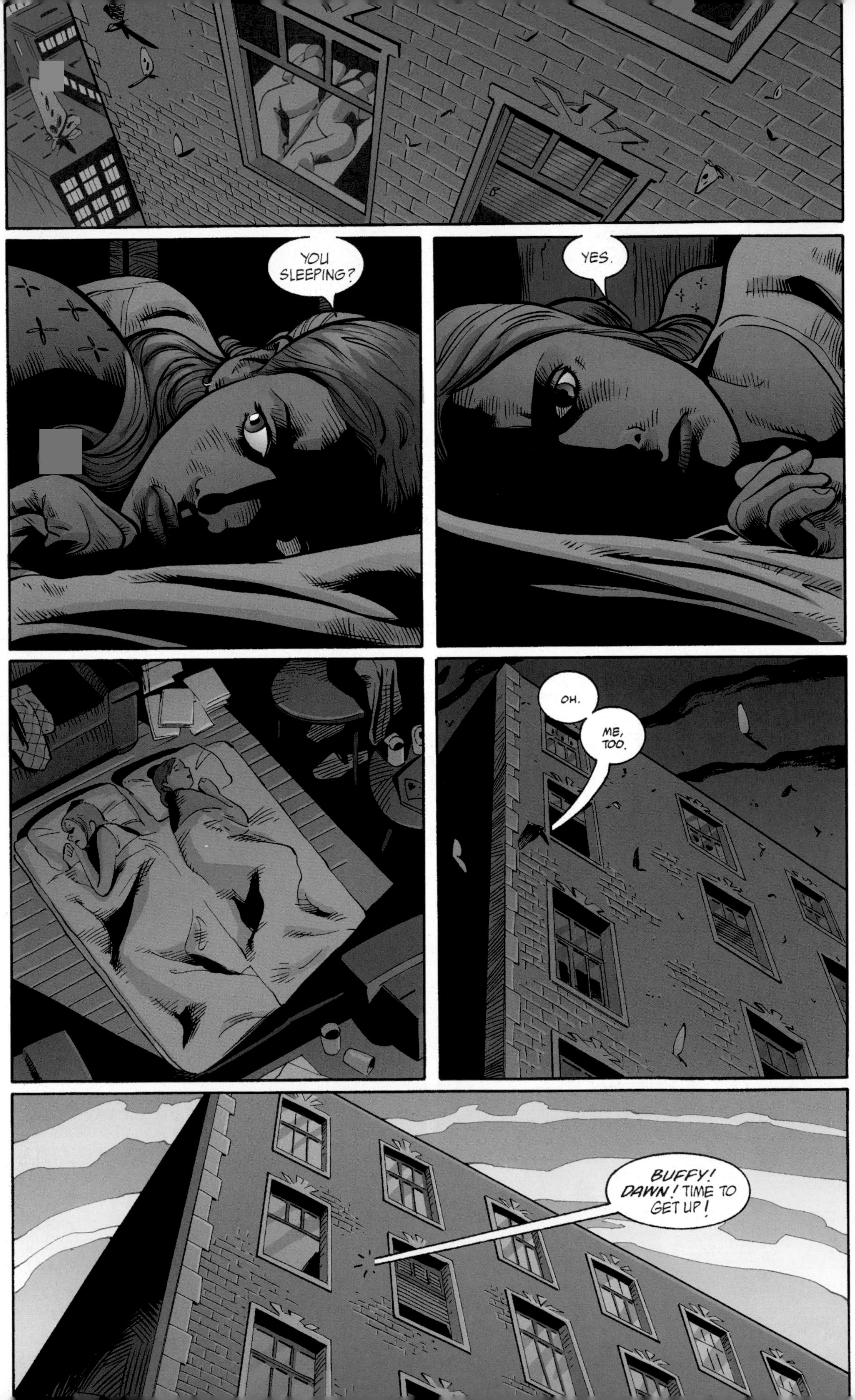
YOU SLEEPING?
YES.
OH.
ME, TOO.
BUFFY! DAWN! TIME TO GET UP!

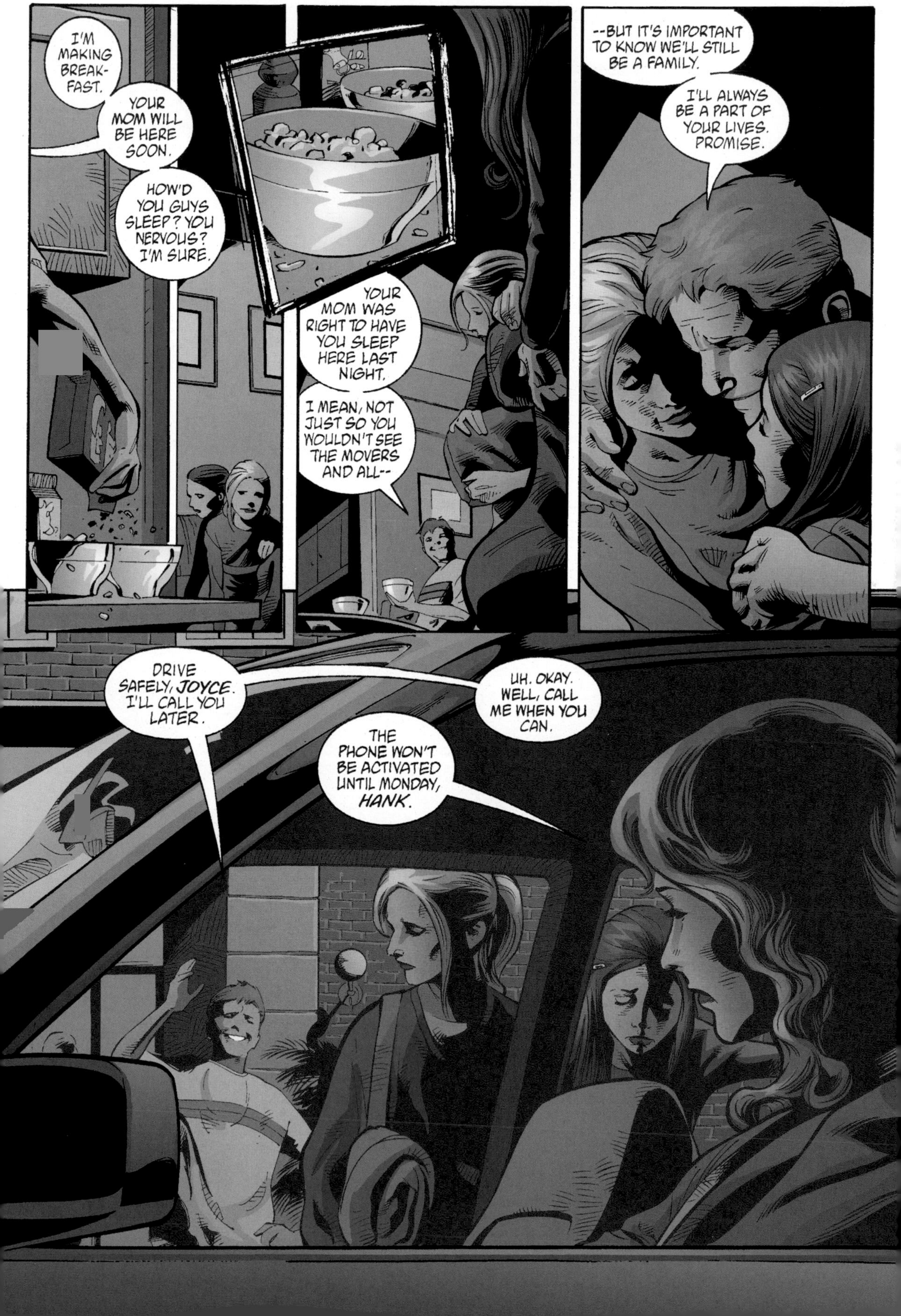

I'M MAKING BREAK-FAST.
YOUR MOM WILL BE HERE SOON.
HOW'D YOU GUYS SLEEP? YOU NERVOUS? I'M SURE.
YOUR MOM WAS RIGHT TO HAVE YOU SLEEP HERE LAST NIGHT.
I MEAN, NOT JUST SO YOU WOULDN'T SEE THE MOVERS AND ALL--
--BUT IT'S IMPORTANT TO KNOW WE'LL STILL BE A FAMILY.
I'LL ALWAYS BE A PART OF YOUR LIVES. PROMISE.
DRIVE SAFELY, JOYCE. I'LL CALL YOU LATER.
UH. OKAY. WELL, CALL ME WHEN YOU CAN.
THE PHONE WON'T BE ACTIVATED UNTIL MONDAY, HANK.

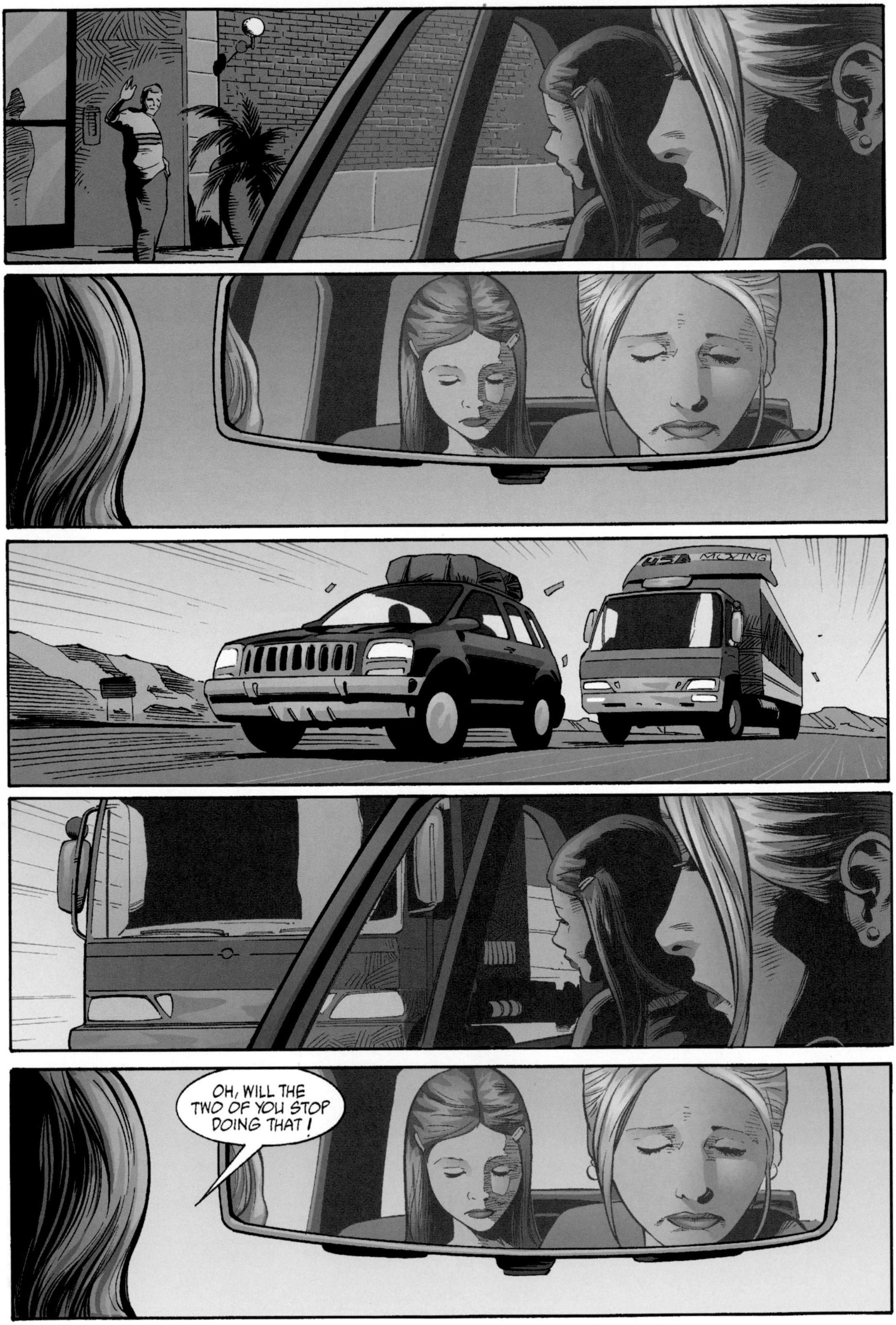
USA MOVING
OH, WILL THE TWO OF YOU STOP DOING THAT!

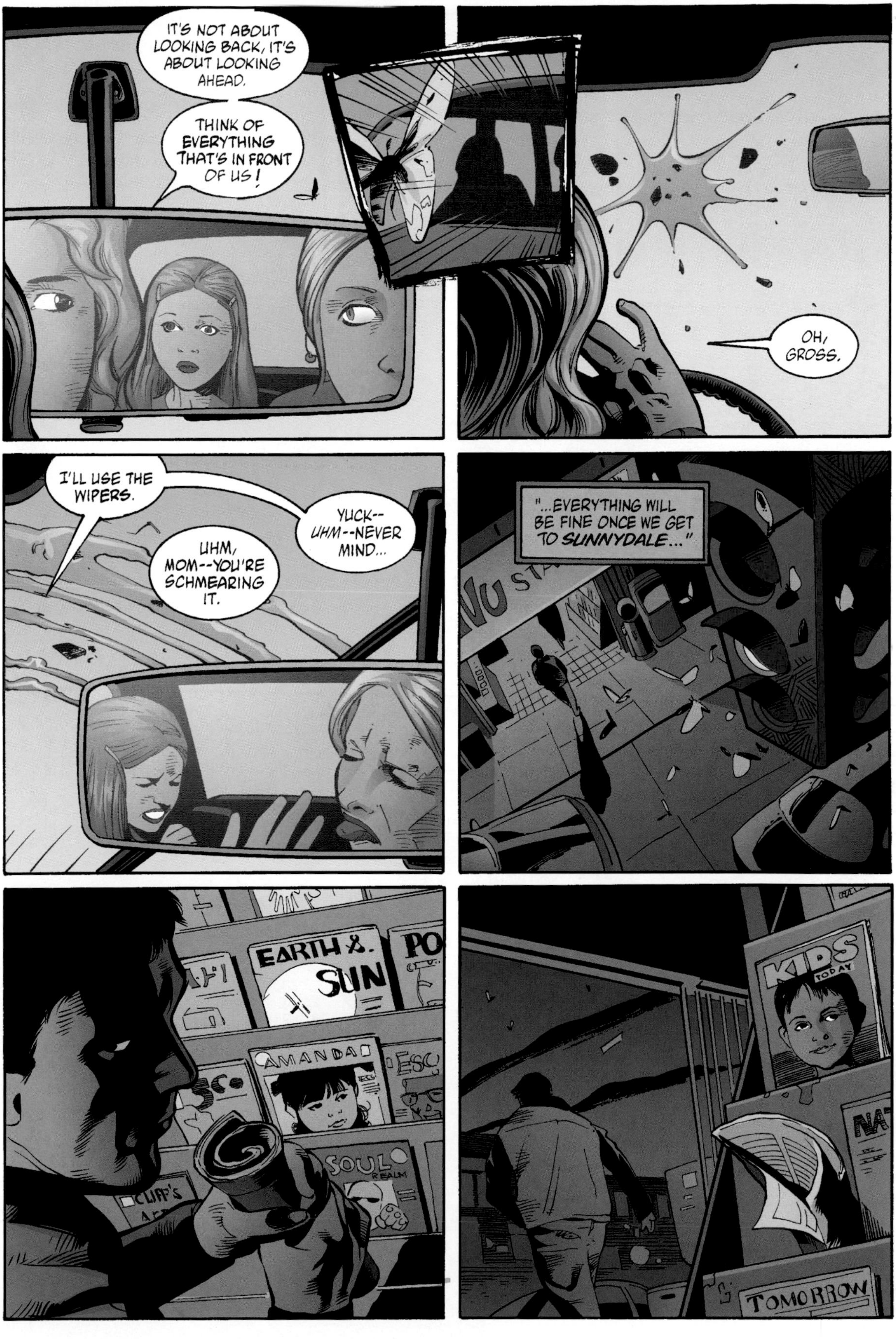

IT'S NOT ABOUT LOOKING BACK, IT'S ABOUT LOOKING AHEAD.
THINK OF EVERYTHING THAT'S IN FRONT OF US!
OH, GROSS.
I'LL USE THE WIPERS.
UHM, MOM--YOU'RE SCHMEARING IT.
YUCK--UHM--NEVER MIND...
"...EVERYTHING WILL BE FINE ONCE WE GET TO SUNNYDALE..."
EARTH & SUN
AMANDA
SOUL REALM
KIDS TODAY
TOMORROW

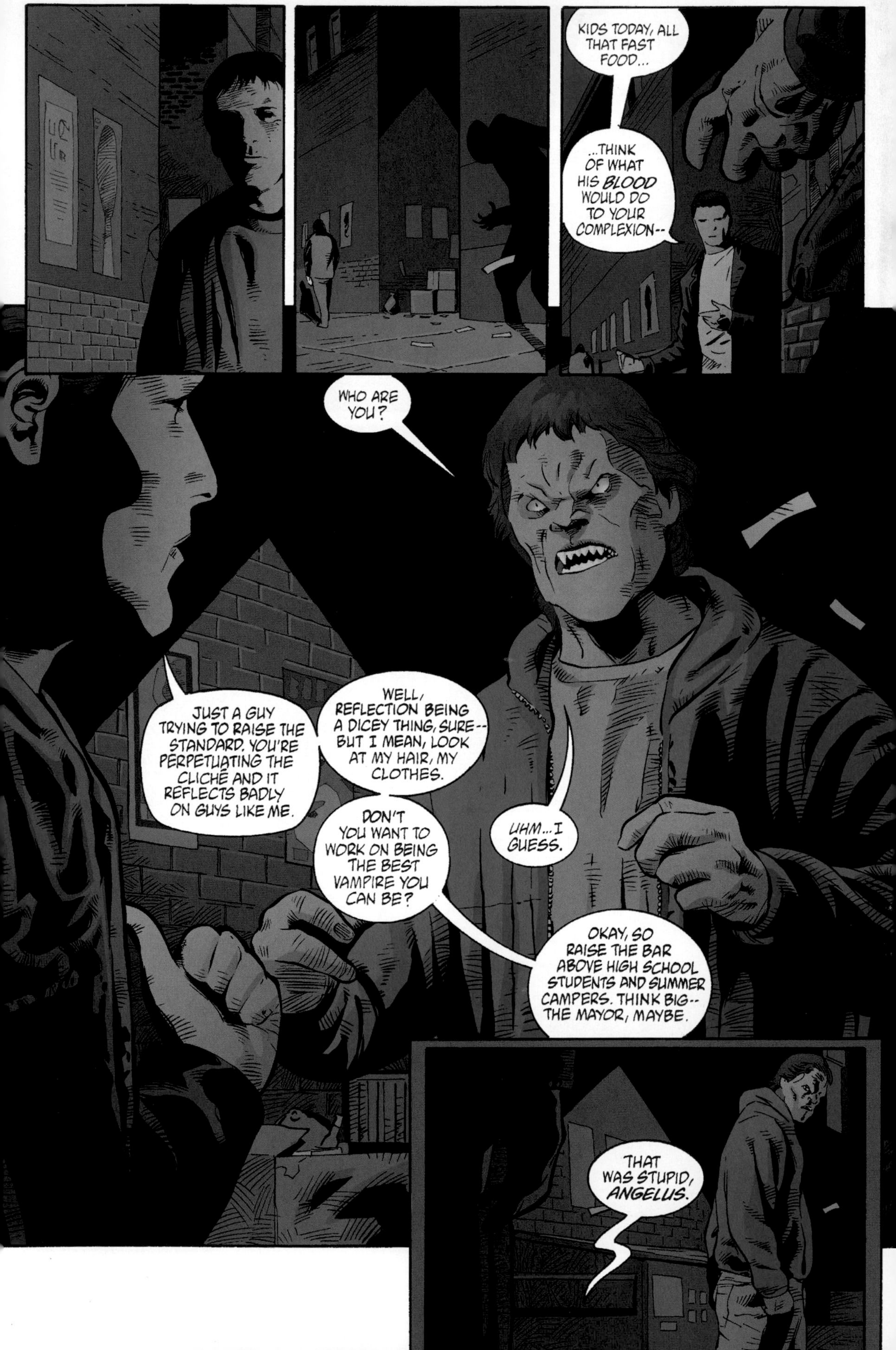

KIDS TODAY, ALL THAT FAST FOOD...
...THINK OF WHAT HIS BLOOD WOULD DO TO YOUR COMPLEXION--
WHO ARE YOU?
JUST A GUY TRYING TO RAISE THE STANDARD. YOU'RE PERPETUATING THE CLICHÉ AND IT REFLECTS BADLY ON GUYS LIKE ME.
WELL, REFLECTION BEING A DICEY THING, SURE-- BUT I MEAN, LOOK AT MY HAIR, MY CLOTHES.
DON'T YOU WANT TO WORK ON BEING THE BEST VAMPIRE YOU CAN BE?
UHM...I GUESS.
OKAY, SO RAISE THE BAR ABOVE HIGH SCHOOL STUDENTS AND SUMMER CAMPERS. THINK BIG-- THE MAYOR, MAYBE.
THAT WAS STUPID, ANGELUS.

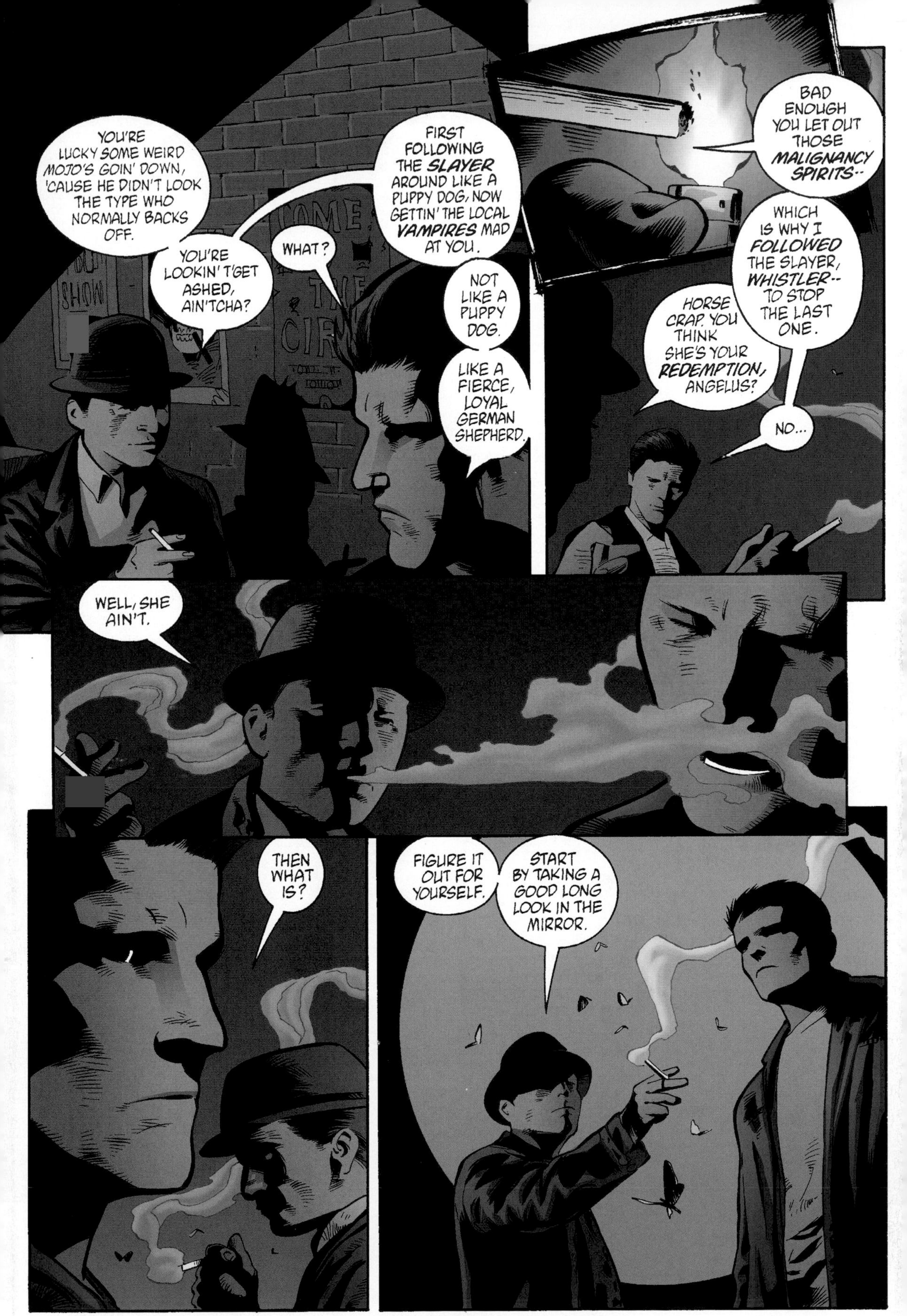
YOU'RE LUCKY SOME WEIRD MOJO'S GOIN' DOWN, 'CAUSE HE DIDN'T LOOK THE TYPE WHO NORMALLY BACKS OFF.
YOU'RE LOOKIN' T'GET ASHED, AIN'TCHA?
WHAT?
FIRST FOLLOWING THE SLAYER AROUND LIKE A PUPPY DOG, NOW GETTIN' THE LOCAL VAMPIRES MAD AT YOU.
NOT LIKE A PUPPY DOG.
LIKE A FIERCE, LOYAL GERMAN SHEPHERD.
BAD ENOUGH YOU LET OUT THOSE MALIGNANCY SPIRITS--
WHICH IS WHY I FOLLOWED THE SLAYER, WHISTLER-- TO STOP THE LAST ONE.
HORSE CRAP. YOU THINK SHE'S YOUR REDEMPTION, ANGELUS?
NO...
WELL, SHE AIN'T.
THEN WHAT IS?
FIGURE IT OUT FOR YOURSELF.
START BY TAKING A GOOD LONG LOOK IN THE MIRROR.

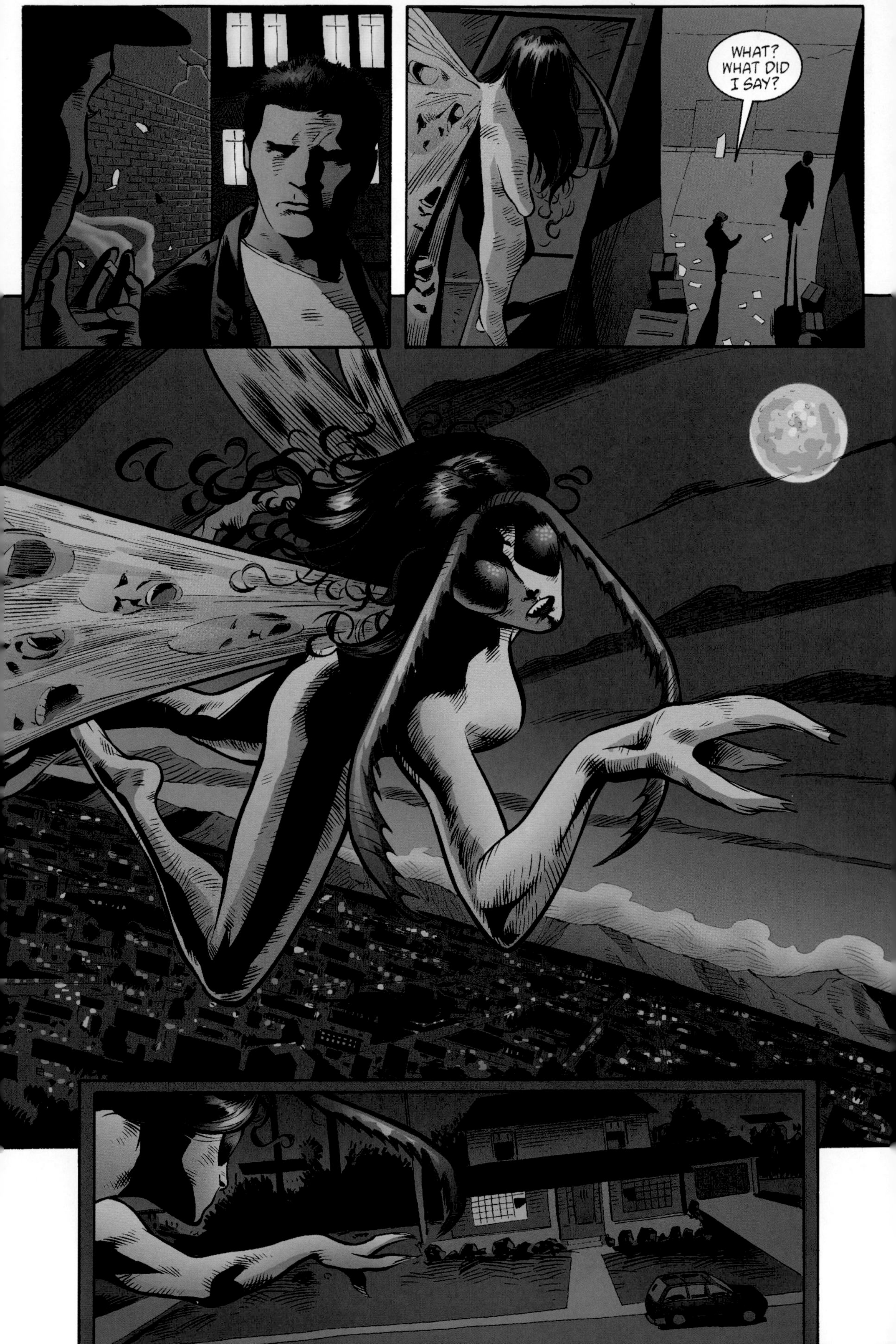
WHAT? WHAT DID I SAY?

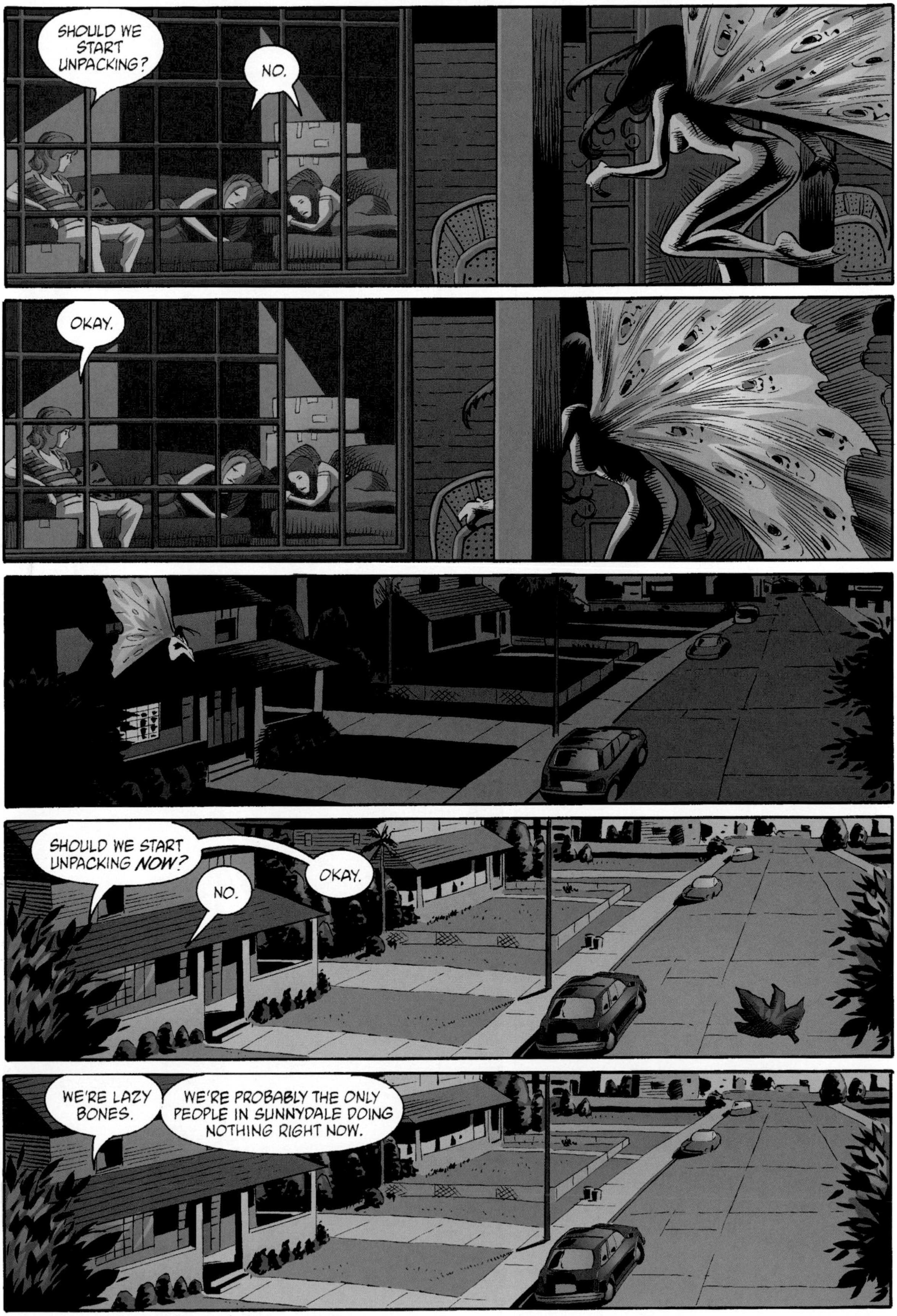
SHOULD WE START UNPACKING?
NO.
OKAY.
SHOULD WE START UNPACKING NOW?
NO.
OKAY.
WE'RE LAZY BONES.
WE'RE PROBABLY THE ONLY PEOPLE IN SUNNYDALE DOING NOTHING RIGHT NOW.

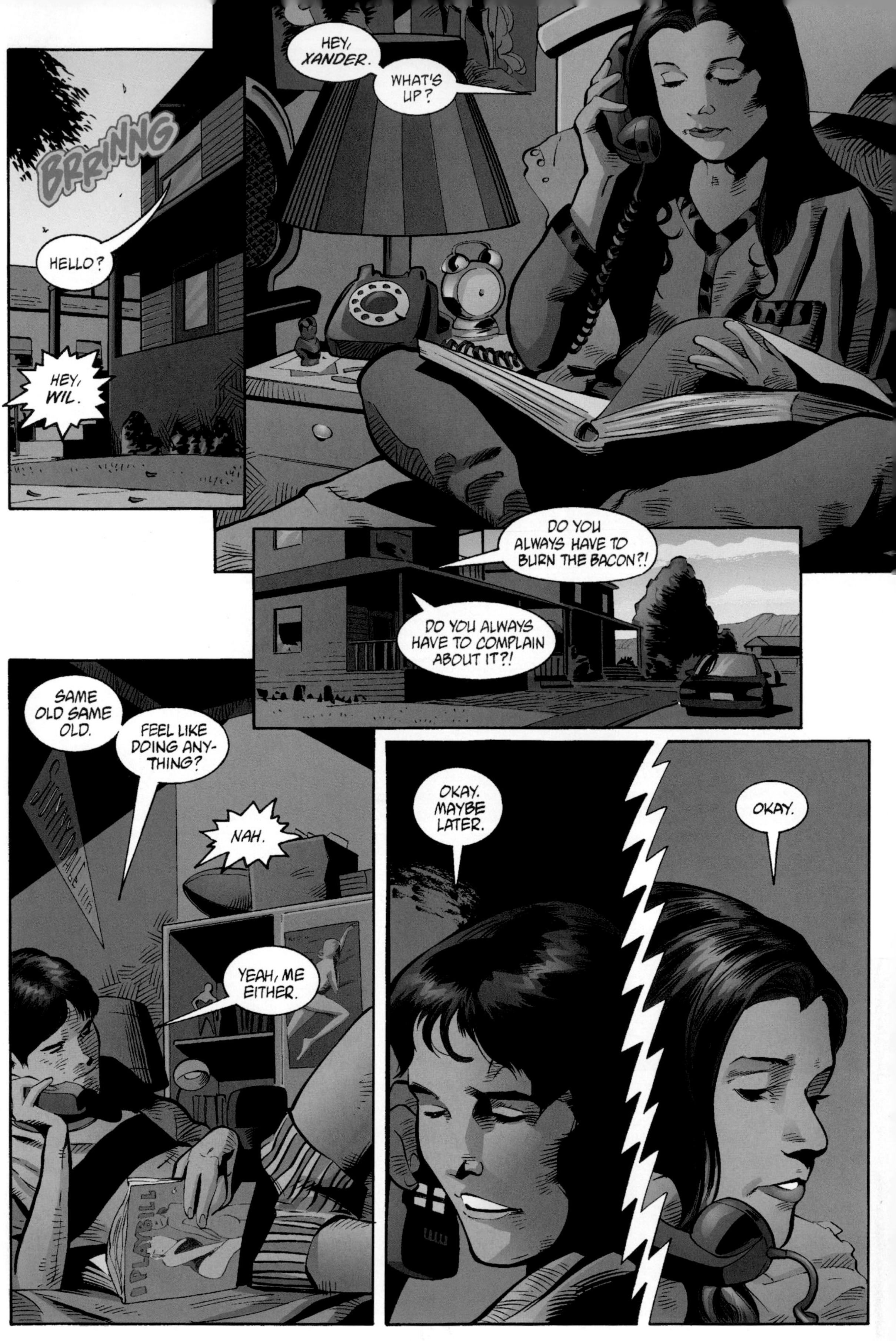
BRRINNG
HELLO?
HEY, WIL.
HEY, XANDER.
WHAT'S UP?
DO YOU ALWAYS HAVE TO BURN THE BACON?!
DO YOU ALWAYS HAVE TO COMPLAIN ABOUT IT?!
SAME OLD SAME OLD.
FEEL LIKE DOING ANY-THING?
NAH.
YEAH, ME EITHER.
OKAY. MAYBE LATER.
OKAY.
PLAYBILL

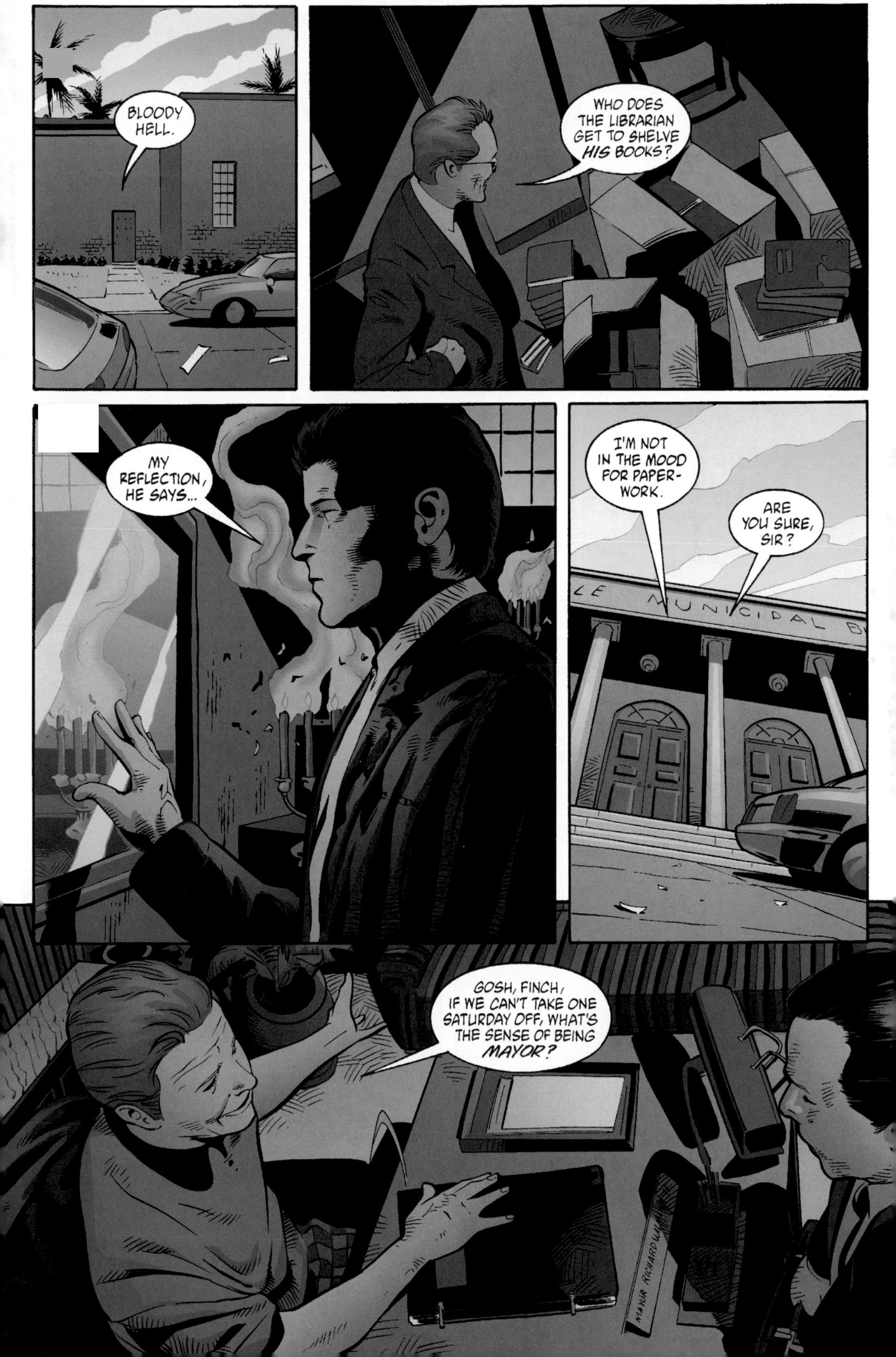
BLOODY HELL.
WHO DOES THE LIBRARIAN GET TO SHELVE *HIS* BOOKS?
MY REFLECTION, HE SAYS...
I'M NOT IN THE MOOD FOR PAPER-WORK.
ARE YOU SURE, SIR?
MUNICIPAL
GOSH, FINCH, IF WE CAN'T TAKE ONE SATURDAY OFF, WHAT'S THE SENSE OF BEING *MAYOR?*
MAYOR RICHARD

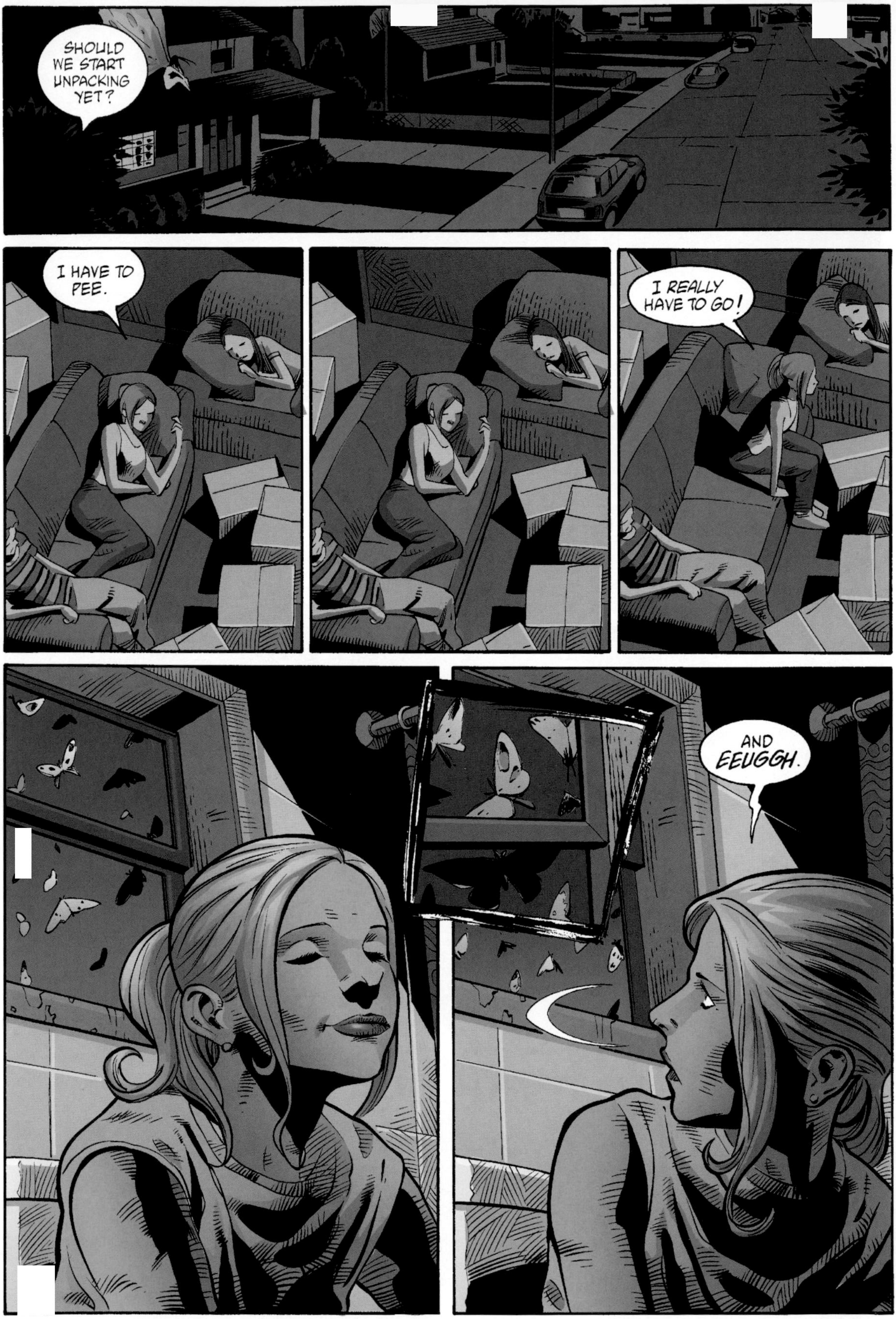
SHOULD WE START UNPACKING YET?
I HAVE TO PEE.
I REALLY HAVE TO GO!
AND EEUGGH.

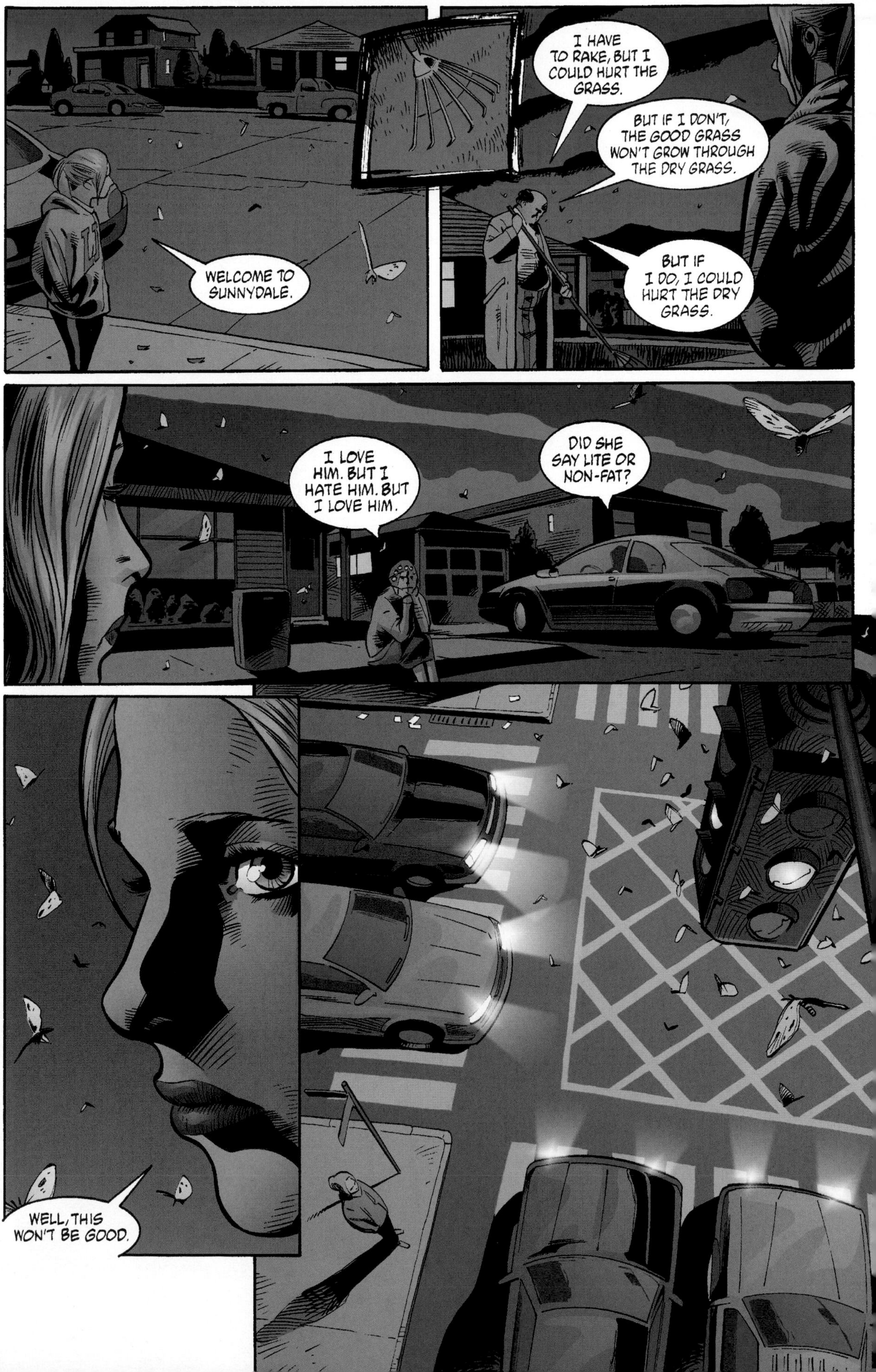
WELCOME TO SUNNYDALE.
I HAVE TO RAKE, BUT I COULD HURT THE GRASS.
BUT IF I DON'T, THE GOOD GRASS WON'T GROW THROUGH THE DRY GRASS.
BUT IF I DO, I COULD HURT THE DRY GRASS.
I LOVE HIM. BUT I HATE HIM. BUT I LOVE HIM.
DID SHE SAY LITE OR NON-FAT?
WELL, THIS WON'T BE GOOD.

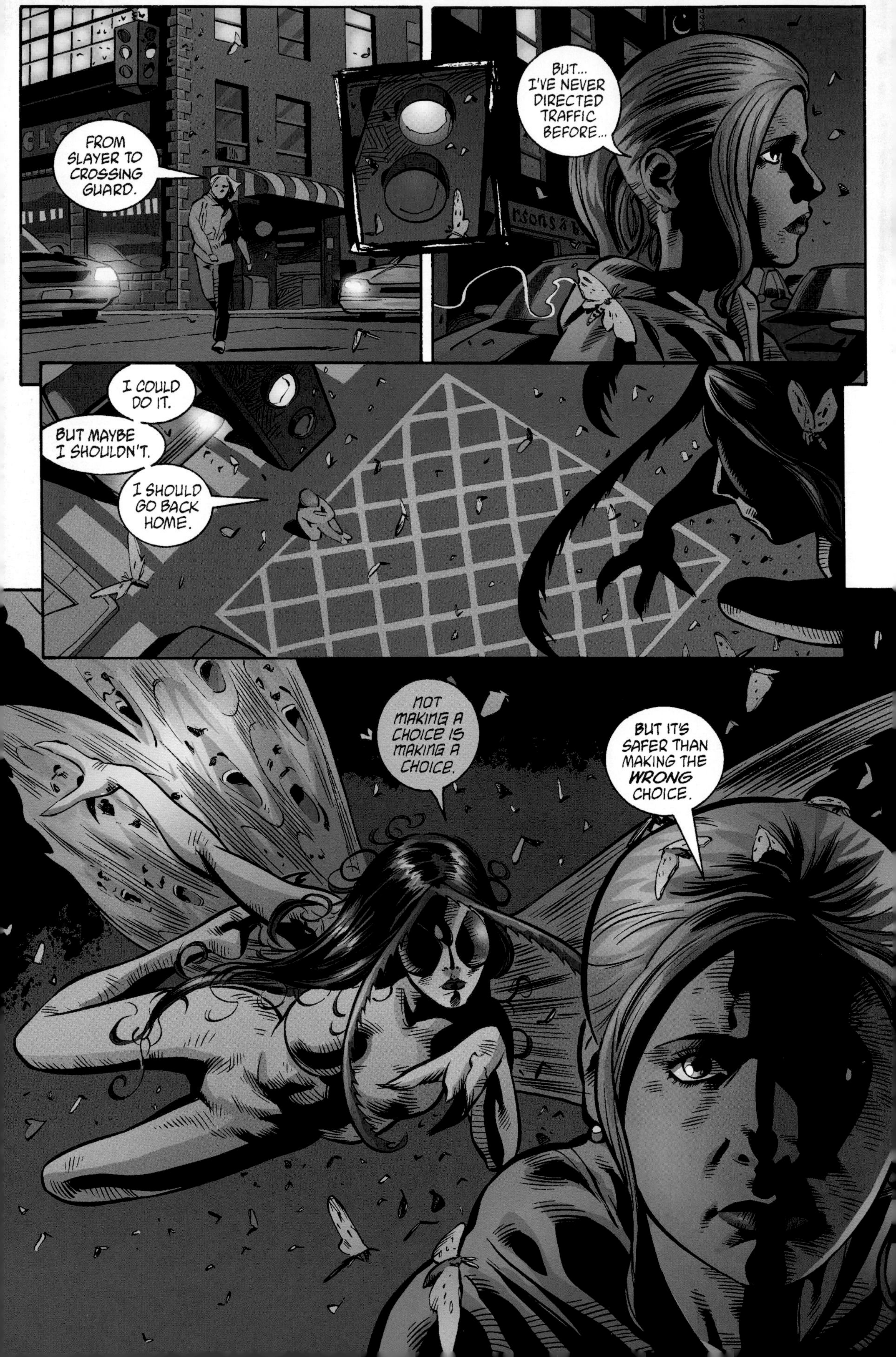
FROM SLAYER TO CROSSING GUARD.
BUT... I'VE NEVER DIRECTED TRAFFIC BEFORE...
I COULD DO IT.
BUT MAYBE I SHOULDN'T.
I SHOULD GO BACK HOME.
NOT MAKING A CHOICE IS MAKING A CHOICE.
BUT IT'S SAFER THAN MAKING THE WRONG CHOICE.

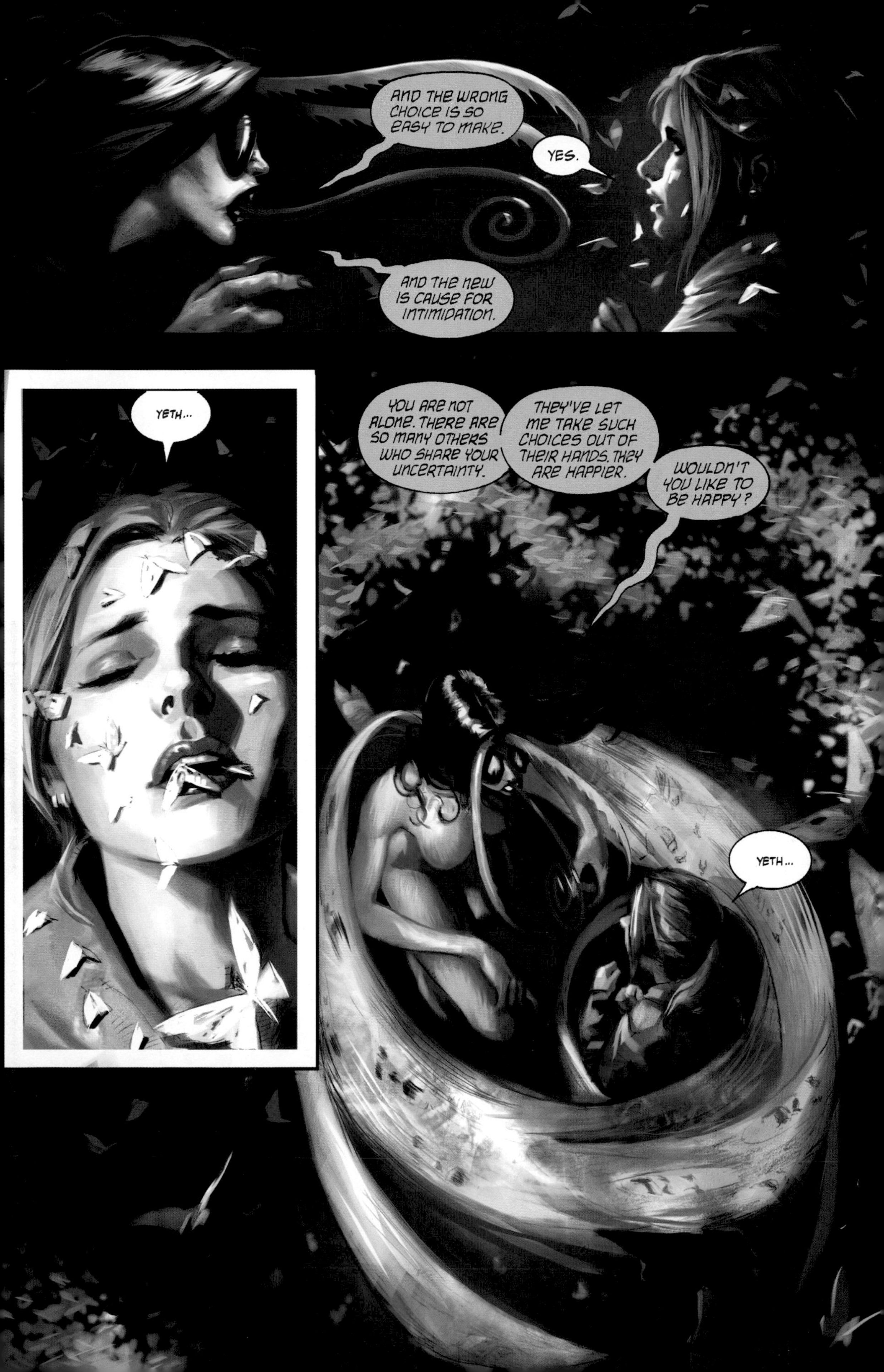
AND THE WRONG CHOICE IS SO EASY TO MAKE.
YES.
AND THE NEW IS CAUSE FOR INTIMIDATION.
YETH...
YOU ARE NOT ALONE. THERE ARE SO MANY OTHERS WHO SHARE YOUR UNCERTAINTY.
THEY'VE LET ME TAKE SUCH CHOICES OUT OF THEIR HANDS. THEY ARE HAPPIER.
WOULDN'T YOU LIKE TO BE HAPPY?
YETH...

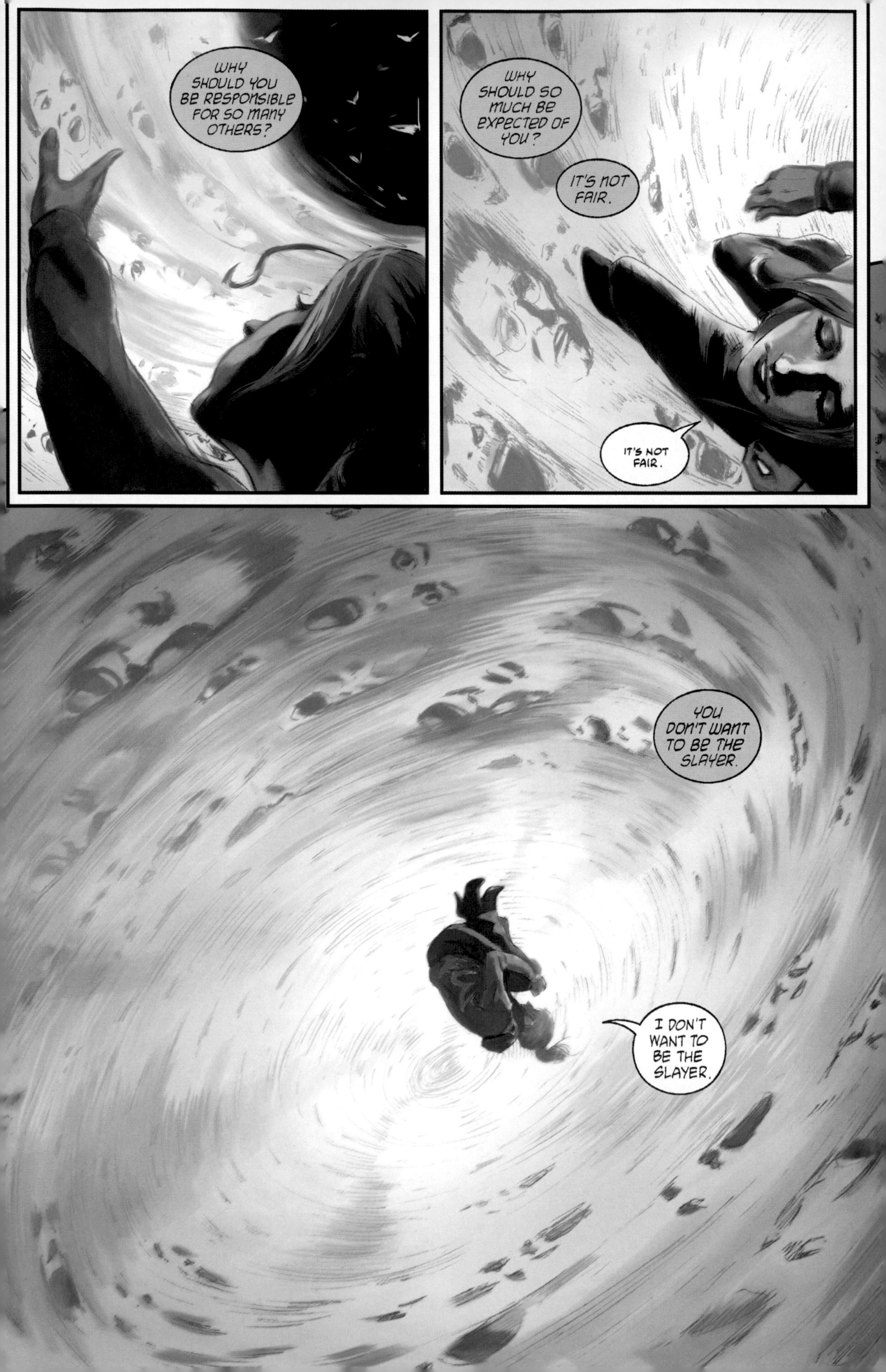
WHY SHOULD YOU BE RESPONSIBLE FOR SO MANY OTHERS?
WHY SHOULD SO MUCH BE EXPECTED OF YOU?
IT'S NOT FAIR.
IT'S NOT FAIR.
YOU DON'T WANT TO BE THE SLAYER.
I DON'T WANT TO BE THE SLAYER.

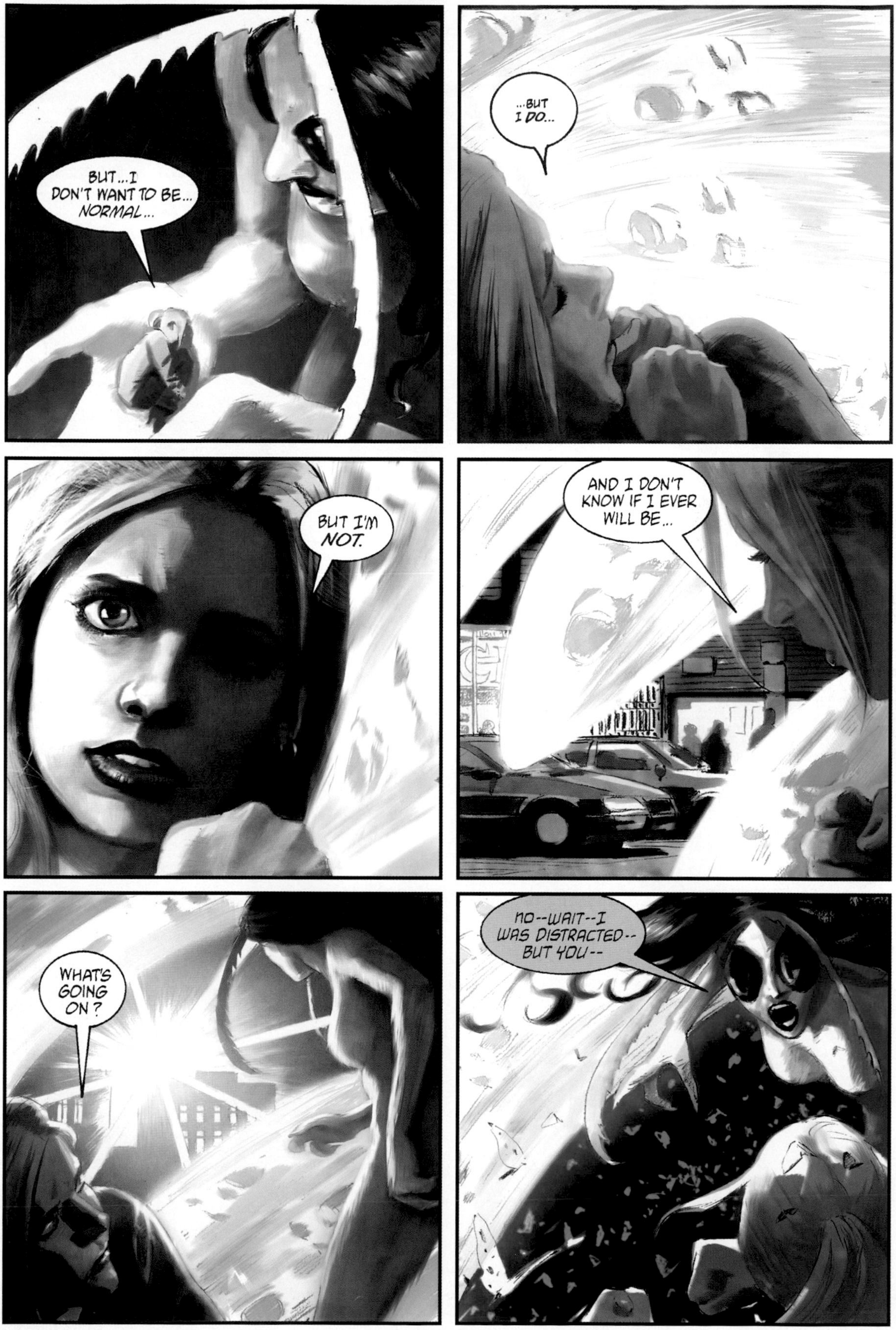
BUT...I DON'T WANT TO BE... NORMAL...
...BUT I DO...
BUT I'M NOT.
AND I DON'T KNOW IF I EVER WILL BE...
WHAT'S GOING ON?
NO--WAIT--I WAS DISTRACTED--BUT YOU--

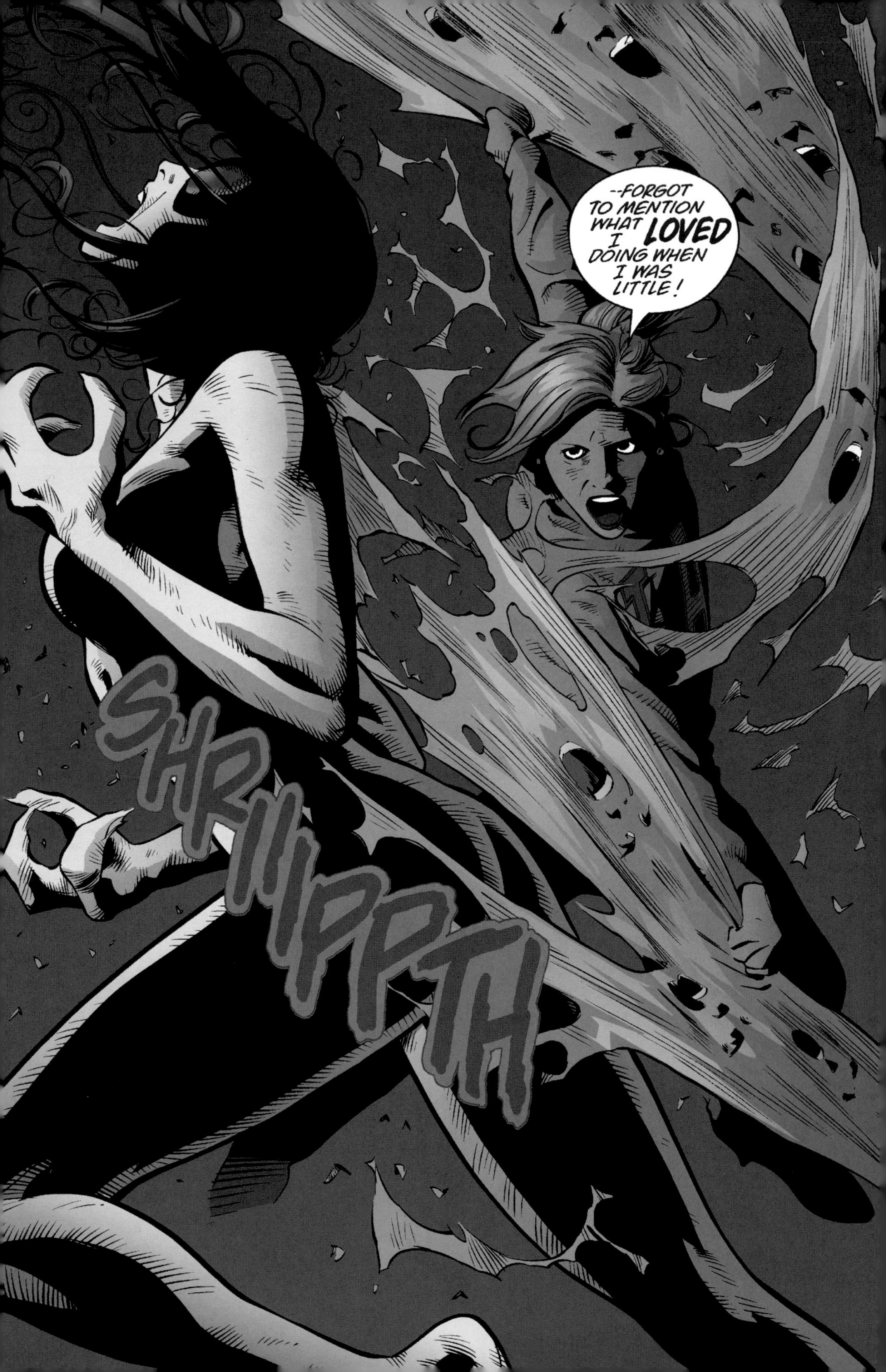
--FORGOT TO MENTION WHAT I LOVED DOING WHEN I WAS LITTLE!
SHRIIPPTH

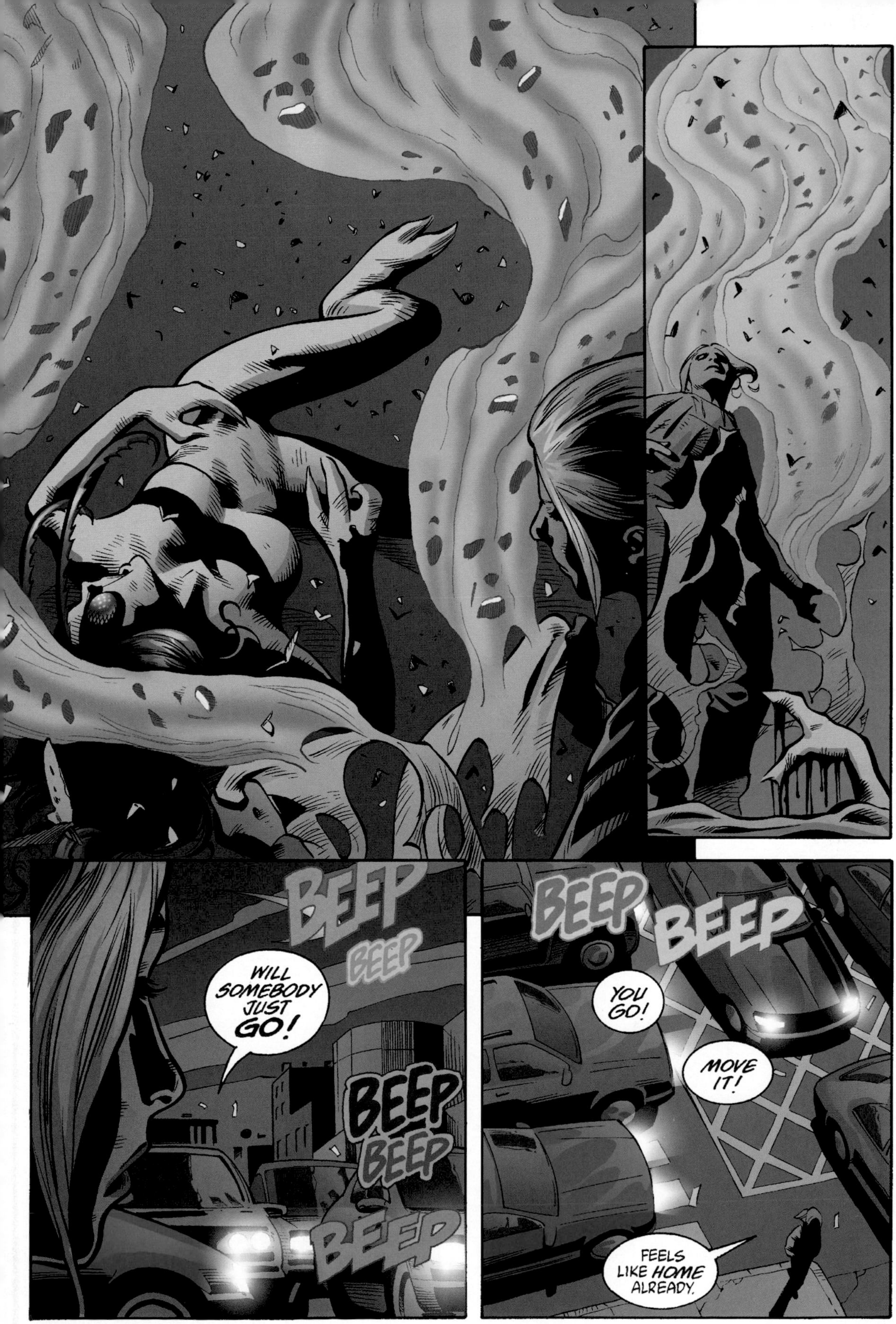
BEEP
BEEP
WILL SOMEBODY JUST GO!
BEEP
BEEP
BEEP
BEEP
BEEP
YOU GO!
MOVE IT!
FEELS LIKE HOME ALREADY.

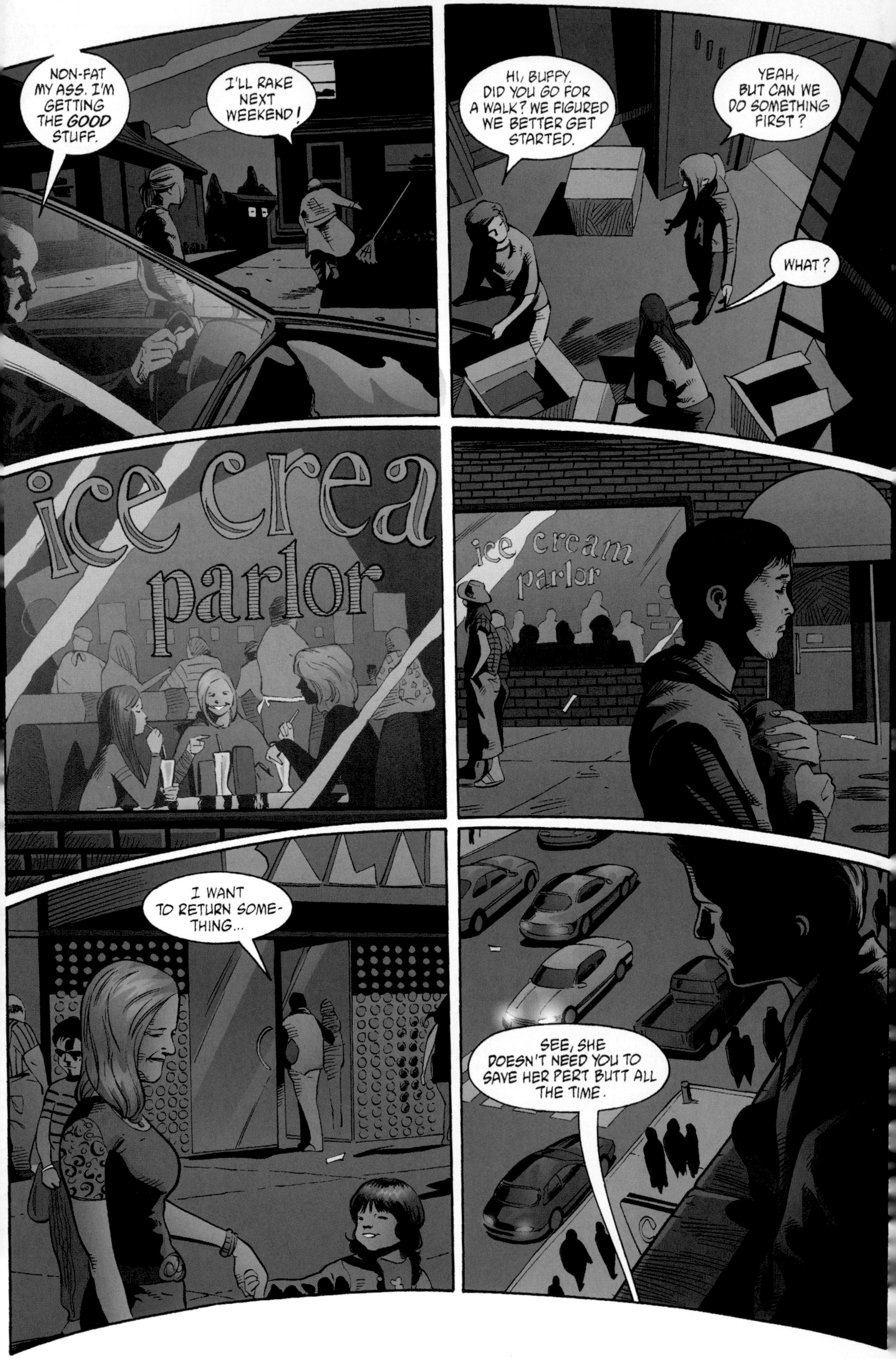
NON-FAT MY ASS. I'M GETTING THE GOOD STUFF.
I'LL RAKE NEXT WEEKEND!
HI, BUFFY. DID YOU GO FOR A WALK? WE FIGURED WE BETTER GET STARTED.
YEAH, BUT CAN WE DO SOMETHING FIRST?
WHAT?
ice crea parlor
ice cream parlor
I WANT TO RETURN SOMETHING...
SEE, SHE DOESN'T NEED YOU TO SAVE HER PERT BUTT ALL THE TIME.

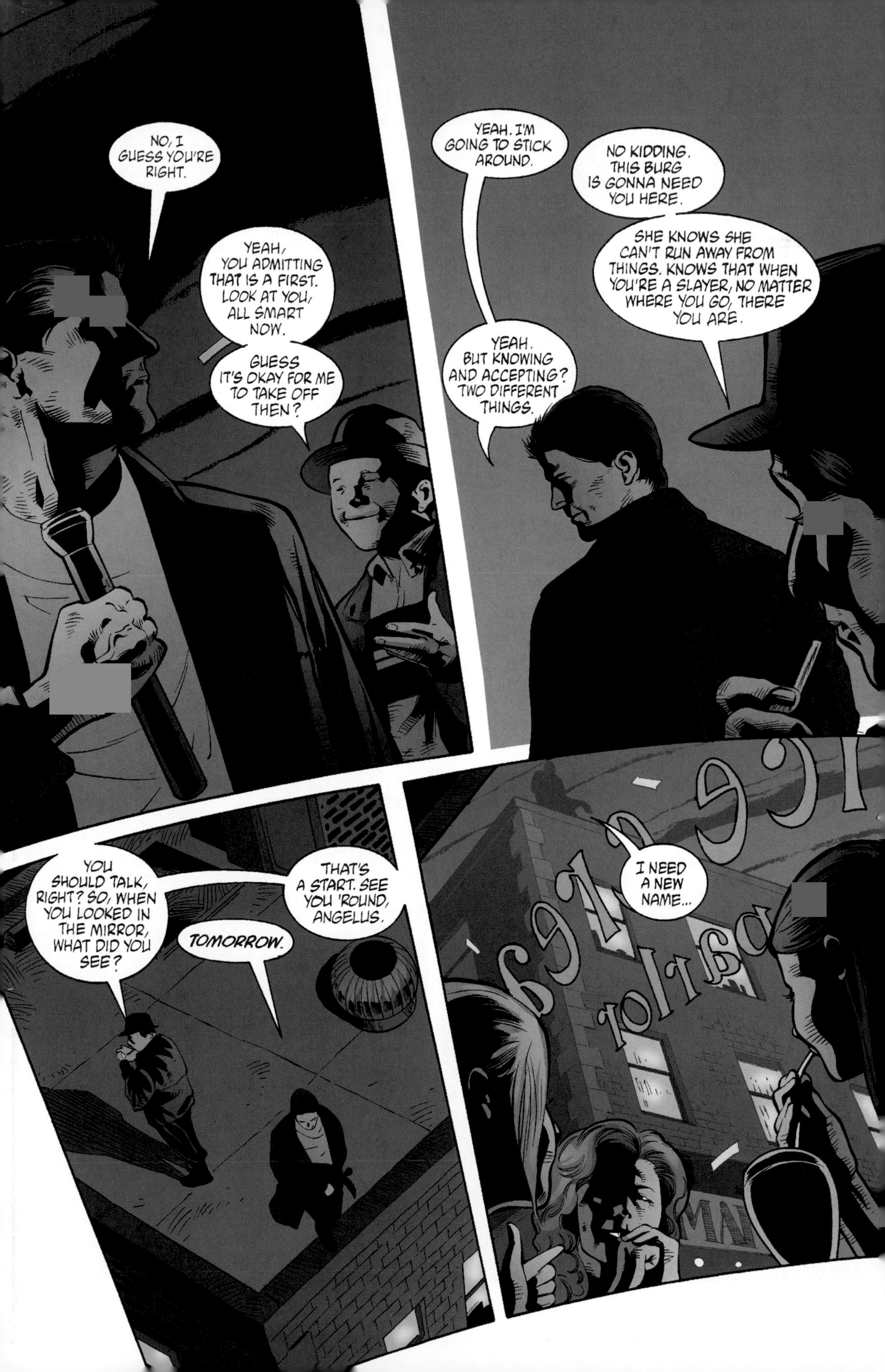
NO, I GUESS YOU'RE RIGHT.
YEAH, YOU ADMITTING THAT IS A FIRST. LOOK AT YOU, ALL SMART NOW.
GUESS IT'S OKAY FOR ME TO TAKE OFF THEN?
YEAH. I'M GOING TO STICK AROUND.
NO KIDDING. THIS BURG IS GONNA NEED YOU HERE.
SHE KNOWS SHE CAN'T RUN AWAY FROM THINGS. KNOWS THAT WHEN YOU'RE A SLAYER, NO MATTER WHERE YOU GO, THERE YOU ARE.
YEAH. BUT KNOWING AND ACCEPTING? TWO DIFFERENT THINGS.
YOU SHOULD TALK, RIGHT? SO, WHEN YOU LOOKED IN THE MIRROR, WHAT DID YOU SEE?
THAT'S A START. SEE YOU 'ROUND, ANGELUS.
TOMORROW.
I NEED A NEW NAME...

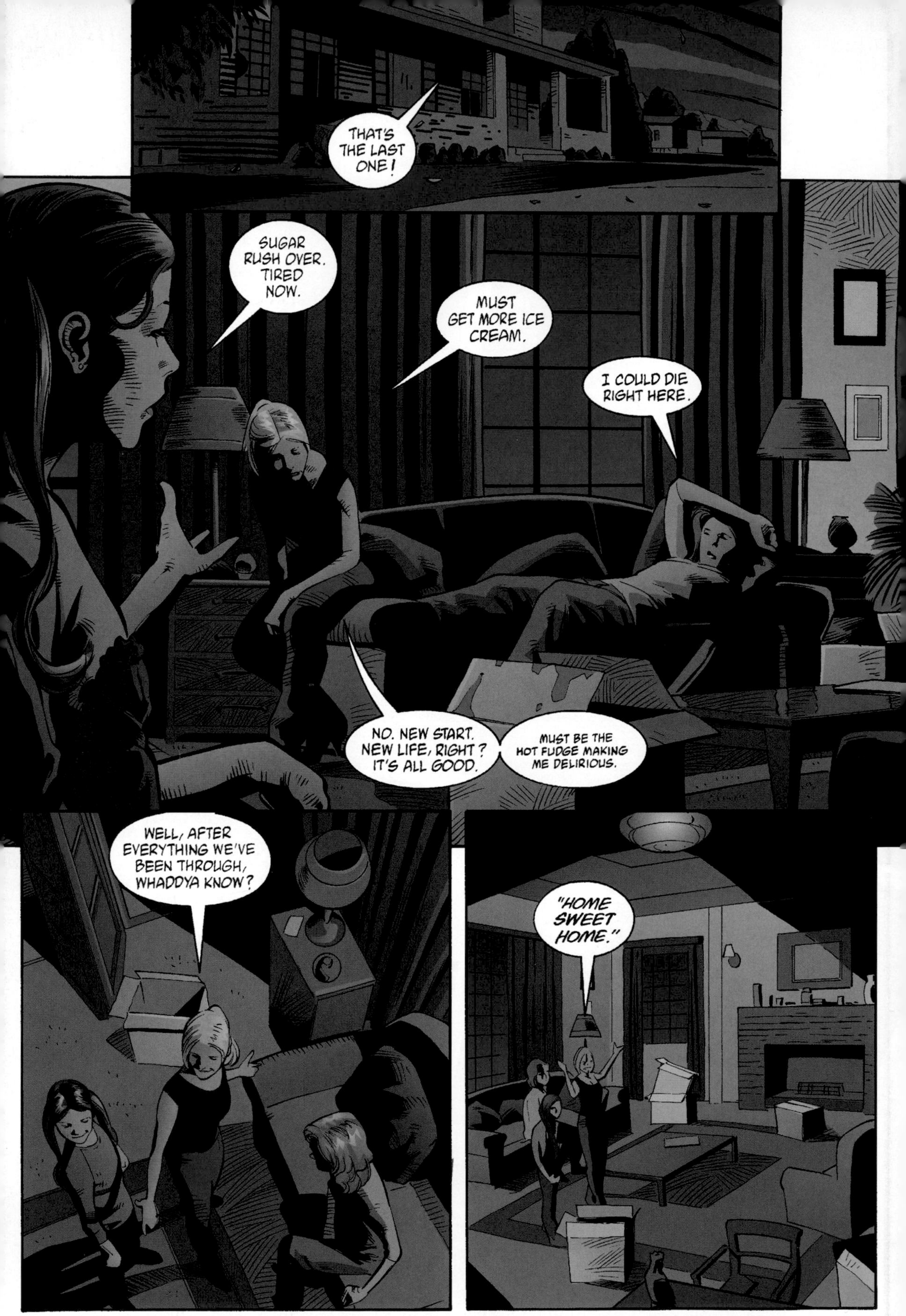
THAT'S THE LAST ONE!
SUGAR RUSH OVER. TIRED NOW.
MUST GET MORE ICE CREAM.
I COULD DIE RIGHT HERE.
NO. NEW START. NEW LIFE, RIGHT? IT'S ALL GOOD.
MUST BE THE HOT FUDGE MAKING ME DELIRIOUS.
WELL, AFTER EVERYTHING WE'VE BEEN THROUGH, WHADDYA KNOW?
"HOME SWEET HOME."

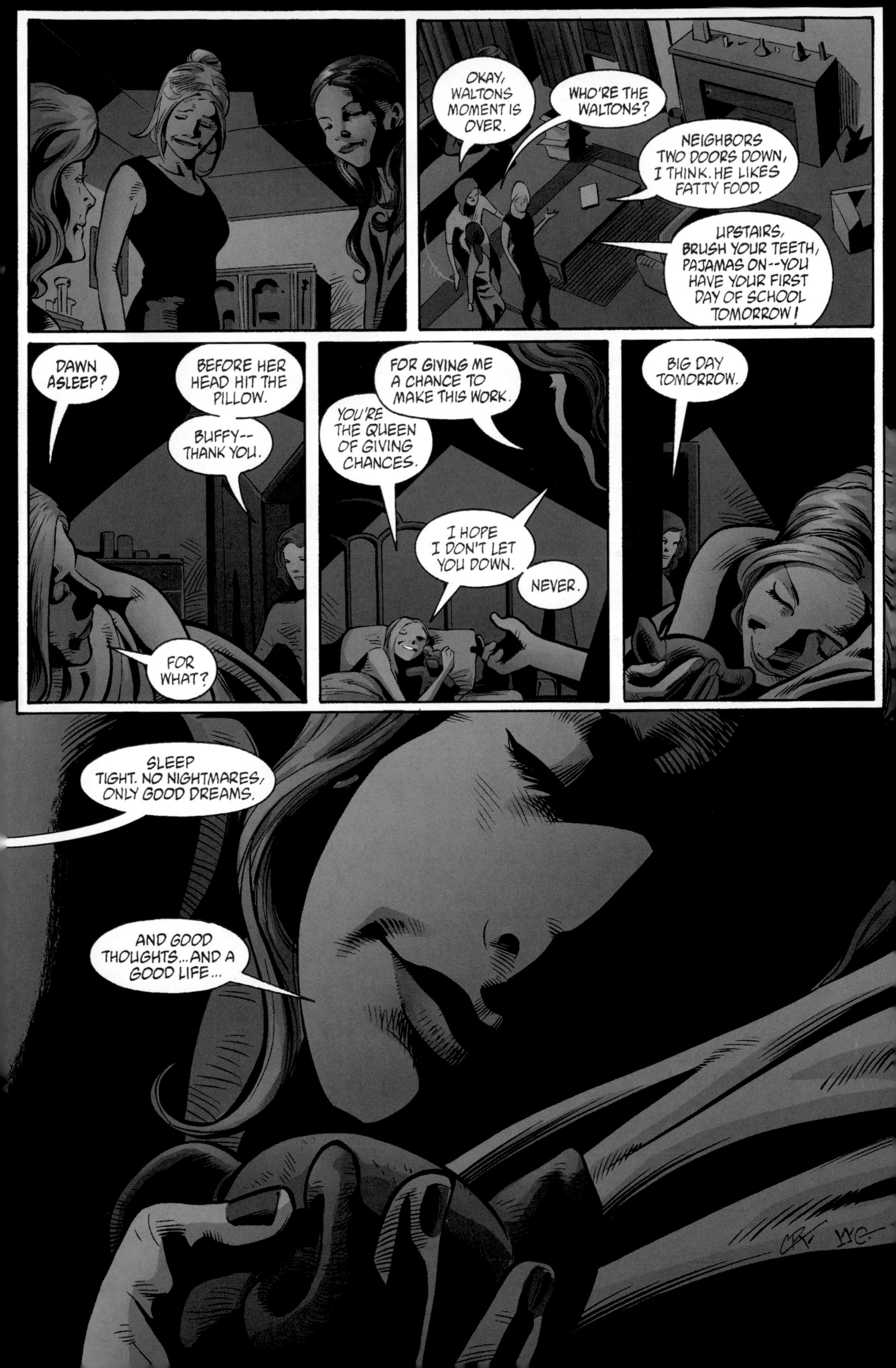
OKAY, WALTONS MOMENT IS OVER.
WHO'RE THE WALTONS?
NEIGHBORS TWO DOORS DOWN, I THINK. HE LIKES FATTY FOOD.
UPSTAIRS, BRUSH YOUR TEETH, PAJAMAS ON--YOU HAVE YOUR FIRST DAY OF SCHOOL TOMORROW!
DAWN ASLEEP?
BEFORE HER HEAD HIT THE PILLOW.
BUFFY-- THANK YOU.
FOR WHAT?
FOR GIVING ME A CHANCE TO MAKE THIS WORK.
YOU'RE THE QUEEN OF GIVING CHANCES.
I HOPE I DON'T LET YOU DOWN.
NEVER.
BIG DAY TOMORROW.
SLEEP TIGHT. NO NIGHTMARES, ONLY GOOD DREAMS.
AND GOOD THOUGHTS...AND A GOOD LIFE...

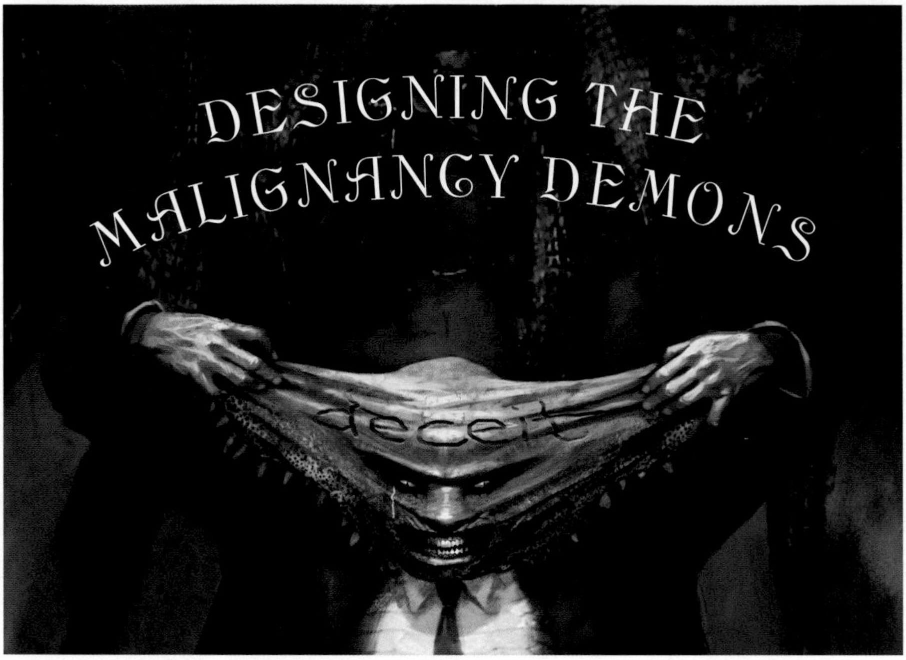
DESIGNING THE MALIGNANCY DEMONS
deceit

For the final story in the *Buffy* monthly comic, Fabian Nicieza called for the creation of four demons who would feed on Buffy's emotions around her parents' divorce. One of Brian Horton's most unique talents is his monster design, which earned him a job with Clive Barker on *The Undying*, so I knew I wanted him to design the creatures. After the very bizarre covers he and Paul Lee had done for *The Devil's Footprints*, we wanted to take it a step further, for a larger audience, and do something very strange, using Buffy as the center of some truly horrific images. Because Paul was busy with work on *Sam and Twitch* and Drew Goddard's Spike and Dru story in *Tales of the Vampires*, Brian tackled the covers for *A Stake to the Heart* on his own. But first he had to work out the demons' designs.

We decided to design the demons before any scripts were written, and this led to one of the most unique things about the story. The text in red is what Fabian provided for Brian, along with the crude sketches.

When Brian designed the first character, he went much more by instinct than by a literal depiction of deceit. This impressionistic approach led to a suggestion which would influence the story significantly.

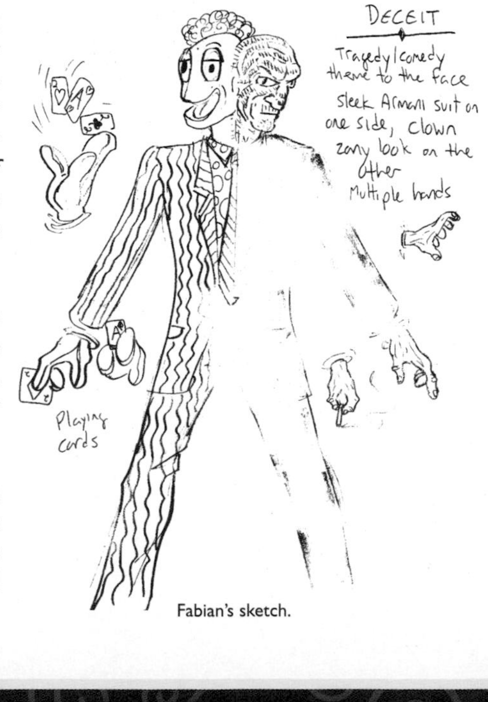
DECEIT
Tragedy/comedy theme to the face
Sleek Armani suit on one side, clown zany look on the other
Multiple hands
Playing cards

Fabian's sketch.

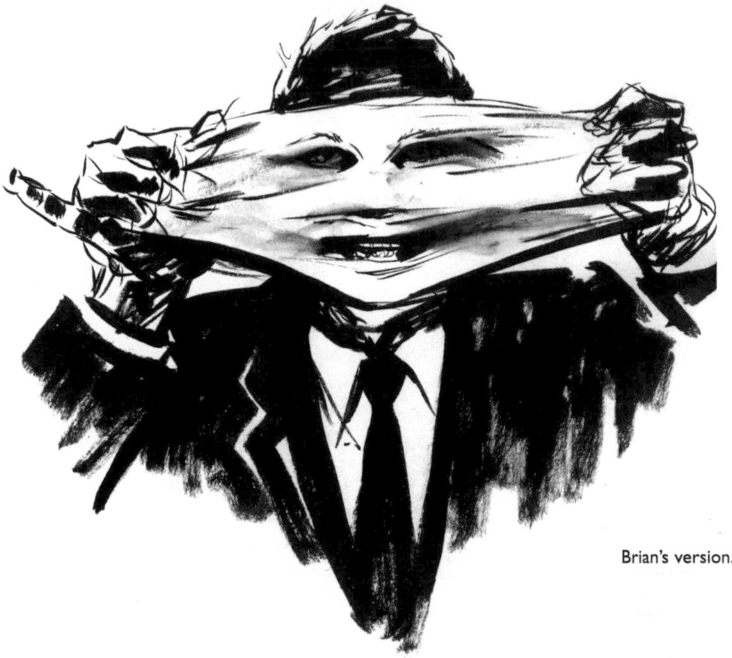

Brian's version.

*The Malignancies are cancers of the soul—emotional tumors that can be manipulated by supernatural means to manifest themselves as living entities. For this story, four aspects of depression are created to reflect themes of separation, divorce, moving to a new home, and the fear of the new.*

*All the characters are meant to have a Mike Mignola-meets-Tim Burton design sense. See my VERY bad drawings attached and laugh. Then read the descriptions below, look at the drawings again, and make them something I'm not a good enough artist to do–make them cool!*

*DECEIT appears as a two-faced creature, both faces melded together like the muses of the Theatre, Comedy and Tragedy. The left side is a stark, featureless HAPPY FACE, contorted to a grin of frightening proportions. The right side is a pained rigor-mortis mask of contempt: frowning, scowling, furrowed brow, serrated ridges along the forehead and nose, drawn, withered skin. Deceit wears a sleek businessman's suit. One side is smooth and pressed, the other is frayed and torn, worn and weathered. He has two arms, but no hands. Instead, SEVERAL PAIRS of hands float around him. Three sets each of Pained Hands and three sets each of ANIMATED-STYLE CLOWN HANDS.*

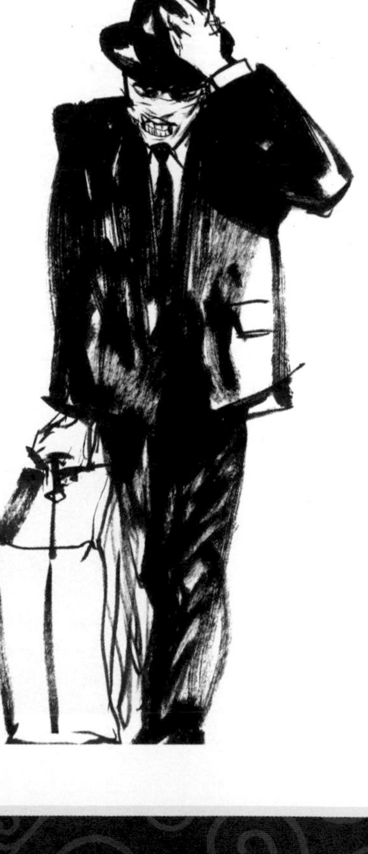

GUILT

Thin, emaciated, hunched, shuffling body.

Head plunged INTO shoulders

"buried in the sand"

dangling keys on tendrils like spider-webs

keys = secrets

spider-webs = time

Brian got so involved in designing the characters, and working out a symbolic approach to the covers—using animal imagery, like the alligator skin on Deceit and the albatross on the Guilt cover—that he proposed what became one of the most unique elements in the story. Each issue would begin with a vignette having nothing to do with the principle characters, but showing animals acting out the theme of the issue.

*GUILT is an emaciated, naked MALE BODY (whose private parts are discreetly kept in shadows), but he has no head—it is not cut off or missing, it is literally PLUNGED INTO HIS NECK like a turtle, creating a withdrawn crater around the open neck area. He wears dangling chains all over his body with KEYS on them, all to lock away secrets. The keys dangle and jangle like eerie chimes.*

For Guilt, Brian stayed much more faithful to Fabian's design.

Fabian agreed to work the animal scenes into the story, and Brian offered to paint those sequences over Cliff's pencils, adding to the mysterious effect, the otherworldliness of the cut aways to the animistic world. For the first chapter, Fabian followed Brian's suggestion and kept it pretty simple, but in Act Three: Abandonment, the animals became more important, with Buffy and Dawn transported to that symbolic world.

*ABANDONMENT is a young PREGNANT woman in full Victorian garb, but the front of her dress is torn revealing a black MAW inside; entrails dangle from this open wound. She is MISSING the baby inside her womb, in its place is a hollow whistle of wind. Baby rattle in hand, her eyes stare off to the side, never connecting, as she shuffles around, looking for her missing child.*

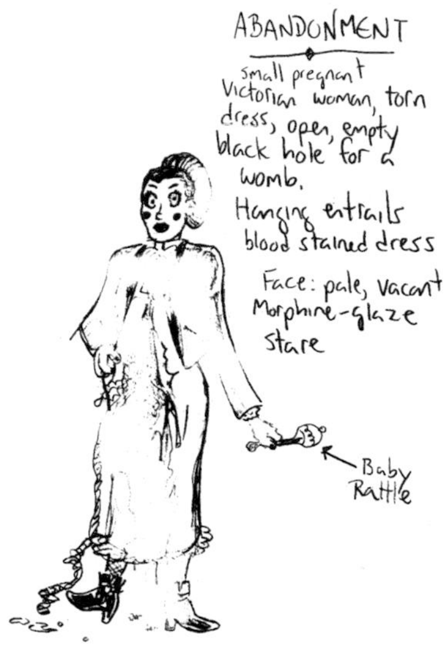
ABANDONMENT
Small pregnant Victorian woman, torn dress, open, empty black hole for a womb.
Hanging entrails
blood stained dress
Face: pale, vacant Morphine-glaze stare
Baby Rattle

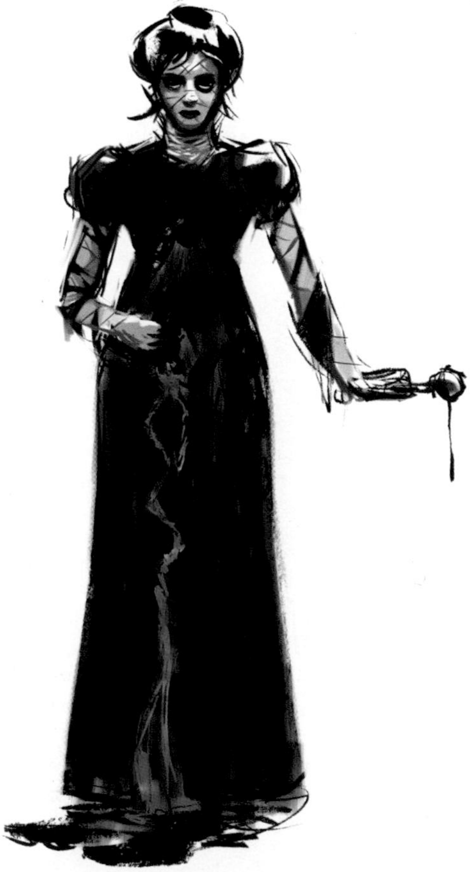

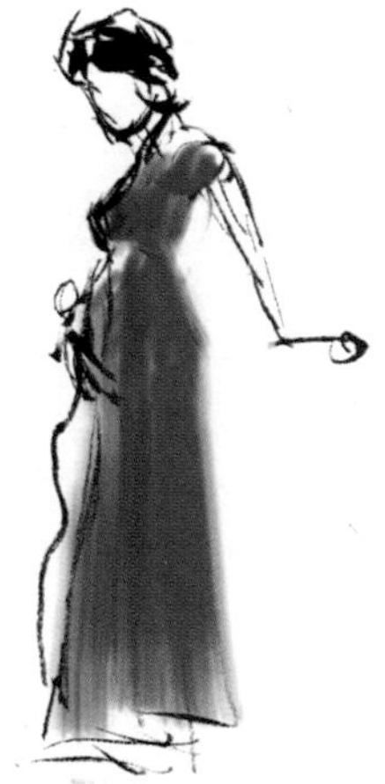

For Abandonment, Brian stayed faithful to Fabian's idea, adding the cuts along the face and arms.

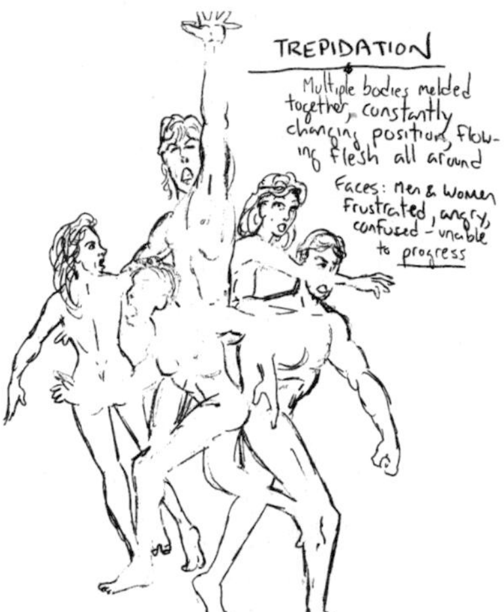
TREPIDATION
Multiple bodies melded together, constantly changing position, flowing flesh all around
Faces: Men & Women Frustrated, angry, confused - unable to progress

For the final Malignancy Demon, Brian took more liberty than before, and used the sort of animal imagery he'd been using on the covers for the body of the demon itself. The wings became a focal point for Fabian's approach to the creature, and for Buffy's destruction of it.

*TREPIDATION is afraid to make a move—it is SEVERAL BODIES stacked one on top of the other, back to back, side to side, in a writhing amalgam of flesh that can't move in any direction without being stalled and pulled in another. Each body covers one of the five senses, blinding themselves individually, hands covering eyes, ears. mouth, nose and one body with missing hands.*

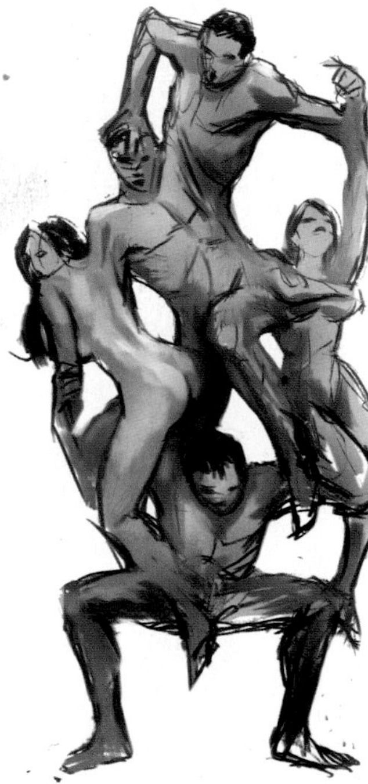

Brian tries out Fabian's concept...

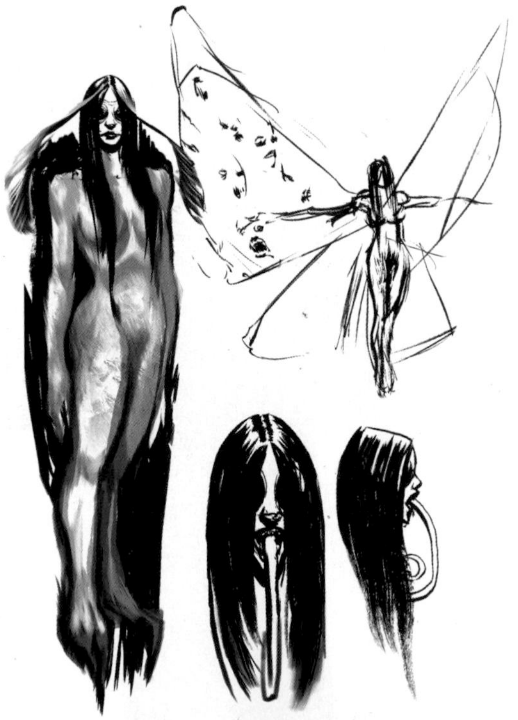

...but abandons it almost entirely.

*A Stake to the Heart*, the last story in the five-year *Buffy* monthly series, was one of the most unique collaborations between cover artist and writer that I've been a part of, and one of the most surreal stories in the *Buffy the Vampire Slayer* canon.

Scott Allie
October 23, 2003
Portland, Oregon